Building a Billion

The Story of John McCarthy

Charlie Berridge

HARRIMAN HOUSE LTD

3A Penns Road
Petersfield
Hampshire
GU32 2EW
GREAT BRITAIN

Tel: +44 (0)1730 233870
Fax: +44 (0)1730 233880
Email: enquiries@harriman-house.com
Website: www.harriman-house.com

First published in Great Britain in 2011

Copyright © Harriman House Ltd

The right of Charlie Berridge to be identified as the Author has been asserted in accordance with the Copyright, Design and Patents Act 1988.

ISBN: 978-0-857191-17-5

British Library Cataloguing in Publication Data
A CIP catalogue record for this book can be obtained from the British Library.

Set in Frutiger and Sabon.

Printed and bound in the UK by CPI Antony Rowe, Chippenham and Eastbourne.

 Harriman House

Contents

Foreword

I first met John McCarthy in the summer of 1972 when I attended an interview for the post of surveyor at his offices in New Street, Lymington. McStone's, as they were known in those days, had very modest offices comprising two rooms and a corridor, which soon became my work place. However, in true John McCarthy style the offices were on the top floor of the building and his own room occupied the majority of that area.

The great attraction for me as a newly qualified surveyor was not the career opportunity but the fact that the company car that went with it was an MGB convertible. In those days John drove a red E-Type Jaguar roadster which I greatly admired. During the interview John seemed a little edgy, cigarette smoking behind his oversized desk. I formed the impression that he was a man in a hurry to succeed and the interview was taking up precious time that could have been better used on that objective.

Rapidly John's talents and faults became apparent. He was always on a mission, looking for the next deal, angling to keep costs down and profits up. John was driven to show his critics, of which there were a number the more successful he became, that he was a winner. John did not have the advantage of a fine education, and when he started out he had no real business training. He had to learn the hard and fast way. He hit the ground running, was good at it and rarely made the same mistake twice.

This book is the story of John's remarkable life: the challenges faced and conquered both in business and sport; and, perhaps most significant of all, the tenacity, passion and self-belief that has carried John from that original little office to his present status. It is a truly inspirational story.

Harry Harrison
March 2011

1. The Defining Moment

In 1977 pre-Thatcher Britain, the housing market was dire and the economy seemed bogged down in Socialist treacle. I was thirty-eight years old. In a pub, the Ship Inn at Keyhaven, down on the South Coast after work one evening I was chatting to a friend. During the conversation he asked me how my new building project for the elderly was coming along. I started talking about it and listening to myself, almost hovering above the conversation like an eavesdropper. It suddenly dawned on me that I'd made it. It was my Eureka moment, my epiphany, the point when the penny dropped. I realised that I had actually cracked it, the numbers game, and I could see my way to a fortune. I'd identified a niche market in the building industry and the chance to create a significant business and make more money than I had ever dreamed of. I'd hit on a scheme for building retirement homes in the private sector and was the first to do it.

The year before I'd bought the old Waverley Cinema in New Milton with a bungalow alongside. Having received planning permissions for a range of uses, from offices to shops and flats, none of these added up to a viable development. It was in danger of becoming a millstone round my neck. I had seen the latest newsletter from the Home Builders Federation which talked about a Government Green Paper and the need for developers to consider building homes for the elderly. I sat on a county liaison planning committee as a representative for the House Builders Federation and I had mentioned retirement flats, or sheltered accommodation as it was called, and that policies needed to be amended to allow private house builders to build such homes. We were eventually granted planning permission for the old cinema site on the basis that we'd only provide one car parking space for every seven flats. The norm was one and a half spaces for each flat. With this change we could build ten times more flats on the site and the project became profitable. We carried out some extensive market research and placed a couple of ads in the *New Milton Advertiser* and *Bournemouth Echo*. The response was unbelievable. We sold all thirty-two units before we'd put the roof on the new building and at a time when the market was as flat as a pancake. We charged just under £10,000 per flat. On the strength of that we bought the doctor's surgery opposite and built and sold another identical thirty-two flats. We charged £15,000 each for those. We turned over less than a million pounds that year. In 2006 McCarthy & Stone was sold for £1.1 billion. As I stood in that pub, nursing that G&T and talking, I could see that I was going to make a lot of money and that kept me completely focused. I had another drink.

2. Birth, Bombs and Billericay

I was born John Sidney McCarthy, half an hour before midnight on 31st December 1939. My mother Helen was a little upset. Another half an hour and she would have probably got her name in Surbiton's local newspaper and picked up the fifty pound prize for having the first new baby of 1940. I was called John, my father's Christian name, and Sidney was my middle name after my grandfather Fisher's first born son who died aged thirteen. Helen, or Nellie as my mother was nicknamed, was a Fisher and was the eldest of Grandpa Fisher's five children. My three uncles and an aunt were to become a big early influence on my life.

I didn't remember grandfather Fisher at all, even though there's a photograph of us together at some family gathering. He was a carpenter by trade and he had his own large joinery business in Kingston upon Thames. He was one of the first to set up a factory to design and build pre-made fitted kitchens and during the war he made the wooden fairings, from the cockpit to the tail, for Hurricane fighter planes and had a very successful business. He must have made a lot of money because he drove an open-topped touring car, which in the 1920s was very rare.

My dad's side of the family came from Dublin. He and his father had come over from Ireland and had worked on the canal longboats that plied the waterways between London, Liverpool and Manchester. I didn't really know anything about my paternal grandfather other than that rumour had it he was a Freeman of Dublin City. My father seemed reticent to talk about him and I sense that strong drink must have something to do with the man's past.

Father (his nickname was Mac) turned his hand to several trades. He worked for the Fifty Shilling Tailors, became an engineer and ended up as the landlord of a pub. As hard as he tried to be successful in business, father never made it, which was a cause of some anguish to my mother. Her father had been very successful and her three brothers had all established businesses and I guess that she expected her husband to emulate them and their lifestyle. This became a real problem in their relationship but as much as Dad tried it was never to be. He was a fine-looking man, standing over six feet tall, with a moustache and he always dressed like a gentleman. He looked the part even though perhaps he wasn't. However, he never seemed to get flustered by anything and least of all by Mum's obvious frustrations.

Mother and father were keen ballroom dancers and met at the Hippodrome and married in 1938. They made a very "handsome couple". My first home was at Elm Avenue in Hook near Tolworth and Kingston upon Thames. It was a comfortable redbrick semi with a big garden and open fields on one side. Dad was working as an engineer in Chessington and Mum was a seamstress. My first sister, Caroline, was born in 1942 and the second, Victoria, in 1945.

The Second World War was the background to my early years. One of my very first vivid memories was of Dad's rifle propped up in the corner of the kitchen and me crawling towards it. He was in the Home Guard. I remember the air raid shelter that Dad built in the garden. An Anderson shelter – the thing had grass turf on its roof and a big step up into it before you went underground. I remember that because one time, when the warning air raid siren went off, I was sitting on the lavatory. I jumped up and banged my head on the loo roll holder but rushed off with my trousers round my ankles to get to the safety of the garden shelter. Such was my hurry to get away from the Germans and, not helped by the flapping trousers, I tripped over the top step and fell headlong down into our back garden bunker.

It was scary with the bombs, especially the doodlebugs. You'd hear the distinctive droning engine and when it cut out there was an eerie silence for some long seconds before the big explosion as it indiscriminately hit the ground. The time between the engine's last splutter and the loud thump of the explosion was a lifetime. The closest one fell about three hundred yards away. We were lucky. It was, I remember, very frightening. I'd look up into the skies above us sometimes and see the dogfights and vapour trails as the fighters twisted and turned round each other. The planes looked like toys but it wasn't a game. Several came down in Chessington. Sometimes there were so many bombers in the air that you couldn't believe the numbers. They were impossible to count. We'd sit under the stairs during some air raids. I mean, how pointless was that? Under the stairs! I guess that if a doodlebug or another of the Nazi munitions was going to get you it didn't matter where you were.

At some stage I was evacuated to Middlesbrough but not for long. On the way back we were waiting on the platform of some station and a train came through full of American soldiers. They threw packs of Wrigley's chewing gum out of the windows for us kids.

Peace came at last and there was a great sense that something bad had ended. Dad took me up to town and we stood outside Buckingham Palace, me on his high shoulders, and joined the throng celebrating. Later there was a street party in Elm Avenue and we all danced for joy. What a relief, no more explosions or worried looks on the faces of my parents. No more cowering under the stairs with a crying sister or falling into the garden underground shelter. No more gas masks. No more blackouts and at last more smiles than worried frowns or real tears. The effect of peace on VE Day, 8th May 1945, was electrifying.

When I was five I started school at Tolworth Boys' School. Punishment seemed to figure prominently in my early education and the cane was the new weapon to be feared. When it found its target it hurt and I cried. Mum had one at home hanging on the pelmet as a reminder. On occasions she'd use it on the back of my legs when she thought I'd gone over the top, but the one at school was swung in front of the morning assembly or class, in public, presumably as an extra deterrent. The first time was because the art master wouldn't fire my clay model of a battleship in the kiln. He said it wasn't any good so I protested by breaking up the piece and several others. The second caning was for running across the road without looking. The traffic didn't get me but the cane certainly did. The third was for not being able to spell the word "off". I was called out to the front of the class to write the word on the blackboard and wrote "of". The master became frustrated and angry because I just didn't get it. I kept spelling "off" as "of". So as he went "off" to get the cane I ran "off" home before he could use it on my backside.

I wasn't academically bright. I was dyslexic which was something that no one recognised in those days. Like a lot of small boys I was more interested in keeping white mice as pets, bolting and building my Meccano and playing conkers. I was competitive and hardened mine up with vinegar or in Mum's cooker before the contest in the street or playground so that I had a better chance of winning.

Dad never hit me with a cane or anything else. We used to go to the pictures on a Saturday morning; Laurel and Hardy or Buster Keaton, black and white flicks in a church hall. During the war years he was an engineer. I used to watch him in the garden shed as he made cigarette lighters as a hobby. When the war ended he lost his job which came as quite a blow to him, especially as the owner was a great friend and the best man at his wedding. But after the war business dropped off and there was little that he could do. He looked for something different and found a small general store in Billericay. My grandmother's sister lived in Billericay and she suggested the move. Her son Fred Jackson was a carpenter and builder who took me out with him shooting rabbits and I experienced the first kick from a twelve-bore shotgun.

We moved there much to the disappointment of my mother. The store was a timber-built building clad in boarding with the shop at the front and our family accommodation behind. It sat on its own between two bridges that crossed the railway line right next to our new home. It had all the basics but an unplumbed-in galvanized bath was brought into the living area at bath time for me and my sisters aged five and two. This was not something we'd been used to. Mum was horrified that we lived in a home like that but I enjoyed it.

I remember the distinctive sound and smell of the steam trains passing under the bridges when the enveloping smoke would swirl around us like a blanket of thick, friendly fog. There was also a special smell from Dad's general store at the front of the building. He appeared to sell everything. Homemade ice lollies for one penny for the children on their way home from school and sweet confectionery, bread and buns, fruit and veg from the early morning market that Dad went to in his old Austin Seven, packets and tins of stuff and clothes pegs, dusters and dish mops. It was open all hours and the "old-fashioned" whiff of all on offer mixed with the smuts from the railway. Sweets in enormous bottomless glass jars, steam railway engines and a small boy aged seven was a union made in heaven.

I walked to school in Billericay. The best thing about school was joining the Sea Scouts and the worst was watching the newsreels they showed us. The piles of dead bodies being bulldozed in Auschwitz were unreal. We watched the jerky black and white pictures with mountains of matchstick people, emaciated and somehow no longer human. I was aghast. It gave me nightmares even though those newsreels were not as immediate as everyday life around me.

3. Bullies, Bottles and Burst Appendix

After about two years we moved from the general store in Billericay to a hardware shop in Ruislip. The shop, called Domestos Store, had a flat above it and this was the new family home for the five of us. Ruislip Lido wasn't far away and we used the outdoor swimming pool with typical British stoicism.

I walked the two hundred yards to the primary school in Ruislip every day where I learned a lot more than I did in Billericay or Tolworth. There was a stage in the large school hall and one day the comedian and singer, Tommy Trinder, came to talk to us. He was the first famous person I had seen up close and you remember your first encounter with "a star". My first brush with the school bullies was just as memorable. There were two of them in particular that used to have a go at me. They would trip me up, barge into me, hit me and generally try and make my life miserable. I told my dad and he said the best thing I could do was to fight back. So the next time they tried it on I turned on them and lashed out, hitting one of them rather hard. After that, they never bothered me again.

Grandma Fisher had given me my first bicycle and I'd cycle with friends out to see the aerodrome at Northolt or into the countryside. Once I threw a brick at a wasps nest and the swarm chased after me. With my short trousers there was not a lot of protection from the furious wasps but I made it home covered in stings and Mum took me to hospital.

After eighteen months of the Domestos Store, Dad had had enough of being a shopkeeper. He found a job in an arms factory near Greenford in Middlesex so we moved to a semi with a big garden at number 74 Millet Road, Greenford. I went to Greenford Secondary Modern for boys. The daily walk to school was now two miles but some of it was through the park. All boys at the school were expected to join the Air Training Corps and this was a real early excitement for me. I thought when I grew up I'd join the RAF as a flyer. I'd seen and heard the planes above us fighting the Luftwaffe and the new Hawker Hunter jet was the dream machine I wanted to fly. I wanted to be just like Biggles whose exploits I read about. But the most we did with the ATC was drill, drill and more drill.

I got my first taste of flying when Mum took me to Northolt one day. We sat in the airport café looking at the planes coming and going. She'd booked us a twenty minute flight in a de Havilland Dragon Rapide and Mum and I, with a dozen or so joyriding passengers, were taken up for a flight. It was way and afar the most exciting thing I'd ever done. The exhilaration of climbing aboard the biplane with its two propeller-driven engines took me almost to bursting point. I had my nose firmly pressed up against the window as we taxied along the runway. Then, throttling up noisily, the propellers spun to a blur and off we went. The struts between the wings trembled as much as I did as we circled over the airfield. The houses and fields below us looked like something out of a model shop and I definitely wanted to join the RAF as soon as they would have me.

The café at Northolt aerodrome became a regular haunt for me. I'd cycle out there on Sundays and pick up the empty bottles left on the tables and help to clear up the used cups and saucers. Each empty pop bottle was worth a halfpenny and some Sundays I'd get as much as five shillings from the refunds. After a week or two the café decided to offer me a summer job and my pay was two shillings and sixpence a day plus all the Lyons buns I could eat. This and being next to the working planes was a dream.

Dad changed his job again and moved from the arms factory into selling ice creams from a van on the surrounding estates. Uncle Lesley had started an ice cream round and Dad joined him. Aged ten I'd sometimes go out in the van and help scoop the ice cream from the tubs.

One day I woke with a pain in my side. I complained to Mum and she eventually took me to see the doctor. After a further visit he referred me to the hospital but there was apparently nothing to worry about. I was very uncomfortable and had to take some days off school but Mum thought that I was faking and trying to avoid going to school. The Eleven Plus exams were looming but I was in genuine pain. It got worse, so one morning she told me to go and see the doctor on my own. I did. The doctor took one look at me and told me to go straight home where an ambulance would pick me up and take me to hospital. I had a grumbling appendix. I got home and when the ambulance turned up Mum felt very guilty. My appendix had burst and I was kept in hospital for three weeks. If it hadn't been for penicillin, I most probably would have died.

The big country house convalescent home I was sent to after hospital was fun. It was full of children like me getting over whatever they had had done to them. There was a sheep, just one old ewe, in the paddock next to the house and it used to chase us when we played football. We used to encourage it of course and laugh loudly at the old thing as it set off after another goading child. Apparently the fleece from that ewe ended up as a jumper for Princess Margaret. I don't know why that stuck in my mind.

The convalescent home taught me my first lesson in not paying for goods until you've got them. I handed over two shillings for a guinea pig I wanted to take home with me. They said they'd send it on but it never ever arrived.

As a result of the time off school and my own lack of academic ability I failed the Eleven Plus exam and was put into the lowest stream, but by the time I left had moved up into the highest even though my mind wasn't really on the job and the teachers didn't engage me. They didn't try to make it fun. The music teacher was a serial beater and his use of the ruler on your bare hands a sadistic affair. The work didn't seem to relate to real life somehow. Algebra, what was all that about? Playing football, or trying to, was painful because of the stupid boots. They were so inflexible and despite ample coats of dubbin they still felt dreadfully uncomfortable.

The best bits about the secondary modern in Greenford were the woodwork classes, the badminton team and the school choir. We had spent hours rehearsing for Carmen and put on a performance but neither Mum nor Dad came to see it, which hurt me at the time. There was too the weekly ration of the ATC which I thought just might help me get into the RAF one day.

What I may have lacked in class work I more than made up for with my extracurricular activities. I became a trader. If anyone wanted the latest cigarette card or Marvel comic or the biggest brightest marble or a particular Dinky toy, then I was your man. I swapped my way to the biggest collection in the playground and became the twelve year old wheeler-dealer king. My over enthusiasm for a deal got me into trouble once when I persuaded a smaller boy to swap some bright new toy cars for something that was really not worth the transaction. The kid's father came round to see mine and the swap was quickly reversed.

Home life was fine. We had a television set and would gather as a family to look at the test card and watch the following black and white, crisp Queen's English spoken news. We always took meals together and Mum cooked while Dad smoked his pipe. We didn't go to church on Sundays although we did do Sunday school for a while. The Father, Son and Holy Ghost meant less to me than my three uncles, Lesley, Alex and Peter. The two older brothers had started a caravan business in Chertsey after the war with their demob money. Called Fisher Caravans, they were building the first touring vans to sell at under £100. I'd visit their works at weekends and in my holidays, driven by Uncle Peter who lived near us. It was simply wonderful to be let loose in my uncles' business. I'd be given tasks, proper jobs, to do. Armed with screwdriver or spanner, saw or chisel, I'd be set to work finishing off some detail or other to the caravan. I was important. I knew what I was doing. I took pride in it. I could see the end result. There was a meaning to it. I was patted on the back for a job well done. It was something I could do and do well. And best of all I got some pocket money for doing it.

4. Wood, Rock and Stone

I must have been about fourteen when I realised that I didn't have the intellect needed to get me into the cockpit of an RAF plane. Sadly I would never do what the "Brylcreem Boys" had done in the skies above me at the Battle of Britain. It was my uncles, and Uncle Peter in particular, who had shown me the path to another career. My new goal was to emulate the opportunities that were there to be had and the idea to run my own business became an obsession. I wanted to be the master of my own destiny. Good or bad.

For some of the time Uncle Peter worked for his two older brothers, Alex, who'd been a mechanic in the RAF and Les, who'd collected some shrapnel while on the beaches at Dunkirk. Peter was the black sheep of the family and I remember that he used to "borrow" equipment from his brothers' workshop to complete the project he was working on behind their backs. Tools and axles for caravans would disappear from Fisher's Caravans and reappear at Uncle Peter's yard at Weybridge not far from Addlestone, where he lived with his wife Peggy. I don't know if his brothers knew what he was up to but I suspect that they did and that rows raged from time to time.

Uncle Peter was the most remarkable craftsman and engineer. He was so adaptable and could design something on the back of a fag packet which when built would run like clockwork. Not unsurprisingly his projects included caravans. He added motor and sailing boats, substantial houseboats for use on the Thames and battery chicken coups for which he devised a production line, eventually selling the rights to his design to his brothers for half a penny a go. This upset the big manufacturers who were making the batteries and they eventually bought out the designs. He put together a production line for garden sheds and mass-produced a range of doll's houses. He also designed and built an aeroplane. Once when I visited his works he opened some double garage doors behind which were stacked wrought iron tables, from floor to ceiling, and for which he still hadn't found a buyer. He wasn't a businessman like his brothers but when it came to making things he could create and make jigs and set up a smooth running production line in no time. I admired his work ethic. He didn't hang about and got things done even if he did get into trouble sometimes with the family, his finances and his women.

With Uncle Peter behind the wheel and me riding shotgun, we'd often deliver the Fisher caravans to their new homes. He'd drive like the wind and once the caravan being towed behind started to snake. Gently at first so as not to cause too much irritation, the swaying from side to side quickly became rather too violent. Despite my warning shouts and Uncle Peter's efforts at braking, the inevitable jack-knife occurred and we snapped to a sudden and ungainly halt spread right across the carriageway like an impromptu and rocking road block, shaken but not stirred that much. He set about decoupling the caravan, righting it, jacking up the bent wheel and cobbling together a spare wheel so that we could continue on our way. He was reckless but he was Uncle Peter and the man who, more than any other, impressed me at that time and was my role model. Dad had got me a new puppy, a sheepdog cross, and I called it Peter. That's how impressed I was by my uncle.

When I was fifteen, our family moved again but this time to the South Coast. We'd spent some summer holidays there in a caravan we'd rented when we lived in Greenford. Dad had moved back into engineering with de Havilland in Christchurch and we bought a detached house in New Milton. It was in Manor Road and had a garden with a greenhouse and orchard. I honed my skill and accuracy with an airgun on the unsuspecting birds that perched there. I went to a new school at Arnewood in New Milton but only for a fortnight. The talk there was mostly about hay and cows or Cowes and farming and I had nothing in common with any other boy there, so I left.

My first job was with New Milton Timber Company in their machine shop in Old Milton which made the beech wooden trays for Lyons cakes, the same ones I'd enjoyed back at the Northolt café. I was paid one pound a week and spent most of the time sweeping up. Needless to say I was there for less than six months.

My second job was with a caravan company, Green Pennant Caravans in Christchurch. I knew all about caravans, or thought I did, from the time spent with my uncles and so this seemed a natural job for me. I was paid thirty shillings a week for five and a half days' work and I gave Mum ten shillings a week for board and lodgings. I cycled every day from New Milton to Christchurch and back again, a sixteen mile round trip. The job involved fitting gas lamps and pipes to the caravans and some days I was the delivery driver's mate. But I was always asking, "What shall I do next?" There never seemed to be enough work to fill the days. One Saturday morning I didn't go in and the following Monday I was fired. I lasted about six months in that job.

It was Mum who took me along to the interview with Mr Briggs the owner of FJ Pearce and Co., general builders in Lymington. She'd seen an advertisement in the local paper for an apprenticeship. It was for five years, learning to be a competent carpenter and joiner. Mr Briggs showed me the workshop and straight away I felt at home. This was just what I wanted and my obvious enthusiasm must have impressed Mr Briggs. I became the new apprentice much to Mum's delight and started right away.

Dad helped me to buy my own set of tools and I soon got used to cycling the ten miles each way with a bag of them slung over the handlebars in the rain and on those hot sunny days. I spent hours in the workshop with two other guys. Mr Tora was a craftsman and used to teach woodwork at the Community Centre in his spare time. He was very helpful and gave me instruction on the machines. He was very kind and a good teacher even though he removed the best part of his hand in the plane machine while I looked on. There was blood and sawdust everywhere.

Some days I was instructed to go out on site doing things like repairing sash windows. I did that at Dennis Wheatley's house. Wheatley's books were selling over a million copies a year and he was a world-renowned author. His was a grand house behind curved old redbrick walls and it overlooked the sea. He was in a vast sombrero laying bricks for the walls in his vegetable garden, just for fun like Winston Churchill used to do. Later on I collected buckets full of gull's eggs from Lymington marshes for him. He took them up to a London restaurant, presumably for the chef to cook for him and his chums.

I was expected to attend the Technical College in Bournemouth for three nights a week and one full day. I travelled on a bus for an hour and a quarter each way and worked out that I was travelling for about forty working days a year which, over five years, was nearly a whole year of non-productive time. I did, however, learn more in the skills and systems there than anywhere else and became a keen pupil. I loved the technical drawing and I was taught geometry and how that related to building construction. What a difference it was to the teaching I'd had at school! What I was doing had meaning, had a use and I embraced this new opportunity with enthusiasm. The tutor spoke to the class carpenters once and said that over 50 per cent of us would go on to have our own business. I was very pleased with that remark and he was proved to be right.

One day some of the other students returned from lunch to announce that the army call up had been dropped by the government. What a relief it was. I was dreading going into the army for two years of National Service. I just missed call up and had I been three months older would probably have spent my time doing square bashing in Germany. Many of my mates did. The possibility of being called up meant that I might have wasted two years before I could go into business which was my new overriding goal.

Most of my fellow students couldn't wait to go home after tuition but I stayed on to colour and enhance my drawings, get them absolutely right and try and make sure of a first class pass in subsequent exams. Actually there was another apprentice at the same firm although he went to study at Southampton. He was the pet so I was a little jealous of him. When, after my extra efforts, I received a first class pass Mr Briggs, my boss, gave me a penny an hour pay rise. The other apprentice didn't get anything. Yes! I thought punching the air. A penny an hour more than him!

There is nothing finer, no nicer feeling than creating things. Most of it was hand work and one day we'd be repairing kitchen cupboards, the next making pews for Wallhampton school; one minute Dennis Wheatley's windows the next Mrs Smith's kitchen drawers or shelves for the local pubs. I was learning a trade, becoming skilled at something I enjoyed. I was a teenager and a paid apprentice and doing alright.

When I was seventeen, the family moved to Lymington which was great for me in two respects. One, the family home was nearer to my work and two, Dad had become the landlord of The Bugle Hotel and that was our new home. I had never drunk beer before and wasn't about to start. Once I had overdone it on rum and coke and had been as sick as a dog so apart from the odd gin and tonic I wasn't really a drinker. I had, however, become interested in girls and music. It was Elvis and the Everly Brothers on the radio and as often as not classical seventy-eights on the hire-purchased record player. I bought a six string Spanish guitar and frequented the local young place to be seen, the café Snappy Snacs, and tried to perfect the chords from the teach yourself guitar book by Bert Weedon.

Acoustic soon gave way to electric and the sound of me practising on my Höfner guitar and Vox amplifier in the roof space over the garage behind the pub would not have been pretty. Soon a band was formed. Brian Pink was my brother-in-law, married to my sister

Caroline, and he played bass. Mike Johnson was the singer and Gordon the drummer gave us the four we needed. The Blue Cats Skiffle Group was the name of our band and we were going to rip up the town.

For £5 a night we played at the Boldre Working Men's Club, Pilley "across the water" in Lymington and at other pubs that would have us. We covered Bill Haley's records with our amplifier set in an orange box and a big "old-fashioned" microphone. Brian's brother Norman joined us with a double bass and our reputation, good and bad, spread locally. We sometimes played at The Bugle, Dad's pub, but he always tried to turn the volume down. We were having fun, making music, pulling the birds and behaving like local "pop stars". Our biggest night was playing at the Lymington Regatta in a stand built on the car park. We also played the Waverley Cinema in New Milton which turned out, some years later, to be somewhat ironic. I started to make wooden guitars by hand from a mould that I'd designed, however after just four Spanish acoustic models realised I was not going to make sufficient money to make it worthwhile, so I dropped the idea.

There was one particular girl from Christchurch, a nurse with a good voice. I chatted her up and she became my girlfriend. Her name was Frankie. She sang with us for a while and we had fun making music together as Frankie and Johnnie. We were so cool!

Once we went to Bournemouth to make a record. We played Rock Island Line made famous by Lonnie Donegan one of our favourites and emerged from the studio session with a handful of black seventy-eight records we'd paid for. We felt like we'd just recorded a number one chart-topping disc. Three of us went up to London to the Two Eyes Café in Soho one evening. We'd arranged an audition at the café which was a hotbed of creative musical talent. It was where Tommy Steele had apparently been discovered so we thought, "Look out, we're the next big thing." We performed and the guy in the suit said to us that he hoped we all had other jobs to go to.

I was getting more into modern jazz, Barney Kessel and Django Reinhardt. I'd started to play with a good pianist and a drummer who had fits from time to time. He was great when he wasn't having fits. There was a rhythm guitar player too and we formed a band called the Johnnie Mac Four and played pubs and clubs from Lymington to Bournemouth.

One morning at the Pearce workshop I was asked by Mr Briggs to go to the Berthon Boat Company where we were doing a job on the roof. I was going to work with another chippy from the firm, someone who had just qualified and who was a year older than me. His name was Bill Stone.

Bill was a tall good-looking fellow. He had black hair and a moustache to match. His wife Janet was very attractive and the couple lived in a council house in Lymington. The two of us hit it off rather well and while we worked I talked about my uncles and their caravan business. It wouldn't be difficult, I thought, for us to build our own caravan and sell it. Bill had a motorbike and the two of us went up on the machine to Chertsey to visit Fisher's Caravans and my uncles. We came away convinced that we too could have a go at making one. It couldn't be that difficult for a couple of guys with the skills we had, could it? We looked at some magazines from America where mobile homes were big business. We drew up designs on the back of envelopes. We thought about the idea and then thought about the reality. How would we pay for it? Where would we make it? How would we sell it?

We went to see the manager at Barclays Bank in Lymington for a loan of £100. The answer, the first of many, was a straightforward, "No". The bank suggested that my dad might like to act as a guarantor but he too said, "No". He didn't do guarantees. After much badgering and pleading from me, my father lent me £40 and Bill Stone did likewise so we had the working capital we needed to get us going. Mobile Homes Construction was born.

A local smallholder we knew, Mr Akeman, had some unused buildings, old piggeries and cow stalls, and we rented them from him. The first job we did was to build a circular saw on site and then we set about making our first mobile home. The caravan was big, not really suitable for towing behind a car but rather one of those mobile homes that need a permanent site. It had a walk-on balcony at one end and slept four with ease, with a kitchenette and a loo. We got the chassis from my uncles and built the rest from wood and aluminium. The interior was finished in oak ply and matt varnish with the outside handpainted two-tone, blue and white. The whole job took us about two months, working evenings and weekends.

There was a petrol station with a large forecourt called Fox Pond Garage near Lymington and we asked the owner if we could park the mobile home there with a "For Sale" sign on it. We were hoping for £400 or even £500 for our efforts. Of course, what the mobile home lacked was a site to put it on. No site meant no sale and the "beast" sat on the forecourt going nowhere.

The local paper saw the "For Sale" sign and decided to write a piece about Mobile Homes Construction. The interview, which appeared in the *Lymington Times*, didn't attract any sales leads but it did grab the attention of Mr Briggs, my employer. I was called into his office on the Monday morning after the article had appeared and he told me that there was only room for one businessman in this company and that was going to be him. I was sacked. I was less than three months away from completing my five-year apprenticeship.

5. Cars, Construction and McCarthy & Stone

The fact that Mr Briggs had decided to get rid of me wasn't really a major blow. He didn't fire Bill Stone, who was mentioned in the same newspaper article, so I guess that Bill was more useful to him or I was given the boot as the ringleader. To give him his due, Mr Briggs did ring me later to say that he would arrange for me to finish my apprenticeship with my next employer. I told him not to bother as I was now underway in my own business. I was already doing work on the side for other builders apart from the moonlighting for our own Mobile Homes Construction. The "beast" we'd built was low loaded off to Uncle Peter's yard near Addlestone. He'd sold it to a friend of his who had a site to park the mobile home on. Actually, Uncle Peter was probably less concerned with his friend's parking site than the space next to his friend's wife. Nevertheless it helped the deal. Bill and I didn't get what we wanted for the mobile home but made enough to pay back our fathers and clear our costs. We started to build a smaller towing van but ran out of cash so the whole idea was knocked on the head. If a project isn't going to work, knock it on the head early. It was good advice then and good advice for later.

George Dunford was the landlord of The Chequers Inn in Lymington. He was a publican and a jobbing builder and I'd helped him out most mornings before going to my full-time job with Mr Briggs. I would arrive at the site at 5am, fix the work from the night before and then go off to my full-time employer in time for the 8am start. It was cash in hand for me and helped me pay for the cars I tried to keep on the road. My first was an Austin Ten for £5. The big ends had gone but I repaired them. The second was a red MG with a soft top, long bonnet and oak chassis. The local garage got it ready for me but before I could collect it the paperwork from the previous hire-purchase agreement caught up with it and the car was repossessed. The law did change but not before I lost my hard-earned £35, and the garage took pity on me as it was partly their fault so they invited me to choose something else off the forecourt. I plumped for a Ford Escort van, something I could get my tools into, the guitar and amp and, of course, a mattress so the equipment wouldn't get damaged!

George Dunford offered me contract work and I helped him out with home extensions and the like for six months or so. I still saw Bill Stone socially and he, his wife Janet, me and one of my girlfriends would all go out together frequenting the bars and cafés in Bournemouth. The world of R&B was all very well but it didn't pay any bills and I found myself thinking more about work and less about play. Then I met Gwen.

I met Gwen at the converted police station in Lymington. She was a waitress in the restaurant that had sprung up in the old cop shop. She had the shortest mini skirt and the best legs in town and she couldn't believe that every Thursday night when I turned up I'd order a well done steak. I plucked up courage to ask her out and we went for a drink at The Ship on the quayside in Lymington. She was only sixteen and her father was a dentist. Sadly he didn't like me from the start. I didn't dress like a teddy boy but I wasn't conventional either. I used to wear one green sock and the other orange. It was a "hip" thing to do and Gwen liked it even if her parents didn't. Her father probably thought that his daughter should not have anything to do with a bloke that turned up in a three ton tipper truck to take her on a date. We'd go out on the promise that she'd be home by 10pm latest. The clock at Highcliffe would often show us that we were already late and the 10 o'clock deadline was rarely adhered to. She had a terrible row with her

father one day. It had been brewing up for some tim
home aged seventeen and rented a bedsit in Lymingto
in a café. Having got her independence it was then th
thought that I was wasting my time and Gwen was gett
my persistent one-track interest in her young female cha
off for Switzerland and became a nanny to a banking fan
wasn't to be that.

Bill Stone followed me from Mr Briggs' clutches after a
months and we started working as subcontractors togethe
1961, January 1st. I was twenty-one years old and determined
a go of it as a subcontractor. I hung up the guitar and put awa
blue suede shoes. Bill was twenty-two.

We had little work, two small jobs, and had to go to Hythe w
they were building council houses to pick up jobs. We kept a little
book that listed all our income on one side and our outgoings on t
other. The toll bridge over the river at Lymington was a halfpenny
time and Bill and I used to argue about how much each of us was
claiming for the crossings. We met up every Friday evening to balance
the book and nine times out of ten we'd end up in heated discussions.
From then until 1971, for ten years, we paid ourselves £8 a week in
cash according to that little red book. As far as I was concerned we had
to do everything to conserve cash for the business if we were to build
it up.

If only all we'd had to argue about was halfpenny toll fees. One
Easter time there was a roof that needed putting on a bungalow with
timber gable ends and boarded soffits. "I'm off on holiday," said Bill,
so I was left to do the job on my own. I did the whole thing, cut the
wood and erected the timbers. It took me five days and when I'd done
it I went to the guy for my money. "You haven't done the double garage
roof," was the response. The whole job was worth £45 and the guy
kept back £15 for the garage roof. The next day we put that on for him
but never got the money because he went bust. That taught me a lesson.
Six days work for £30. That didn't seem right or fair somehow. As

ontractors we really struggled with some silly jobs at silly prices.
were expected to do the second fixings, the doors and skirting
rds for peanuts. We were getting all the rubbish and Bill couldn't
that there was any future and he grumbled about the lack of
portunities. I was the optimist. If Bill said "No", I'd say, "Yes". But
ould see that we needed to move up the food chain. We needed to be
e contractors not the bloody subbies.

I heard that George Dunford had quoted a farmer for the building
of a bungalow in Pilley. We went in for the job and tendered at a price
of £1,400. We were expected to build a three-bedroomed bungalow
with a garage from scratch on a green field site. We discovered later
that George Dunford's quote had been for £3,200 so it was no surprise
we won the contract. I had little idea how to estimate a job and had no
experience of costing so £1,400 was more of a guesstimate, a finger in
the air exercise rather than anything more precise.

We set to and took on Bill Stone's brother-in-law, Paddy Matcham,
who was a jack-of-all-trades. He could lay bricks and plaster walls and
the three of us put up the bungalow in five or six months with some
other small jobs running alongside. When we'd nearly finished the job
the farmer complained about the garage doors. He didn't want to pay
his bill or was acting like a tight farmer. We'd fitted the ones he had
specified and we were in no mood to argue with him. A local estate
agent, Donald Blatchley, was asked to come in and act as a mediator.
"You've ripped these guys off," he said to the farmer who then
reluctantly paid up. We made less than £100 profit on the job but it
kept us in work, kept us afloat.

Our office was still in Mr Akeman's piggeries and cow stalls, the
place where we'd built our ill-fated mobile home. I was beginning to
realise that in the contracting business the money was made in the office
every bit as much as it was made on site. We ticked over with various
projects and in 1963 our bookkeeper, Mr Watson, a fellow who used
to collect butterflies, suggested that we form a limited company. Our
annual turnover was about £7,000 and he thought that it would be

"expedient". McCarthy & Stone Limited was duly registered with Bill and me as equal shareholders. The economy was OK with low interest rates and a forecast that 400,000 new homes should be built in Britain each year. We got a board made up with McStone emblazoned on it. This was the new trading name for the two of us.

One day Mr Akeman came to see us to tell us he'd received planning permission for the site we were occupying and he wanted to develop it so could we please move? I sensed that we could make something out of this situation. Why could we not take on the whole project? We offered to buy the site. Have you got the money asked Mr Akeman without telling us the price? But Mr Brown, the manager at Barclays in Lymington, said, "No". I worked out a deal that would give Mr Akeman £740 per plot on the seven buildings approved. He'd have to accept the money for each one once we'd built and sold them. Our £740 offer was better than the £500 he could expect for a straight sale but there was a risk attached: we might not be able to pay him.

Mr Akeman agreed to our terms and Barclays agreed to a £500 overdraft with our personal guarantees for working capital and off we went building one property at a time. The bank manager, Mr Brown, visited the site one Sunday morning while I was painting. I remember his remark: "You shouldn't run before you can walk." Many years later when we floated the company I wrote to him and said, "We are no longer running. We are at full gallop."

We started on the bungalows, architect-designed and properly costed, and we sold the first one for £3,500 to a painter who worked with me at Mr Briggs'. Cheekily I used to say to him when I was an apprentice, "Watch what you say to your future employer!" Little did I think that he'd be our first customer for a bungalow. The deal with Mr Akeman went like clockwork and just before we finished the last house, the land next door came up with planning permission for fifty-five homes.

Bill and I went out and bought brand new Ford Zephyr 4s. Mine was cream and Bill's was green. Being self-employed was not straightforward and balancing the books not an easy task. One day we had a visit from the bailiffs and nearly had the cars repossessed by the hire-purchase company. I had to rustle up some cash to stave off the heavies. If it wasn't the bailiffs after the cars it was the narrow lanes between Lymington and New Milton.

Once I was racing a few friends back from a pub outing in Burley. We were heading for some skinny-dipping on Milford beach. We didn't overdo the drink but neither did we worry too much about the consequences of drinking and driving. I had Tim Ham, a close friend, and his girlfriend Heather in the front on the bench seat with me and we sailed round a bend to see a friend's car slewed across the road in our way. I swung the wheel violently and ducked off the road, narrowly avoiding a telegraph pole, but clipping the kerb which flipped the car into a roll, ending on its side in the middle of the road. I was flung out without a scratch. Tim was still in the car and trying to kick out the windscreen. I went and opened the available door for him and pulled him and his girlfriend out. We then got the car back on its feet and pushed it out of the way just as a motorcyclist came haring round the narrow bend at such speed that had we not moved the car he would have hit it full on and probably died as a result. Next day I found my little-used guitar in a nearby hedge. Like me it had been thrown clear from the Zephyr without any harm. With every panel on the car bashed and dented and the roof pressed down so far that it nearly touched the steering wheel, I nevertheless drove it back to the suppliers in Surrey. The wheels were so out of line that by the end of the journey the tyres were completely bald. Unbelievably, they repaired it.

We really wanted to get hold of the Buckland Park project, as we called it. We knew the vendor and had done a bit of work for him before. He had outline planning permission but the access to the site from Ellery Road was difficult and the council had him over a barrel. He had to pay £15,000 over the top for the "ransom strip" which gave access to his land and this was fairly common practice. If the council could screw you, they would. The new access, however, meant that we could build another bungalow on the Akeman site, one we hadn't planned for originally, so it was a bonus for us. Once again we went cap in hand to Mr Brown at Barclays. The answer was again, "No". This project demanded more serious investment and we turned to the financial magazines. We found an investment adviser who put us in touch with a merchant bank, an offshoot of Julian Hodge, the Welsh Bank. We were looking for £80,000; £50,000 for the site and construction of roads, drains and houses and £30,000 as working capital. The investors came to see us and looked at what we'd done on the adjoining site. We got the money at 12 per cent p.a. over three years. I'd done my sums and as they lent on 100 per cent value of the land and 70 per cent of the building costs, I made sure that the building costs would cover the lot. I inflated them to ensure that we had 100 per cent of the total we needed. This of course was helped by Bill and I doing a lot of the work on site ourselves. The lenders did not seem to have any idea of costs. It was also a matter of timing between the work being done and the receipt of payment from the backers. We agreed a price for each stage of the building, like the foundations, superstructure, roof, plastering and second fixings such as the doors, kitchens and bathrooms. The final completion was therefore fixed at a price before we'd started and once the job was done then payment was made. The same deal applied to the road works and drainage. We'd got the backing we needed. The McStone sign went up on the site in Lower Buckland Road and off we went.

We'd watch every penny with the sort of care a lioness has for her cubs. Sometimes the cut and thrust of doing the deal reminded me of that small kid in the playground at Greenford, the one who'd swapped his prize Dinky toys for not a lot in return. I nailed one local sparky and his mate to wire up a complete bungalow for £47. The poor buggers wouldn't have made a penny out of that. Maybe I was being too hard though. It was no good frightening off good people and no good upsetting those you loved either.

In our temporary wooden office that Bill and I had built at the Buckland Park site I borrowed a typewriter from Dad so the temp we took on could do our letters for us. There was lots of paperwork with detailed planning permission applications going backwards and forwards between us and the council and us and the architects. I can't remember why but Dad and I were going through a rough patch, probably something to do with the black sheep of the family, Uncle Peter. Anyhow Dad asked for the typewriter back. I said, "No" but he came and took it when we weren't around. I reported the theft to the local police and told them that I thought I knew who had done it. The machine was returned but my dad didn't speak to me for months. It was a bloody silly thing for me to do and I couldn't blame him really. I thought business was business and sod personal relationships. How wrong I was. It was something I very much regret, a heat of the moment, knee-jerk bad decision on my part. It did, I think, help the learning curve going forward. It was a vital lesson in understanding when to button it and how to engage the brain before opening the mouth.

There was one occasion when, even after twenty-four hours of reflection, I still spoke my mind. Tim Ham was an electrician doing a bit of subcontracting for us and someone we'd socialise with after work sometimes. He told me that he'd been to see his bank manager and told him he was doing some work for McStone. The manager said to him, "If you're working for the Skiffle King of Lymington you'd better be careful." I double-checked the story with Tim and its implication and then made an appointment to go and see the manager of the Midland Bank in Lymington. I'd also heard that he was keen to take on our business so I waited in reception like any prospective customer and was eventually called into his office. He asked me to sit but I stood in front of his desk and leant over it.

"If I hear one more word from anyone that you are badmouthing me I'll knock your bloody block off." I was still a little cross.

The manager grabbed the phone and before he could use it I swept it off his desk and on to the floor, turned and walked out.

I never heard another word from the bank or that manager again.

I'd be dressed in a Burton suit one minute and in my working overalls the next. The pinstripes for the bankers, architects and estate agents and the dirty overalls for the lorry-load from the London Brick Company that needed to be unloaded and stacked. We employed half-a-dozen workers including Paddy Matcham and Frank Totterdal and we took on the son of the guitarist from the old group, Mike Base, as an apprentice carpenter. I would still roll up my sleeves and get stuck in alongside them laying Tarmac or pouring concrete. We'd invested in some machinery too, a couple of tipper trucks and an Allis Chalmers tracked digger to dig the drains and excavate the foundations. On Sundays I would go down to the site on my own and bulldoze the roads and accesses and inevitably finish the day with the machine bogged down and stuck in the mud. The guys could always tell I'd been using it.

The Buckland Park project took about three years to complete, with two-thirds two-bedroomed bungalows and a third three-bedroomed houses. The price for a house was under £5,000 and a bungalow about £3,000. I'd meet up with our estate agents, Donald Blatchley and Jerry Clark, from Hewitt and Co. every day to see how they were getting on with sales. Financing the job was easy with the way I'd planned it and we built the properties in batches, watching the costs at all times. We used concrete blocks with render rather than bricks when they weren't on show, and our gable ends were single-skinned concrete block walls, something that today would not get approval. We complied fully with all the building regulations but cut costs to the bone. We were determined to make money.

It was a big blow when in 1967 our merchant bank, as they were called, went bust. It was a bigger blow when the liquidator tried to consolidate the bank's losses by lumping our debt in with lots of others. I argued strongly and he agreed to finance the completion of the development but that any surplus cash would remain on deposit to be paid to us at the end of the job. By 1969/70 we had completed the development and sold all the units, however, the liquidator went back on his word and decided not to pay us. We decided to sue but had to prove that we were in possession of the site before we had signed the contract agreement and payment of the first money from the bankrupt bank. I looked through all the invoices and found one from the London Brick Company proving that three loads had been delivered and unloaded on site. If they had inspected the site as they claimed, they could not have failed to see the stacks of bricks which should have put them on notice. The Chancery Division of the High Court heard the case in 1971 and we won on the basis that we were in possession of the site and that the bankers should have known this. The decision created case law. There was £35,000 on deposit which came as a welcome boost to our finances.

6. Sons, Separation, Gabbie and Gwen

President Kennedy was shot in November 1963, the same year I met Eileen. I was twenty-four and she was twenty-one. I was mostly working with very little time for play but one evening I met her at a dance in Fawley, near Southampton. One thing led to another and Eileen became pregnant. We got married in 1964 even though my dad warned me against it. Mum didn't say a word. The ceremony was at a church in Pennington, near Lymington and my best man, Tim Ham, delivered his warm-hearted speech to the forty or so guests. My uncles were there to see me on my way and a jolly time was had by all. When the family got together we did have fun and even Mum enjoyed more than a glass of sherry and her usual Babycham.

I bought a condemned house in Buckland Road not far from the building site. I paid £900 for it. It was a two up, two down affair with an outside loo and no bathroom. Even though this was my first move away from home, I had to return to The Bugle if I wanted a bath. The house was right on the roadside and if you opened the front door to step out you'd have to look out for the passing traffic.

The guy who sold me the condemned home, Walter Symons, was on the local council and he sat on the planning committee in Lymington which was to prove very helpful. Despite all the stories that are bandied about concerning planners and the talk of backhanders in brown envelopes, I never encountered anything like that from Walter Symons, or any other councillor. He was as straight as a die and seemed genuinely keen to help out a pair of young, hard-working, local builders.

My first son, Clinton, was born six months after we were married and we really had to move to somewhere more suitable for a young family. I bought a plot of land in Pennington on the main road and built Orchard House, a three-bedroomed, detached home for us to live in. It was not without problems and the next-door neighbour insisted that the foundations we were digging out one Saturday morning were too close to the boundary. I told him he was wrong and that we were pouring the concrete that morning. The police and the local authority arrived after we had started pouring the concrete. I threw my hat into the mix in exasperation and told the driver of the pre-mix lorry to continue to pour out his load. I said to the officials that if I was proved wrong then we would dig out the concrete. We were later proved right but we had fallen out with our neighbour.

Shortly after I caught the local news on the TV about a homeless family who had arrived back in Britain and were finding it difficult to get a roof over their heads. I offered them the condemned house in Buckland Road. It had been good enough for me. We agreed a rent of £4 a month and then they went to the rent tribunal to get it reduced to £1 a month. That dented my belief in human kindness. When they moved out I sold the place for £3,000.

My hasty but well-intentioned marriage to Eileen was hitting rocky ground. We'd had three boys in four years; Clinton was followed by Spencer and Scott. Eileen could not have found it easy to be a new mother to three babies in such quick succession. My full-on working life building my business didn't help either. My father's words of warning about the relationship hit home on New Year's Eve, my birthday, in 1968. I had been to see Mum and Dad at the pub and arrived back home to a major row, the inevitable culmination of our increasingly ugly relationship. I couldn't believe what Eileen was telling me anymore and any respect we had for each other had evaporated. I walked out and went back to The Bugle for the night. I was very depressed and close to a breakdown. I just had to get away.

The next day I moved to London and rented a room from my friend John Colwell in the house he'd inherited in Edgware. John was a surveyor for Taylor Woodrow. I had got to know him because he was the boyfriend of Gwen's girl friend Jane and we used to drink together in The Angel in Lymington High Street. I guess that I'd never forgotten about Gwen and our earlier relationship. I had been living in the bedsit in Edgware for about three months when I met Tim Ham who told me that Gwen had returned from Switzerland and was working in London. The news was music to my ears. I was determined to catch up with her again. I really wanted to. I needed to get a life back and just the thought of meeting Gwen, the girl I had lost and the girl I was immeasurably in love with without knowing it, gave my life new purpose. How had I been so stupid in the past and allowed myself to get into a relationship on the rebound with the wife I was now divorcing?

My next-door neighbour at Standsmore in London was a lawyer. Gabriel Moss, Gabbie to those that knew him, specialised in divorce so I took him on. His advice to pay a lump sum with accommodation for my ex-wife and family as a settlement seemed sensible. It did take thirteen years to reach an agreement though.

Fighting on three fronts stretches the resource but strengthens the resolve. Divorce, banks and new developments were all demanding but I set about handling all three with equal zeal from the company's office, Newcourt House. We'd built the office in New Street in Lymington in 1968 after complaints the secretary made about walking through the mud on site to the timber cabin I had built as our first office. We took the top floor of the building renting out the two below us. From here I was able to develop my architectural skills and planned further developments in New Milton, Christchurch and Sommerford. From here I spoke to Gabbie about my ex-wife and from here I planned my new life with Gwen.

Gwen had been working at the American Forces Hotel and Club in London, became pregnant and been left in the lurch. She had reluctantly decided to have the baby and put it up for adoption. Gwen had a job but her parents had disowned her. I reappeared on the scene, Gwen had her baby in London and I was at her bedside with a bottle of bubbly acting like the father. We both agreed that we'd get back together. I was not that well off, what with the bank in trouble, a problem with the company not being able to obtain its investment deposit and the divorce. After the birth of her son we travelled to Weymouth where the baby boy was adopted as planned. It was a day in November 1968, the day of the adoption and the first time Gwen met my parents. I told them that she was just a friend. I moved back to the South after six months of living in a bedsit in London and I bought into one of the company's developments of one-bedroomed flats at the Hamilton Court development in Milford on Sea. Gwen joined me later.

Eileen and the boys lived in a large Victorian house I had acquired but it caught fire and was badly damaged. She then moved into one of the flats we had built at the original house in Grosvenor Mews on Lymington Road. I later bought my sister's house in Broad Lane, Lymington and they moved there. The boys visited Gwen and me regularly so our relationship was out in the open but Eileen's antics didn't make life easy for any of us.

Despite Gabbie's help and advice my divorce took a very long time to sort out. Eileen was forever changing her mind and her lawyers so the process would stop and start all over again. It took thirteen years until the final deal was struck between me and Eileen's solicitors in the corridors of the High Court in London. In 1979 when we were due to finally face each other a message came from the other end of the corridor and once again she asked for more. I'd had enough. I marched down and confronted her legal team. I started to take my shirt off telling them that enough was enough.

"You may as well have the shirt off my back," I said in frustration, "There's nothing else left." We settled and I gave her a big detached house in Pennington, £40,000 as a lump sum plus a monthly payment for the children. That, at last, was that.

Although getting involved with Eileen had been one of the most unfortunate decisions of my life, we did have three wonderful sons. Meeting Gwen and getting back with her again had been one of the best decisions I'd ever made.

7. Sites, Suites and Sheer Hard Work

We couldn't let the grass grow under our feet and had pushed on with other new developments. In late 1968 I bought a strip of land from three people in Church Lane in Lymington. There was plenty of room to build six bungalows. The land had covenants which allowed for only four. Dennis Wheatley had the benefit of the covenants and as I knew him I approached him to release them for a consideration so that we could build the two extra bungalows we wanted. The other owners went mad and tried to insist that we paid them more than what had been already agreed. We hadn't signed contracts but they were under a time constraint over their agreement with Dennis who had already agreed the deal with us for the extra two units. We would not agree to their request. I remember the local estate agent, Tony Elliot, saying that we'd get a bad name locally if we didn't offer more money. It didn't worry me. I was spending more time away in London and was in fighting mode with the divorce on my hands too. Perhaps I was a little over the top but that was the business we were in; we had seen the opportunity and were not prepared to share the spoils. Why should we increase the purchase price? Perhaps their advisers had not given their full attention to the opportunities that we had seen. Anyhow, the contract was duly signed at the original price.

It was at about this time, the Summer of Love, that aged twenty-nine I realised I was a millionaire. I'd looked at our assets versus our liabilities and on paper anyway I'd made the money. It was the sort of calculation that I'd do every now and then, like counting the pennies in the money box when I was a child. I was on the road I'd planned and nothing was going to stop me. I'd ticked off two ambitions. The first was to make a million before I was thirty, the second was to buy the new E-Type that Bill and I used to drive past on its revolving stand in the car showroom in the Square at Bournemouth when the two of us used to go there for coffee in our vans. I was now the proud owner of the twelve litre red E-Type Jaguar with a soft top. It leaked like a sieve and I had to drill some holes in the footwell but I put up with that because the car was great for the girls. An E-Type turned their heads. I bought it for £1,500 and sold it for the same price five years later.

We had several sites on the go: Highcliffe, New Milton, and Walkford Park which was a disused gravel quarry site I bought from a Bournemouth car dealer. I attended a meeting at his house with lawyers to finalise an agreement that had been dragging on for months. I was learning that most car dealers and farmers wanted their pound of flesh. After about two hours of haggling I decided to leave so I got up and walked out to my car. I was sitting in it talking to my lawyer about the frustration, when, as I expected, there was a tap on the window: he'd followed me outside, keen for a deal. We agreed to toss a coin for the last five thousand pounds that had become the sticking point. I won and we built sixty homes on the site.

Other sites included Christchurch, Brockenhurst, Sway and Hamilton Court at Milford on Sea and were all funded by new backers we had found called Old Broad Street Securities, a merchant bank. I didn't see the trouble just around the corner or understand that a blow-up in the Middle East could cause ripples in Hampshire that would hit us all. The 1973 Yom Kippur War put shares into a nosedive and drove many investment banks to seek shelter.

Our new backers were put into the "lifeboat" as part of the £500 million to secure merchant banks. Old Broad Street Securities came to see me and basically asked for their money back. Their portfolio contained a high proportion of property developers and house builders. They wanted us to stop all work as they didn't have sufficient funds to keep going. Northern Developments, the largest builders in the UK at the time, were being backed by Old Broad Street Securities and were causing them difficulties. They had persuaded a local company they were also funding to go into liquidation, telling the owner that he'd be paid a lump sum for his trouble in preference and outside the other creditors; a course of action that was illegal. They wanted us to do the same.

We had £50,000 on deposit in our clearing bank which they knew about. In exchange for us agreeing to their "deal" and therefore giving them the £50,000, they'd make sure our guarantees to the bank were torn up and that Bill and I would end up with a "few thousand pounds" in our pockets personally. I said we'd think it over but I had no intention of playing their game.

I stalled but they insisted on coming to my office to see me. By this time I had started recording all our telephone conversations. There was a piece of kit that sat on top of the phone and when they came to the office they saw it and asked if I'd been recording their calls. I replied, "Which ones?" and they immediately left looking worried. I was summoned to London to their city office. They wouldn't let me take my briefcase into the meeting which was probably just as well because it was bugged and once in the room threatened me with bankruptcy, told me they'd sue the company, not advance any more funds and make it very hard for us to deal with the city again. I played it dumb, didn't say a word. I knew that they were on the hook. They knew they'd been caught out with some dodgy dealing and there wasn't a lot they could do about it.

The final deal fell into our lap when their team arrived at our lawyer's office, Moore and Blatch, in Lymington. The original two directors who knew we had £50,000 in the bank and who wanted that as part of a continued business deal with us, didn't attend the meeting. It was 1975 and things had come to a head with Northern

Developments, one of the largest house builders at the time, and the two of them had to go north for a meeting with the intention of putting Northern Developments into liquidation. The crew that did turn up made no mention of the £50,000 we had talked about before. We couldn't believe our luck! We certainly didn't mention it. Here were our backers agreeing to a deal that wrote off £100,000 worth of debt, continuing to finance our projects going forward and with no demand for the £50,000 we had in the bank. Mike Crosby, our lawyer, drew up a letter of agreement which we signed that day, breathing a big sigh of relief that their underhand activity and incompetence had played into our hands. They had to continue to fund our developments, reluctantly and all, because they'd been caught out. Funnily enough, had they called my bluff about the recorded telephone conversations, they would have found that I had no incriminating evidence on them at all. I met one of their key players about fifteen years later at a NatWest Bank luncheon. He had found a home there as a director. We did a double take in the gents and I'm not sure who was more surprised at the urinal encounter. I expect he was. He turned as white as the porcelain he'd been pointing at.

In the early 1970s banks were falling over each other to lend money. They really couldn't give the money to developers fast enough and provided you'd got your sums about right and they could see that you were competent builders you'd get the money. Of course when things went bad they went bad quickly and a lemming-like economy of boom and bust became a challenging background in which to grow a business. Old Broad Street Securities went bust in 1974 because they over-lent money with insufficient security.

If it wasn't tussling with the finance for a project and bank liquidators it was overcoming the logistical challenge. On one site where every local developer who looked at it thought that it was impossible to build anything of any use there, we designed a thick retaining wall and built six three-bedroomed houses with garages below, but needed a tower crane to do the work. Once we'd finished the job we couldn't get the thing out and so had to hire another vast crane to remove the first. We learnt a lot from the scheme and over the following years had the biggest number of self-erecting cranes in the UK.

At a waterfront site on the quay, Admirals Court in Lymington, we built a mismatched complex of shops, offices and flats. The design was not what I would have chosen but it fitted in with the planners' requirements at that time. We'd bought the site from the boatyard owner and Tim Ham who had a shop there. We were concerned that our excavations of the old boat yard might interfere with the neighbours' garden land. They had of course expressed their concerns to us as most neighbours do when applying for planning permission. We had to knock down the existing buildings right up to the boundary for the new construction and it would have been easier to get access to our bit by going on theirs and using retaining shuttering. This wasn't an option as they refused. There was a risk that the work would disturb the neighbours' land but it was a risk I was prepared to take. The site had cost us £30,000 and we needed to get on with its development. I went to see my lawyer and asked him, what was the worst that could happen?

"They could sue you for damages to their gardens," he said. Armed with that advice, Bill and I sat in The Ship public house opposite, sipping a pint, and looked on as the digger went to work. Sure enough, the ground started to slip and the neighbours' land slid unceremoniously into our site. The avalanche was quickly followed by a similar fall of legal letters in the in-tray. We had to repair the damage with eight foot of topsoil and some new trees. It was worth the effort and we built the twenty-two foot retaining wall. If we'd dilly-dallied around the project, worrying about the consequences of our action, we'd still be standing, dithering on Lymington quay today. You can't be faint-hearted about being a property developer.

Gwen took on the chandler's shop, Quayside Chandlers, at Admirals Court, the completed quayside development at Lymington with flats, shops and a restaurant and boatyard. Gwen had grown up in Salcombe and knew a thing or two about sailing. Bill Stone had the flat above the restaurant. Sadly he had left his wife and the space was ideal for him. We hung on to the freehold of the whole site, including the boatyard and shops.

Despite being next to the sea I'd never really been tempted to use it for recreational purposes. On one occasion there was a bit of salvage work that Tim Ham and I got involved with. We watched the delivery boat from the Mew & Langton's Isle of Wight brewery unloading its cargo of beer on to the quayside at Lymington. A pallet laden with bottles of beer slipped from the grip of the cradle lifting it from deck to quay and the whole lot dropped into the harbour. There was much head scratching from the crew before the boat pulled away leaving the submerged cache. Tim and I retrieved it all and what we didn't sell we used at the various parties we'd put on. It was free beer for a month or two!

There was, of course, swimming and fishing but I'd never really thought much about boats. Gwen thought that I should learn.

I had persuaded John Colwell to leave Taylor Woodrow in London and come and join us in the South. He sold his house in Edgware and invested the money with us in sites at New Milton, Shenstone and another called Robin Gate which proved successful. Adrian Otten, a civil engineer we'd taken on when building Admirals Court, got on well with John and for six months or so we worked reasonably as a team, as a new working partnership. However, I could tell that Bill Stone wasn't happy with the new arrangement and we had words. John and Adrian felt they were being held back so decided to go it alone and set up Colten's, their own building development and construction business which is still going today. I couldn't blame them and sometimes wonder what might have happened if the four of us had stuck it out.

In 1969 John Colwell had the idea to buy a sailing boat. We chose an Enterprise dinghy, buying it between us, and we went sailing, or at least we tried. We ran aground in Lymington river right in front of the Royal Lymington Yacht Club and, much to our consternation and the amusement of the watching members, leapt out of the dinghy into the cold water to push the craft back into the river. We must have looked like a right pair of novices. We could, of course, have backed the sails to get away but we didn't know anything about that then. Little did the members realise as they laughed into their gin and tonics that they were watching the first steps of a future yachting world champion floundering in the mud and water.

8. Fast Cars, Fast Yachts

My uncle's caravan business had folded by 1969 and Alex, after a brief time making cricket bats, and Les had acquired a garage in Byfleet. It was the sort of place motorists used for fuel, servicing or repairs. I went up to visit the Motor Show in Earl's Court. While admiring the De Tomaso stand I saw, right opposite me, one of my local building competitors, Morris Warry, doing the same. Without hesitation I skipped over the red rope guarding the magnificent De Tomaso Mangusta from the passing public, grabbed the attention of the smart-suited sales executive, inspected the silver grey sports machine and bought it there and then. It felt good to be beating Morris to the post. My new car was one of only six that were imported into the UK and I paid £7,000 for the privilege. It was barely waist-high and looked every inch the "super car" of its day. Mangusta is Italian for mongoose, an animal that can kill cobras. It was named as such by De Tomaso because Ford had apparently promised the engine for the new car which then went to Shelby Cobra instead. They built four hundred cars between 1967 and 1971. The V8 engine gave it a top speed of 155 mph. At the back, over the mid engine and boot space two doors lifted like gull wings. Its ground clearance was so low that sparks would often fly off the scraping sump. It was very nearly an uncontrollable beast but I had to have it.

I drove onto the forecourt of my uncles' garage in my new car.

"You're going too fast," was the comment they made. I didn't know if they meant me and the car or me and the life I was leading. It was probably a gentle warning about both.

In 1971 I sold the small, one-bedroomed flat at Hamilton Court that the company had built and Gwen and I moved to Hurst Barn in Raven's Way, a great property at Milford on Sea overlooking the sea front. The property had access to some land behind it that we later developed as Westover.

In 1972 the business bought a site on the corner of Osborne Road and New Milton High Street and we built Osborne House with four shops and flats over in a four-storey building. There was a suite of offices on the first floor and we moved our office into one half and let out the remainder. A chap called Newton took on the space but pretty soon fell behind with his rent. I got fed up with trying to extract it from him so one day we had the only entrance door to his offices sealed up properly with all his kit inside. Young Mr Newton soon arrived to complain. I told him that if he paid his rent he could get into his office. He left in a huff. The following day he came back with a solicitor who told me that I was going outside the law by impounding Mr Newton's gear and preventing his access to it. I told both of them the same thing: Simply pay what you owe and I'll let you back in. Off they went again. A couple of days later he turned up with his father and a henchman from a Southampton liquidation specialist who threatened to wind us up as a business and bankrupt me personally. I gave them the same simple answer as before.

During this coming and going we had discovered that Mr Newton and his father were not all they said they were. They were trying to sell sheep to the Arabs among other "funny" deals and their activity had caught the attention of the press. In particular Roger Cook from the BBC was very interested in the Newtons. Allegedly, both father and son were serial fraudsters. I passed all correspondence and information we had on to the TV investigative journalist and Cook did one of his Cook Reports, tracking Newton down to his caravan in Brockenhurst. When the TV show was broadcast Roger Cook knocked on the door of the mobile home to be confronted by Newton junior. When asked where Mr Newton senior was, a clear voice in the background could be heard saying, "Tell 'em I'm not here son." Our wayward tenant eventually paid up with interest and we put all his equipment down into the street where it was picked up.

In 1974 we had our own first run in with the media although, thank goodness, not of the Roger Cook variety. It was over a leaking roof at Grosvenor Mews. The Georgian-style building had been designed with parapet walls at roof level and finished in such a way that water had unfortunately leaked into one of the flats and its incumbent reported the mishap to the agent on site. He'd certainly not handled the incident as he should have. Unimpressed by the lack of response from us, she took her grievance to her MP and the press. The Tory MP in question was not one of my favourites and he probably took great pleasure in having a go at a property developer. I remember that he was rather a pompous arse by the name of Robert Adley. The local press got hold of the story and they came down on us like a ton of bricks. We discovered that the subcontractor had skimped on the job. After trying and failing with lead, we had to replace the felt with hot bitumen asphalt that did the job. We also had to pay out compensation so the mistake cost us thousands. We were in the wrong but it taught us to double-check everything. It was the hard way of introducing us to a system for quality control. It also taught me that good press fills column inches with very little beneficial effect, whereas bad press of any degree does so much damage. In a parade of marching soldiers you only ever notice the one out of step, not the hundreds marching perfectly.

An ambitious young man can feel claustrophobic in that little piece of Hampshire that runs between Lymington and New Milton. I was hemmed in. I felt like a ship in a bottle. Everyone knew my business and I knew everyone. The local boy and ex-skiffle-king-made-good wasn't to everyone's liking. If we were going to make the big time, we had to break the glass and set sail. So I did on land and at sea.

My early dabbling with sailing had sparked an interest. From the Enterprise sailing dinghy I moved in a bold jump up to a thirty-two foot Nicholson which I bought from the MD of Sellwoods, the plant hire company. The boat was called Tresillian, after the Cornish village, and I needed help to sail her. Gwen and I went to learn about basic navigation at the Lymington Community Centre. Tim Ham came to my aid and helped me find a mooring too. David 'Daisy' May, the owner of the Berthon Boat Company, just along the front from our Admirals Court development, asked me to go and see him. I thought it was about a piece of land we were interested in buying, a coal yard, on the harbour front next to his business. It wasn't. Being a commissioner for the river, he wanted to know how I'd managed to get a mooring for my new boat within three yards of the end of his pontoon when there was a long waiting list. 'Daisy' May, as we called him, suggested that I had obviously slipped the Harbour Master a backhander, thus pushing me to the top of the waiting list faster than a distress flare. I expect that Tim Ham may have had some influence along the line but I totally denied any skulduggery and suggested that Mr May might like to study the waiting list and, by the way, did he want to sell the land adjacent to his boat yard. He didn't. He sold it instead to the local council for the car park to be extended.

I joined the Lymington Town Sailing Club, whose HQ was a whitewashed art deco style building that looked rather grander than its brick-coloured Royal neighbour across the car park. The two club buildings stood adjacent to the same site where we had played our music for the crowds at the Lymington Regatta when I was a teenager.

I started racing Tresillian, which was hardly a racing boat at all, being built with a deep keel for cruising. It was very handy having Gwen running Quayside Chandlers with access to all the spares and gear I needed to fit the yacht out. I could also dry dock the yacht right in front of Admirals Court and leave her on the quay to dry out so we could work on improving her underside by sanding it down back to the gel coat and glass fibre. With no anti-fouling we were hoping for more speed through the water at the regattas held by Lymington town. We performed well and won the odd race but in the main were beaten by the more modern boats built for more speed than we could achieve. I did get to know the Western end of the Solent like the back of my hand. I found out the hard way by going aground and discovered where the tides were strong and the bottom shallow.

Once I invited some new friends down to Lymington for a sail. After lunch in Yarmouth, we sailed down towards Cowes but unfortunately went aground on Hampstead Ledge. It was a spring tide and the boat was stuck fast and started to lean to about sixty degrees. The friends started to panic especially as one of the women was heavily pregnant. At one stage they were waving frantically to a passing helicopter, which just ignored us, as he would. We sat it out and after five awkward hours the tide came in sufficiently for us to sail off and back to Lymington. We never saw our guests again. I had learnt about another pitfall in the Solent.

I sold Tresillian and bought a brand new Holman & Pye thirty-two foot and called it Solent Saracen. Still really another cruiser, the design was used for racing and I had a new set of Hood sails which gave me the confidence for my first offshore race under the Royal Ocean Racing Club, the "Channel Race". The new Yacht Haven Marina had just been built and I heard from Tim Ham that there were two debentures left. I rushed down to the marina with my chequebook in my hand and signed up for both of them at £5,000 each, one for me, the other for Bill. This bought us a twenty-one year lease on a thirty-six foot pontoon with all services included. It was a fantastic deal. Its value was to increase by over ten times. Later I was pressurised by the owner, Dirk Carliss, to sell them back to his company but I refused. After twenty-one years, the asking price for a ten-year lease with a lot of strings attached was £36,000 per mooring.

I was asked to chair a committee for the keel boat racing at the LTSC and my first job was to persuade the yacht club to become more professional about cross-Channel racing. We needed to make sure that there was someone the other end of the race to clock competitors in across the finishing line. Gwen volunteered for the task and travelled to Cherbourg ahead of the sailing competitors. The race set off from

Lymington towards a turning mark, one of the buoys off The Needles at the Western end of the Solent, before crossing the Channel. Unfortunately, in my effort to turn at the buoy, I touched the mark therefore disqualifying us from the race. I returned to Lymington having lost before we'd really started. I knew the next day there was a race around Alderney so the crew and I agreed we'd enter it. We left that same day for the sixty-mile trip to the Channel Island. I was unable to contact Gwen in Cherbourg who was rather alarmed when we didn't turn up.

There are significant tides that run around Alderney. The race started from the breakwater and the idea was to go off with the tide and through the Swinge, the furious piece of water between the southern part of Alderney and Burhou, and then on up through the channel called the Alderney Race, between the island and the French coast and back to the finish. I was the helmsman and navigator and we went through the Swinge so fast, sailing at six knots with six knots of tide under us, that I had a job to know precisely where we were. However we were first to the bottom part of the island but the tide was against us and we came to a stop. We were stuck and other boats arrived so that we were all lined up across the Alderney Race waiting for the tide to turn. The last boat arrived just as the tide turned and took full advantage of the non-standing start, getting well into the lead ahead of the rest of us. I was following closely behind Paul Elvstrom, the well-known Danish yachtsman with four Olympic gold medals to his name. Unbeknown to me he had sailed over a submerged rock that my boat smashed into with great force. We managed to sail back into Alderney and a diver's inspection confirmed that a chunk of lead, nine inches by six, was missing from our keel. The keel bolts were unaffected thank goodness and we sailed back to Lymington, once again out of a race. If the damage to the boat wasn't bad enough, Gwen's welcome home didn't make us feel any better. She'd been worried sick about our AWOL state and we hadn't even returned with a winner's cup to fill with champagne. We didn't have another volunteer race official to check us in at the French finishing line either.

I persuaded the committee to introduce yacht racing at the end of the season. After Cowes Week, from September to November, there was little or no racing and I convinced Jim Lazenby who worked as an insurance agent for Manulife, the insurance company, to put up funds as sponsor for a new trophy designed by Bournemouth College. The series was run from the club in the western end of the Solent on a Sunday morning and finished in time for a visit to the bar. I organised the whole event from my office. The first year we had an entry of fifteen yachts but by the time I handed it over to the club after three years there were up to one hundred and twenty five yachts and seven hundred yachties. There were two bars opened in the club and the income generated for the club was significant.

I'd put together a reliable crew made up of locals all from the Lymington Town Sailing Club, except for one, and we were, with practice, becoming quite proficient on our mid-week evening run. We did have occasional lapses. One such was after taking on too much alcoholic refreshment in Yarmouth. We determined to return home to Lymington and in manoeuvring the yacht under sail from its quayside mooring out into the channel, we hit and holed the moored lifeboat. I owned up and sent them the money for a repair job. Some months later we saw the same lifeboat at a local regatta and they hadn't bothered to repair the damage. Gwen asked the captain what had happened and was told that some drunken yachties had run into them.

I wanted to move up a class and into more of a racing machine. Jeremy Rogers, a successful boat builder in Lymington who sadly went bust in the mid 1980s, was building a new American designed Doug Peterson boat, a one-tonner. I went to see him and persuaded him to let me have the third boat out of the moulds. The first was going to the Rogers team and the second to a New Zealand team who had won the previous year. Because I was keen to get on with the new boat, I took the hull back to my house and fitted it out myself. I thought, having looked at the Rogers boat, the support for the keel looked a bit on the light side. I decided to reinforce the strength of the support beams, which was just as well as during one of the selection races the Rogers boat 'Gumboots' had to retire with its keel bolts coming loose after they started to pull through their supports. The boat was designed to be handled by a crew of seven so I fitted four gimballed bunks and a Portaloo upfront. A small engine with a folding propeller would give us six knots. The gimballed stove was just big enough for a brew up. I kept all the kit to the minimum so we'd have a lean mean racing machine.

We entered into the UK National Championships from which six out of twenty boats would be chosen to go forward to the World Championships held that year in Torquay. I was new to this game but had no qualms about tacking to the lee of a competitor and forcing other boats to tack away. I didn't know that we were up against Olympic helmsmen and top quality crews. I crossed swords with Daisy May once again. I got into an appeal against him for a port and starboard incident and ended up at the hearing in the Royal Thames in Knightsbridge. It was pretty obvious from the opening remarks that I was going to lose when the bumptious Mr May welcomed the committee as "Sir" this and "Sir" that. He knew them all personally as fellow members. I lost the appeal on the basis that there had been no collision notwithstanding that I had to tack away to avoid one. As the starboard boat I had the right of way but this point was ignored. I learned something about the unpleasant side of yachting politics.

It was 11pm one evening and a surprise when I received a phone call from Alan Green, the sailing secretary, at the Royal Ocean Racing Club telling me that we'd been chosen as one of the six to represent the UK. We were over the moon at having been selected. I immediately contacted the team with the good news, waking some of them up. Tony Blatchford was our tactician and second helm. He was a tall, jolly fellow but could get quite intense. David Worker was a great navigator. He never got seasick, which was just as well because he spent most of the time poring over his charts below deck. He was also the ship's cook although we didn't do much eating when we were out racing. Bill

against nineteen nations and we won the long race overall spending two nights at sea. On the eve of the third night, and to fireworks, with our nearest rival, Ron Holland another well-known yacht designer, half a mile or so behind us, we came home with double points and the championship in the bag by a fair margin.

The racing took place off Hanko Island, which was one of the homes of King Olaf of Norway. The big, balding, jolly monarch presented us with our winning prize, a telescope trophy, which we couldn't use or keep. He'd won a gold medal for sailing at the 1928 Olympics in Amsterdam so could appreciate what we had achieved. Nevertheless, he was the only one who enjoyed a celebration drink of beer while the rest of us had to make do with ghastly-tasting local parsnip schnapps.

We returned to England as heroes but not before we'd been held up by Her Majesty's Customs and Excise officers who decided to search the van and the crew with a thoroughness that showed we had five cigars too many between us. Nobody owned up to them so I paid the duty and kept them. Actually, two of our crew, Tony Blatchford and John Baddock, had been former policemen but that didn't seem to count for anything. The fact we'd just won the World Cup for three-quarter ton yacht racing for the UK didn't mean anything either. The law, it seemed, was the law, with no room for six local heroes or five cigars. Gwen had arranged a welcome home victory party and we all ended up in the swimming pool at Hurst Barn in Milford on Sea.

My reputation in the sailing world was growing. One of my crew from the early days, Jason Holtom, who had been sailing in the prestigious Admiral's Cup Series, asked if I would like to skipper a yacht in Australia. He introduced me to Ron Amey, of Amey Roadstone Construction, who was quite a character. Ron took me out to lunch and we travelled in his Rolls. He called me "the chippy" and although he was a very overbearing man who ran things more with the stick than the carrot, I didn't take much notice of his ways. I actually ended up staying with him on his honeymoon so it's probably just as well I didn't take too much notice. He had lent us his skiing lodge in Chamonix when unannounced he arrived having just married his secretary. He owned a boat called Noryema that had performed very well sailing for Britain in the Admiral's Cup. He asked me if I would skipper his boat in the 1975 Southern Cross Series in Australia, part of which is the Sydney-Hobart race. I agreed. I went to the Southern Hemisphere for Christmas and New Year in 1975/76 and in our first race came second to a boat called Prospect of Puffin designed by a twenty-one year old, Bruce Farr. He invited me for a sail on her and I was very impressed. Ron Amey didn't pay my fare. He got away with that. Even though he'd sold out to Consolidated Gold Fields for a fortune he was as tight as a tick. He nearly had a heart attack when his crew overfilled the kettle for a brew up. It was a waste of gas.

There were three boats sailing from Great Britain. The others were Buttercup, owned by the man with the biggest butter mountain in Europe, and Chris Dunning as captain of the team in Marionette. The second race was a medium offshore race which meant at least one night racing at sea. Come night-time we were in a commanding position and according to our dead reckoning we were some fifteen minutes ahead overall. I went off watch down below, handing over the helm to David Holiday. I was not long in my bunk when I heard a crashing noise, the sort that told me we were going about. I wondered what the hell was happening and went up on deck to find the boat had indeed turned around and was retracing its course. They had decided to change the headsail and a wave had taken one of the headsails away. The cash conscious owner, Ron Amey, had insisted that the boat went back to look for it. It wasn't as though the particular headsail was of any great value. It was only a reacher of doubtful origin and the chances of finding the thing in the dark at three in the morning were pretty slim and in any case it would probably have sunk by the time we had got anywhere near it. I immediately gave instructions for the boat to get back on course, and much to the consternation of the owner, we did so. I pointed out to him that he had spent thousands of pounds getting the yacht out to Australia to race and he was worried about a bloody headsail that had probably cost less than two grand. Talk about spoiling the ship for a halfpennyworth of tar. I reckoned we had lost about twelve minutes over this fiasco. We came second by two minutes in the thirty-six hour race and I was bloody livid.

The last offshore race, which counted for double points, was the tremendous Sydney to Hobart run, which we did in three days and two hours, covering over six hundred and thirty miles through seas in the Bass Strait the size of which I had never seen before or since. Some of the waves were as big as twelve-storey buildings and I'm not exaggerating. They were taller than anything I'd ever built back home. When I went out on watch, the first twenty minutes were very scary. The next twenty were exhilarating and after that I was just hanging on for dear life. It was two hours on and two hours off, shared between me and the second helm, David Holiday. No sooner had I put my sodden head down to grab some sleep after my strenuous two hours on, than it seemed I was being shaken awake to go back on deck again. It was like some rollercoaster ride in a wet hell where rest was impossible and it was all that we could do to cope with trying to sail the sixty-foot yacht which behaved like a fourteen-foot dinghy all down wind. We did it though. We got through that immense sea and arrived in the calm waters of the Derwent River. Kialoa III from the USA had won the race in a record time that wasn't going to be beaten for twenty-three years. Out of 102 boats that started 99 finished and we came first in our class.

Tasmania's welcome was as loud as the sea had been, with the whole island turning out to greet us with honking and waving to every yacht that came safely into berth. Then it was a chaotic procession down to the pub to try and break the last record of glasses of beer drunk in one day after the previous race. There were several lines of glasses stretched out across the bar and the beer was fed into them from a hosepipe, constantly flowing with foaming lager. When a police car arrived on the scene to try and calm down the beer-drinking competition, the gathered partying crowd lifted it up and carried it off down the road. The police thought better than to get involved and left us to our celebrations. It was New Year's Eve and my thirty-seventh birthday.

I'd sold Saracen III to a buyer from Hong Kong in September and the boat had been shipped out by road and sea to compete in the China Sea race. I don't know how it performed but it was the only boat I ever built and made a profit on. I needed a replacement so chose a Bruce Farr design. He had impressed me out in Australia so I bought his design. At 21 Bruce went on to be one of the top yacht designers in the world. I rented a yard in Lymington from a friend, Chris Carrington, and built two yachts, one for me and one for Bill Stone. These were thirty-six-foot one ton yachts and this time it took us six weeks from start to launch for both of them. We used Carrington's labour to help us lay out the glass fibre and Uncle Peter, his son Mark and I did the rest. I offered him my De Tomaso Mangusta car as an incentive to get the job done on time. He earned it.

Both boats looked identical, with the same paintwork and consecutive numbers, one ending in eight and the other with nine. The plan was to confuse the opposition so that they wouldn't know which boat was which when we were out racing together for the selection trials to represent the UK. We even had the crews dressed in the same kit. Sadly, Bill's boat did not qualify for the British selection of boats for the 1976 World Championships, that year held in Marseilles.

Gwen launched my yacht, Saracen IV, in Lymington and we went on to do very well, winning the Solent Point Series, a competition over the year held among all the clubs in the Eastern and Western parts of the Solent. We won the Royal Ocean Racing Club point series, the Dinard Cup and all the races at Burnham Week and Cowes Week in our class.

The 1976 World One Ton Cup, International Cercle de la Voile de Paris, was to be raced in Marseilles but it was not a successful chapter for Saracen. I had decided to race the boat in the Cowes-Dinard race and afterwards had it picked up by a low loader and trucked down to Marseilles. We did in fact win the race overall, although Ted Heath picked up the wrong gold-plated trophy for his efforts. He had only won his class. Although I wrote to him asking him to return it to us we never received a reply. While in Dinard we had to transfer the yacht to the marina in St Malo. We left the Dinard marina under full power to make the lock that was about to close to the St Malo basin. Unfortunately, in our haste, I tried to cross an underwater ledge which was put there to keep the water in the Dinard marina at low tide. With the French crowd on the shore shouting and gesticulating at us, I thought they were cheering when in fact they were trying to warn us about the underwater hazard. I hit it with a big thump but we got over it, made the lock and tied up in the St Malo marina. When the yacht was lifted out onto the waiting low loader we could see that the keel had bent by four inches about halfway down. This was obviously going to make a considerable difference to the performance of the yacht.

The crew and I left from Lymington towing a caravan behind my new Jaguar with a load of gear to try to rectify the bent keel. Halfway to Marseilles the Jaguar broke down with gearbox trouble. What a headache that saga turned out to be. Trying to get the car fixed in France and returned to England was tiresome. Trying to get compensation out of Jaguar was like trying to get blood out of a stone. I never bought another Jag. I hired a van and continued on our way. We parked up in a car park and I took the crew out for a get together dinner. When we returned the van and caravan had been broken into and a considerable amount of gear had been stolen. We told the local Gendarmes. A further crew member, Brent Strickland, had arrived in his car and the following morning we found the rear window had been cut out and further gear stolen right alongside where we were all sleeping. By the following midday we had fixed the keel as best we could, although it was far from perfect, and we had taken the yacht out for a trial run. When we got back to the caravan we had been broken into yet again, although by this time there was very little left to be stolen. I complained to the organisers that we had been robbed three times within twenty-four hours. What the hell were we doing racing in crime-ridden Marseilles? One of the race officers took pity on us and put us all up in his chateau.

Apart from the thieving, the racing was not going too well either. On the final long offshore race we sailed into third place, only to lose it when we passed a nudist colony and some of the naked incumbents swam out to meet us. For some inexplicable reason we slipped from third to tenth. Then we hit a heavy wind known in the Mediterranean as a mistral. The turning mark was around an offshore lightship which, unfortunately, we could not find. After sailing a reducing square, a French frigate came up to us and gave us the co-ordinates we had already gone past. After the race I found out that the lightship gave out weather forecasts on the hour every hour on a particular short wave signal which we would have been able to zero in on to the null as navigation. This was way before GPS. At the pre-race briefing the race committee had omitted to give this information out. The only ones who knew of it, of course, were the French yachtsmen who came first, second and third. Untrustworthy on land and sea, this was a series best forgotten.

As if to rub French sea salt into our wounds, as we were driving away from Marseilles, two of the crew saw a Frenchman ambling along with one of our very brightly decorated sail bags slung over his shoulder. They had been made especially for us for use in the series. They accosted him and told him they were going to take him to the Gendarmes. Unfortunately they did not know the way to the police station whereas the Frenchman said he did. He led them a merry dance and eventually ended up in some back alley where he called out to his friends for help. The crew made a hasty retreat not wishing to add injury to insult.

When we got the boat back to Lymington, Peter came down and within five minutes had thumped the keel back into position with a sledgehammer. We needn't have bothered with all the kit we'd taken to (and had taken from us in) bloody Marseilles.

The new Farr boats were fantastic to sail and they had what's known as three-quarter rig. We did not point so high into the wind as other full mast head-rigged yachts so we would duck to the leeward side of any boat that we were trying to overtake. If a yacht is sailing to windward, into the wind, it can only sail twenty-five to thirty degrees to the true direction of the wind. When a boat is on starboard then the true wind direction is coming from the right. For another yacht to pass to the lee of this one, it would have to pass on the yacht's left and therefore become blanketed by the sails of the yacht being overtaken. This would slow him down. If the overtaking yacht has sufficient speed, he can break through the wind shadow and the yacht being overtaken cannot take action to stop the manoeuvre under the racing rules. The extra speed we achieved by not pointing so high was fantastic and we inevitably would overtake the opposition. It was doubly satisfying doing it this way as we would have to sail through the lee of the opposition yacht. This did mean we would have our wind blanketed for a bit but it also meant that the opposition could not stop us.

Downwind, the yacht was even faster. I remember rounding a mark off Cherbourg called CH1 with an opposition yacht nearly on the horizon in front of us; within one and a half hours we overtook him. It was incredible and, not only that, it was a very cheap yacht to build.

We won lots. At the end of the year presentation at the Grosvenor Hotel, Solent Saracen was declared by the Royal Ocean Racing Club the "Yacht of the Year 1976". My first and last visit to the Royal Squadron in Cowes was to pick up a silver cup for some race well won. Gwen and I went into the building but Gwen's attempt to get in through the front door was stopped by a steward who told us that women were only allowed access to the place via a side entrance. She didn't grumble so I went one way and she went the other. Pompous, puffed-up Ted Heath was present along with the smart row of red-trousered attendants standing in starchy formation with their caps held smartly under their arms. When my turn came to receive the award I stepped up to the Commodore and was told, "Here's the cup, it is insured but make sure it is returned here by this time next year." There was no, "well done old chap", or other niceties. There wasn't even a celebration drink, fizzy or otherwise, and no hint of a piece of pineapple and cheese on a stick. It was one of the most unfriendly and pretentious places I'd ever been to. Gwen and I left, each by our own doors, and never went back. The headquarters of the serious yachting world didn't do itself any favours at all. Maybe they didn't want people like me. I certainly didn't want people like them.

9. Moving into Shelter

We were always in a hurry to get on with the next deal or win the next race. But it didn't always work out as we wanted.

In 1971 we took our architects, Burley, to court over an issue with drainage pipes at a site in Milford on Sea. Basically, the architects had designed the drainage to be laid with a fall of 1 in 40 and they had not surveyed the land properly. This cost us an extra £10,000 due to hitting running sand. We said that modern pipes could be set at 1 in 80, thereby reducing the depth of the dig and not hitting the running sand. Anyhow, the judge agreed with the architects and we lost on a technicality. At a face-to-face with the architect, prior to the meeting to try and resolve our differences, he left the room for us to confer. I noticed that on the mantelpiece, behind a clock, was a recording device. He was hoping that we would say something that might assist him. We upped and left, remarking into the microphone, "Goodbye. See you in court." We didn't use that firm of architects any more.

I did encounter the same judge in court eight years later over the sloppy finish of the paintwork on my Ferrari and the undertaking they gave me to buy back the car at the same price two years later, provided they serviced the car, which they had. However, on the return after a service, they had not checked the wheel bearings despite my having brought the problem to their notice. I had my own mechanic, Paddy Matcham, who took it out for a run and he agreed that the bearings needed immediate replacement, which he did that same day. Luckily we kept the records and the old bearings. Ferrari claimed that we had not fitted Ferrari parts. We produced the old bearings in court and showed them to the judge. They were the same, made by Volkswagen and had been fitted by Ferrari when I first bought the car. Case proved. I won and with it £52,000 plus costs which was more than double what the car cost originally. The owner of the garage said that he was not in the country when I arranged the deal with the salesman. The judge asked him to prove where he was with the dates supported by credit card bills, flight tickets and receipts. He wasn't able to do that and the judge then recommended that he be committed for perjury. You don't try and trip up the law when you haven't got a leg to stand on and, like an elephant, the judge remembered me and the drainpipes.

In 1973 with the onset of the Yom Kippur War, the housing market collapsed and we nearly caught a serious cold. We had been trying to develop a site at the Amberwood in Walkford, New Milton. This was a block of land with no access to it that was going to auction. The only way we were going to be able to use it was to buy a bungalow that fronted the site. I went door-knocking and offered options to all the occupiers of the twelve bungalows that might give access. Another developer was trying to do the same so I paid him not to bid. We were successful at the auction. We obtained planning for over fifty houses and even though the council wanted us to remove a large oak tree, we appealed to the planning committee who agreed with us it could stay even though it restricted the sight line into the development. It still stands today. We started to build the new homes, having demolished one of the bungalows we purchased under option. We'd put up about a dozen new homes and had sold four when the financial storm clouds got very angry and the housing market crash dived. Thank God the Government put up funds for local authorities to buy up completed new houses from house builders at a discount. Iris Nedderman who was chairman of the Hampshire Housing Association and a councillor and colleague of Walter Symonds on the New Forest Council, persuaded the council to buy the completed houses and the remainder of the site to build council houses. We had to buy back the four homes we'd already sold and we just came out of the deal by the skin of our teeth, clearing our costs and making a small profit. Iris, like Walter, was conscientious, as straight as a die and a very helpful person to know especially in those dark days of 1973 and 1974. The deal probably saved McStone's bacon.

There was a car dealer and retired farmer who lived at Westover House on the front in Milford on Sea. The place was an extraordinary old pile and we thought that we could pull it down and redevelop the site and its large garden to the rear. Part of the deal was to build for the owner, Mr Knowleson, a bungalow with an extra large room for his snooker table but trying to get him to agree to the finalised deal was a lengthy process. By the time contracts were exchanged the market was in decline and we were short of funds to complete the second part of the contract. We must have been backwards and forwards to see him at least a dozen times over a year or more and he talked about everything except the deal. When at last we had concluded what we thought were workable terms, the planners gave Westover House listed status. The inside was indeed rather special with ornate wooden panelling, some splendid carved doors and German silver door furniture, stained glass and an impressive staircase. The old place had associations with Lord Nuffield. Mr Knowleson had filled the cellars up with masses of junk he'd collected from years of auction sales and his capacity for accumulating junk. We couldn't get out of our protracted deal with him but eventually sold the building for use as a hotel. We did, however, obtain planning for the extensive garden overlooking the beach some hundred yards away. There is a framed description of the faded place's history hanging in the vast hall. It lists all the good and great occupants and includes a line to the effect that local builders McCarthy & Stone once tried to knock the place down. Time will soon tell if that wasn't the kindest thing that could have been done to the rather faded building.

Next door to Westover House, down Raven's Way, was the first proper family home for Gwen and me. I had bought the property to give access from part of the garden to the land at the rear of Westover.

We'd moved there in 1971. Hurst Barn was a decent sized place with a swimming pool and panoramic views out towards the Isle of Wight. My growing boys came to see us there and learned to swim and enjoyed the pool when they could and the English seaside when weather permitted.

Father had moved on from The Bugle Hotel and taken on The Three Choughs at Blandford Forum. When he finally retired in 1974, after seventeen years as a publican, he flirted briefly with the idea of moving to Malta. Mother and father went out there for a holiday and stayed for six months. At their request I went out to see them. They'd found a place they wanted to settle in but I wasn't keen. There was a problem with flying leases where you never really knew who owned the space above you. Malta was a shabby island where the tangle of overhead wires had replaced the trees. I didn't like it and so put him off the scheme and offered him and mother one of the bungalows I'd bought that backed onto the Amberwood site.

Dad was depressed. Being retired probably didn't suit him. The two of us took off for an impromptu holiday in Ireland. We grabbed a flight from Bournemouth to Belfast, hired a car and drove west. We found a hotel and booked in and ended up stopping there for ten days. It was the longest time the two of us had ever spent together. We took a rowing boat out on the neighbouring loch and fished for trout. We landed on a tiny island to brew up a cup of tea with the kettle borrowed from the hotel. In the evenings we drank Guinness and Jameson whiskey and chatted to the other guests and the local policeman who turned up most evenings at midnight for his drink on the way home. It was a good time for a father and his son.

One Saturday night I went off to the local village with someone I'd befriended at the hotel. The two of us trawled the local bars where every other building in the main street seemed to be a pub. The place was packed with locals all drinking and smoking their hearts out. The thick blue tobacco smoke curled its way from the open doors like a smothering fog into which we sailed blindly. In a scruffy-looking wooden shack was the local dance hall, with the women lined up on one side and the men on the other, eyeing each other up like the potential buyers of stock at a cattle market. The Irish country music was the key for both sides to come together and the surge of couples in the old hall made the floorboards creak with their Saturday night fever. When the music stopped the girls and boys would retreat to either side of the room, just like the parting of the Red Sea. There wasn't a punch thrown or an ugly scene that I saw, but rather good old-fashioned Irish horseplay.

The owner of the hotel would always ask us at every meal in his friendly heavy Irish way, "Now Sirs, have you had sufficient?"

We could honestly answer that we had. Thinking back, maybe my dad and I could have done with some more. Just some more time, like those rare happy carefree Irish days spent together.

My father's 70th birthday celebration was in the summer of 1978.

It was a surprise do at the Westover House Hotel and I arranged for all the family and friends to be there. The apple of his eye, my sister Carol, had moved to Australia with her husband Jack Warren. I paid for her to come back for the party. She had been married to Brian Pink, a fellow member of my skiffle group and the one who played the double bass tea chest. They were divorced in January 1975 and had two boys, Jason and Stephen, and a daughter, Justine. The boys stayed with their father when Carol went Down Under with her new husband, Jack, and Justine. In 1977 they had Jacquelyn.

I picked Father up from Amberwood and when he saw his daughter there were lots of tears. Carol didn't want to go back to Australia after that so I arranged for Jack to come home as well. The two bought a house in Broad Lane, Lymington, which I later acquired for my ex-wife and the boys to live in.

My younger sister Vicky was at the party. She was probably more like me. She was good at sport and ran for the county. She had more of a money-making head on her than Carol and got into the hairdressing business. Vicky had a baby daughter on the quiet. She had become involved with a plasterer called Sam Crouch, who was quite a lad, before meeting and marrying David Chadwick, the Southampton footballer. The couple then had a son, Andrew. David's football took him to Middlesbrough and then back to Bournemouth. He ended up in the USA after divorcing Vicky who got involved again with Sam which resulted in another son with him called Paul. Vicky opened her hairdressing business, 'A Cut Above The Rest', in New Milton and then in Ashley. She remarried in 1982 to Robin Harvey and they had a daughter Kimberly. Four years later he was kicked out after Vicky discovered he was having an affair.

Sadly Father died from cancer of the lungs in 1988. He had been confined to his bed for two weeks when I received a call from his doctor to come immediately. I was at his bedside when he passed away.

Not far from the top end of New Milton High Street the Waverley Cinema was becoming a pain in the portfolio. We had bought the site in 1974 for £20,000 from Mr Plank, the cinema owner and the man who not many years previously had agreed to my band, the Blue Cats Skiffle Group, treading his boards. He also ran the local travel agent and was a good friend of Walter Symonds. We'd bought a bungalow on the site for £5,000 and that gave us the space we needed for our new development. Our in-house architect, Robert Young, drew up some plans and we applied for a mix of four shops and offices, then four shops with twelve flats over, but by then neither of the schemes stacked up financially.

Many of the buyers of the bungalows and flats we had already built at developments like Grosvenor Mews in Lymington were elderly and the area around had what could be described as a greying population. The South Coast was a magnet for retirement. The trouble with the old cinema site was that we couldn't build enough traditional flats with the required car parking space to make the development a financially worthwhile proposition. There was something going on in my mind that kept telling me that the older generation was where the money was and that played a big part in my thinking.

I had my epiphany while reading the latest newsletter from the Home Builders Federation. It asked builders to consider specialised housing for the elderly. I hit on the new idea of turning the Waverley development into sheltered accommodation for the over fifty-fives. Robert Young and I discussed what form this should take and he then drew up plans for thirty-two flats. The extra flats were made possible by the decrease in demand for parking. Retired people didn't have as many cars as families and because the flats were close to the facilities of central New Milton many wouldn't need a car at all. The elderly drove less and, with failing faculties and the increasing cost of motoring, it was important that homes for the elderly were within walking distance of the shops and on bus routes. The more I thought about the idea the more it seemed to me that we could do more than just build homes for the elderly. We could create a living space with some shared facilities and we could design it in such a way that the elderly would enjoy living there. Further, and most importantly, once the children had left the nest parents could trade down from their larger houses into more manageable accommodation. Research showed that many had paid off their mortgage so were cash positive in their move. We could provide an on-site live-in warden, later to be known as a House Manager, to keep a watchful and helpful eye on things. We could restrict the accommodation to those aged over fifty-five within the terms of a lease with a ground rent and an annual service charge on top. I wasn't going to provide nursing homes but I was going to cater for a growing greying population which perhaps wanted the security of communal living and independence without the heavy overhead or inconvenience of running an entire home.

I carried out a significant amount of research into what my potential new customer would require. I built up a very compelling case to show to any doubting planners. I really did my homework to present a watertight case. Age Concern, Help the Aged and the Building Research

Establishment were just three of the bodies that provided useful information about the likely requirements for older people. Some architects were already thinking about the design for living for an ageing population and their ideas on paper were useful to see. Even the NHS were talking about the need, with increasing numbers of old people being found dead in their unsuitable homes with friends and neighbours often unaware of the problem until it was too late. I read report after report and at the turn of every page became more and more certain that sheltered housing was the way forward for our business. My target customer was going to be the widow aged over seventy who had recently lost her husband. As plans progressed 80 per cent of our customers fell into this category with 15 per cent as couples and 5 per cent as widowers. The first advertisement in the local paper confirmed that there was indeed a willing and ready market for such schemes. We sold all thirty-two flats before we'd even put the roof on the building.

The name of the game, as far as construction was concerned, had to be standardisation. I'd learnt enough from my uncles to realise that if we kept things simple and produced them as if they were on a production line then we'd control costs and minimise errors. Measure it twice, cut it once was the old chippy dictum. I was going to measure it once and make it once and that once would work for all. If we were going to build lots of sheltered homes and we had worked out the right formula then standardisation would be one of the vital keys to profitability. I set about this task with vigour and the way in which we built our sheltered homes was a key to the success of the whole venture.

Every unit was built and every aspect designed with the elderly in mind. The space of 450 square feet allowed for a one-bed flat. We coined the phrase "bed space". A two-bed space was 550 square feet. The kitchens were given special attention with an eye-level cooker and grill, a small fridge and space for a freezer. The work units were all narrower than the norm to allow for easy access to the back. The wall cupboards were fixed at a lower height than normal. The fully-tiled bathrooms had a low-level bath with a near to hand push button alarm on the bath panel. We increased the size of all the doors to provide enough access for wheelchairs. All the taps were lever taps for greater ease of turning on and off and there were clear hot and cold markings. Even the hanging rails in the bedroom cupboards were set at a lower height to better suit the occupant. All the electrical sockets were set up the wall rather than at skirting board level, while the spy hole to the front door was set lower. A central laundry room was purpose built in each scheme with high level access to the washing machines and dryers. This became a social meeting point for the residents. We thought of every possible angle that would be of help to the elderly in their everyday life. There were, of course, alarm pulls in every flat so that help could be summoned as soon as possible.

On one particular occasion the alarm was raised and the house manager went off to the particular flat to investigate with a pass key only to find that an amorous couple had inadvertently become tangled up with the alarm cord which hung over the bed. The gentleman had got his big toe caught up in the little triangle at the bottom of the emergency cord. It certainly wasn't a cry for help. It was reassuring to know that the elderly still enjoyed their active sex lives.

Eventually the alarm system from each flat connected to the "Bunker", a concrete encased structure that was half buried under the ground and built on my instructions in New Milton in 1987. It was designed to be like Fort Knox and was the control centre for all the sheltered housing schemes in the country. The Bunker held the computer log containing details on every resident. It was manned twenty-four hours a day, seven days a week, by trained staff who knew how to respond to any emergency call for help, whichever site it came from.

In dealing with the elderly we had to make sure that everything they were going to come in contact with was suitable. This meant that things like the heating controls couldn't rely on the twenty-four hour clock, a concept of timekeeping that some of the elderly just didn't grasp. The main water stopcock had to be hidden and made inaccessible from the flat after I discovered on one visit that a resident had obviously turned the water supply off even though he swore that he hadn't touched the tap in his airing cupboard. All heating was by electric night storage heaters which we found cheaper and more practical than gas. Because each flat only had one external wall, heating costs were kept to a minimum. The communal corridors were heated and we put lifts that could accommodate four people and would cope with wheelchairs into every scheme. We eventually bought Liftwise, a firm in Ringwood that made the lifts, reorganised it and sold it back to its management in 1990.

A fully furnished communal lounge was provided as a meeting point for each development and these proved very popular focal social points. There was a small office in the entrance to each building for the house manager who would either be provided with a two-bedroom flat on site or who came in daily from somewhere nearby. A guest bedroom was provided, particularly for use by visiting relatives of those occupying a one-bedroom flat. The guest room was reserved for those visitors who may have an ill relative. Kitted out like a hotel room, there was a minimal charge for this and the income generated was used to offset the service charges.

Car parking spaces were not allocated apart from those smaller ones exclusively used for electric buggies. The scramble for a space as near to the entrance as possible caused some local difficulties and the misuse of the free car parking so near to the town centre often proved a temptation to those who had no business to be there. We studied the car parking issues carefully and employed a system to count the vehicles in and out over an extended period. We needed this information to justify the number of spaces we were providing because less car parking meant more flats. We had to justify the numbers on several occasions to local planning authorities who would often try and use the car parking issue as a means to object to schemes. Despite opposition to our claims we won numerous appeals and costs after public enquiries because we had done our homework so thoroughly. The national average for success at appeals was 33 per cent while ours was 75 per cent. The car, or rather lack of it, was our ally in justifying our housing density plans. What I had realised early on sitting on planning liaison committees was that the car park was a means of controlling housing density. Over the years many authorities had increased their requirements from one space per dwelling to two or more. We had identified that a quarter of a vehicle per flat was more than adequate to cater for the private transport needs of our elderly residents.

It became apparent that we had not only identified a niche market which had not been exploited, but that there was also no competition in the housing industry for our specialist housing for the elderly. We started to expand the previously local schemes, New Milton to Bournemouth, out to Winchester outside what we initially thought was a southern phenomenon of retirees to the South Coast. Further research which I undertook showed the whole of the United Kingdom was the market place. Our first regional office was in Eastbourne, which proved to be a phenomenal success. How were we to take advantage of this market before others realised? The only way, we quickly realised, was to open up regional offices across the UK. This required finance, hence the flotation of the company to raise funds which I refer to later, and secondly how were we to manage such a quick expansion while maintaining the quality of the product and the brand that we intended to build?

Head office was to be the catalyst to grow the regional centres to a degree where they would become self-sufficient. This meant a policy of buying property in regions that we had identified as prime locations with the ability to enable an area to be serviced in terms of: (a) land opportunities, (b) sufficient elderly residents, (c) communication and (d) employment.

Once a region was commissioned it would take two years before cash started to roll in from sales to enable expansion to proceed apace. The strategy, policies, cash, designs and strategy of planning applications were items strictly controlled from head office, with the regions carrying out the implementation of the architecture on a local basis. The same would apply to the specification of the product with some central buying functions of items supplied UK wide. The manufacturing, for instance, of the numerous concrete staircases were delivered from our factory at Stem Lane, again to fixed standards and complying with building regulation requirements. This applied to many items that we manufactured. Delivery was by our plant company who also installed and serviced our tower cranes across the UK. Sales and marketing strategy was managed from head office as well as legal, city and public relations. Regions would eventually have their own board of directors consisting of construction, planning, finance, sales and marketing, with its chief executive meeting once a month at head office to evaluate changes and ideas that would be chaired by the group chief executive. Each year a plan was agreed of development budget for each region. This was in fact the land buying which would not come on stream for at least two years for sales; this was the main catalyst for expansion or downsizing depending on the main board's evaluation of the economic market.

Uniformity became a key to success with each construction. I eventually made good use of a computer-generated design system and we bought the state-of-the-art kit from Prime Computers in America and set it to work in a new extension to our Stem Lane New Milton office in 1980. Our in-house architects worked on a three-shift twenty-four hour rota so that there was always somebody responsible for overseeing potential building plans as they came in. The fax machine was a new toy and each regional office had one so that each potential new development would have its details sent straight through to head office. Plans would then be drawn up and faxed back so that the region concerned could start the planning process. The benefits of this system were immeasurable. We could overlay plans floor to floor and iron out any potential hiccups at the first stage. Standard windows had become a key element in building to a common blueprint and these could be planned in with precision from the start. The external detail for each development had to fit in with the surrounding environment and this was the only area where simply pressing the photocopy button wouldn't do. A village location would differ from that in the middle of a town and if plans were drawn up in a conservation area then we needed to take account of that with our external designs. We had to prevent our architects from redesigning the wheel and by 1984 we employed twenty-two. I was not going to give them a free rein in their approach to design and I certainly didn't want artistic interpretation left to run wild on the drawing board. The simple rule was to get as many bed spaces in a development as possible while producing a building in a landscape that would be acceptable to the surrounding environment and to the planners.

Standardisation was critical. Internal designs could not be changed. Windows to the bedroom, kitchen and lounge were all of the same standard size. With a frontage of only ten metres there was no room for mistake. All the fire escape staircases were built in modules and we manufactured them in batches in our factory in Stem Lane so that the two or three required for each scheme would fit perfectly, be they full length or half space staircases. The space under the stairs was utilised within the building to give extra saleable space, so precision was vital to good economics. Corridor length was determined by fire regulations but we were able to work within the regulations and use the space to best advantage thus maximising bed and saleable space. Fire hydrants had to be planned in and these were expensive so we developed a standard approach in planning for these. From day one we used pre-stressed floors and produced them in such a way that the underside, which was the ceiling to the room below, didn't need to be plastered. Artex could be applied directly which saved a lot of time and money. The building inspectors were concerned about the sound insulation quality of the floors we were using and so we put on top of the screed of the floor a carpet material which we sourced in Belgium. We called it "sonic cord". This absorbed the sound and deadened it considerably. We employed Southampton University to do sound testing and they conclusively proved its effectiveness. It was so apparent that we went to see the manufacturers in Belgium and arranged for delivery direct to all our schemes. The sonic cord also acted as an underlay for any carpets fitted over it. Some residents left it as it was. Actually the cost of the sonic cord material caused our accountant a problem later on when the VAT man claimed it was underlay for carpets and not a vital component as part of the construction. We won that one on appeal. The walls between flats were nine inch concrete blocks that had to be improved for sound with plasterboard and insulation. Once again, Southampton University helped us prove the point that the steps we had taken were effective. We didn't want to leave anything to chance. Nothing was left to guesswork. Nothing was done by the seat of our pants. Everything was planned. My visit every day to our first development at the Waverley site ensured that I covered every issue as it became apparent.

All these additions and improvements became part of the Prime system of computer design. With greatly improved technology the centralised computer design facility was changed in the late '80s to a CAD (computer aided design) system that allowed those architects employed by each region to design the proposed developments within set down parameters. This meant writing off one million pounds of costs but it had to be done. Control of the software remained a head office function but the fact that the regions could be masters of their own design destiny speeded up the decision-making process. Even so, each scheme was not allowed to be deposited with the Planning Authority until it had been approved by head office. The control for this was that the application fee was to be made out by the group. Initially I took on this responsibility. Later, and once we had agreed the key issues, I handed this over to Gary Day, the director of the Planning Department. I always believed the first profit was made from the design. It was vital to ensure that the optimum value was obtained for each scheme. This was very much controlled by the policy of the sales criteria. Margin was all important and it was of little use that we were the brand leaders if we did not have that extra return which I valued at an extra 2 per cent. Early on we found that some regions started to deviate from our standards. While freedom of design was encouraged these had to be costed and approved before implementation across the group.

We became very proficient at designing products for standard use in our schemes. Wooden window frames were not ideal and from 1980 we were one of the first to pioneer the use of uPVC as a material for making pre-built window units, the insulation and maintenance being of paramount importance. These could be "popped" into place after the building had been completed and would fit like a glove. We developed a system of preformed frames around which the brickwork was constructed so the window frames could be put in after the building was roofed. This saved in cost and damage during construction. The uPVC material was low maintenance and saved on future servicing charges. Each would come complete with its double-glazing already fitted. We purchased our own window making company in 1983 to satisfy our demand for quantity and quality, and once the market caught up and we were able to outsource supply, we shut it down. We were one of the first builders in the UK to use this system and it has since become a standard practice for most of the industry.

We thought carefully about the design for carrying all the interior paraphernalia such as water pipes, electric cables and telephone wires for each flat. This was via a standard suspended panel in the ceiling of the corridor of each building and special blocks with holes for the services were manufactured at our factory.

All our flat doors were two foot nine inches wide rather than two foot six for easier access and we manufactured our own doorframes with standard architraves until we could outsource them. Fire doors and frames too were specially made and there were handrails in all the corridors. There were two sets of double doors to the main entrance of the building to preserve the communal heat, and a TV camera connected to each flat so the occupants could see via their TVs who was coming and going and each had the ability to allow welcome visitors access to the property at the touch of a button.

After our first developments we set up our own staircase manufacturing production line. The concrete stairs were pre-made in heated metal formers which saved so much time, effort and money on site. We didn't need the armies of concrete gangers and form setters that we used at Waverley where we built the stairs in situ. The stairs for other sites were delivered as made to measure units ready to fit into place. We did need tower cranes and Paddy Matcham, who had become something of a welder for us, became our lifting expert. He went on a crane course. We needed cranes to lift the pre-built stairs and landings into place, floor slabs, concrete blocks and beams. We created our own glass fibre moulding plant, for special baths and dormer window cheeks. With assistance from Help the Aged we designed suitably adapted baths with seats. We also fashioned the cowling for the vents fixed in place on the top of the building. We also built at our factory all the portable cabins and loos that we needed for use on our building sites. Before they were made by speciality, third party companies.

Uncle Alec became the plant and production manager at the site in Stem Lane at Numbers 9 and 11. In 1982 we eventually took the lease for Numbers 1 and 3. He, more than anyone, understood the working process we were keen to adopt. He was the ideal person I could entrust to get the job done right. Later Roy Garret took over Construction Services as plant manager.

I had overseen the day-to-day development at Waverley personally. I was there with the fifteen subcontractors and had a hands-on approach to every aspect of the work. I watched the budget like a hawk and learned from the start the right way to proceed to make the very best use of standardisation. I could see that we needed to pre-make the stairs and the windows. I could see that we needed a production line mentality to get the job done. The process for building my uncles' caravans wasn't that much different from building a block of flats for sheltered housing. I wanted to think like Henry Ford. I wanted to build on a production line like him where customers could have anything they liked as long as it was a Model T.

The elderly of the area loved what we were doing. We had queues of over fifty-fives signing up for the 120-year lease with ground rent and service charges on top. What we'd done from the start was right.

We identified our customer and their needs, giving them exactly what they wanted with our bundle of USPs or Unique Selling Points. We sold all thirty-two flats at the Waverley before the roof had been put on the building. Each flat went for £10,000. We immediately bought the doctor's surgery opposite and built another thirty-two flats putting the price for each at £15,000. They all sold like hot cakes. We'd hit a jackpot and one that was showing us a profit and a very healthy gross margin of nearly 50 per cent and a net margin of over 30 per cent. This was the highest in the house building industry by a long way.

In December 1977 Counsellor Iris Nedderman cut the ribbon at the entrance to our first scheme, the new Waverley building called Waverley House. We had a memorial bench seat made to mark the occasion and this was something we went on to do for every development. It was also the opportunity to invite planners and local dignitaries to view private sheltered housing and get them on our side. On the opening of Waverley one of the new residents said a few words about how wonderful it was to have such a well thought out home to live in and her words brought the residents to a standing applause. They also brought a genuine tear to my eye. It was a great day. Twenty-five years later the Beverley Sisters, with their high kicks and melodious sound, attended a celebration to mark the opening of the first scheme.

Things were only going to get better. I'd made a million on paper by the time I was twenty-nine. I'd damn nearly lost the lot by 1973 and, as a result of the Waverley idea for private sheltered accommodation, in 1977, I had discovered the means for getting back on top.

In the late 1970s we purchased Peverel and Company, an estate agent in New Milton, for about £45,000. The idea was to start our own sales department giving a particular focus to the sales side of the business. I knew the firm and had been dealing with them for a number of years and found them professional with some useful people on board. We took them on and they then only handled McCarthy & Stone properties exclusively. The owner of Peverel was Trevor Foan and he joined us as Group Sales and Marketing Director. Trevor also took on land buying. Buying the right land became a major key in the profitability of our schemes. We'd perhaps look at one hundred sites to find one that worked. We never bought on the assumption that the price would go up and only paid the price as it was valued on the day. Speculation was not the job of the land purchasing department.

We'd find sites by advertising and by blitzing an area. We'd take a team and go "spotting" for suitable brown field sites or buildings that could be redeveloped. In Oxford, for instance, we spent two days giving presentations and a lunch to local estate agents, solicitors and planners and we had six guys walking a town just looking. The exercise normally resulted in finding at least two sites.

I was back on track to making my fortune.

10. Stormy Waters

Success on the high seas was always paid for by success back on dry land. In the same year I had won the Yacht of the Year accolade, 1976, our business had developments in New Milton and Lymington funded by Barclays but the bank was in difficult times and calling in loans. I was summoned to a meeting at their Southampton regional office and the local manager, prior to the meeting, seemed to be on my side. Once in the meeting, however, he turned against the company and sided with the local director. I lost my patience and got up and left the room, slamming the door behind me. I later found out that the director was under a lot of pressure from above and that his wife had just died from cancer. He resigned from the bank the following week but the damage had been done. I needed to find another bank to work with.

At the same time as falling out with Barclays Bank, I met David Giddings from NatWest. He was the loans manager for the Bournemouth region and a keen sailor like me. He knew that I had just won the World's three-quarter ton yacht racing championship in Norway and I asked him to accompany me to the London Boat Show and introduced him to a few people. With Barclays being difficult I asked David Giddings if he'd like our business even though our borrowing was seventeen times our net assets. Without a second thought he said, "Yes. We lend to people we respect". He'd take on all the loans we had with the other bank and continue with all the schemes. This was another example of it's not what you know but who.

I made an appointment to go and see the manager of Barclays in Lymington and after waiting to see him I was called into his office. I simply leant over his desk and told him what to do with his banking in no uncertain terms, not just for the company but for me, my wife and family. He looked taken aback and asked what the problem was. I replied that if he didn't know then he was in the wrong business. We transferred all the accounts that day to NatWest.

The sailing business wasn't without its dangers. We had just completed a racing week at Burnham on Crouch in which we won every race and picked up shelves-full of cut glass as prizes. We then competed in the Burnham to Ostend race, which we won, and while on the homeward voyage towards Lymington, with only three of us on board, and one of those was a young French hitchhiker, we hit a furious gale. With the wind whistling in the rigging we tried to make Dover but because of the Goodwin Sands and the size of the sea we were forced to tack offshore and turned for Calais but couldn't get the yacht in there either. A violently swinging boom whacked into the ribs of the competent crewman and he went below with the travelling Frenchman who was no help at all. We tried again to get into Dover. I was helming and the only one on deck, clipped on by my lifeline to the weather rail. The yacht was battened down when I glimpsed over my shoulder a massive wave which enveloped me and the yacht, knocking the boat flat and flinging me into the water. The lifeline saved me and as the yacht righted itself, I was dragged from the water into the leeward lifelines. I was then able to scrabble back on, grab the tiller and carry on sailing. The two below were totally unaware of what had happened. Little did they realise that for a brief terrifying few moments they had been abandoned by their skipper. The winds were gusting between forty-five and fifty knots with foam on the sea. It was the shortness of the seas due to the depth and the sands that caused the problem and on more than one occasion I didn't think that we were going to make it. However, we did and eventually got into Dover and called home telling them that we were alright apart from one of the crew who broke two ribs. Actually, I confessed to Gwen that for a brief moment out in that rough sea I didn't think I'd be seeing her ever again. In 1974, Ted

Heath's yacht, Morning Cloud III, sank returning from the same race with the loss of two crew members.

I was a member of the Royal Ocean Racing Club and after the Southern Cross Series I was invited to dinner at the St James's headquarters. Around the table were some of Britain's best yachtsmen; Robin Aisher the Olympic helmsman. The owner of the Prospect of Whitby, Arthur Slater, was a very capable one-legged sailor. Chris Dunning of Marionette was the famous captain of the British Admiral's Cup team and from the RORC, Alan Green and Mary Pera, the secretary. There was an empty space on my right but we started the dinner and the talk was about the Onion Patch Series in America and the selection of yachts for this race. After the first course had been started and finished Ted "huffy" Heath, at that time Prime Minister, arrived and sat down next to me having come straight from the House delayed by a vote. The discussion continued about what size of yachts should be representing the British team organised by the Royal Ocean Yacht Club in the USA and I was of the opinion that at least one yacht should be relatively small, thirty-six to thirty-eight-foot, with the other two forty-five to sixty-foot. Ted Heath was against this, believing that all three should be large boats as the long offshore race was very important, worth double points, with bigger boats more suited to such racing. I pointed out to Ted Heath that a certain boat called Morning Cloud, one of thirty-two feet, had won the Sydney-Hobart race four years ago and was helmed by him. He replied that this made no bloody difference and that big boats should be sent to America. He was a pompous arse and, needless to say, one with a big boat.

The topic of financing the venture was discussed and the cost of shipping the boats to America and the expenditure. Robin Ashier of the Marley Tile Company thought that the finance could be raised. It had been for the Southern Cross Series in Australia and he saw no problem with suitable sponsors coming forward. He asked if I would be prepared to take my planned new one-tonner to the series to be held in 1979. I was reticent. He said the money would be there in time and

I needed to agree then and there. Put on the spot I said that I would take part. In the event, there were no funds so I had to dip my hand into my own pocket and finance my own trip. Ted Heath didn't participate. Chris Dunning did and so did the yacht Buttercup, owned by the butter king of Europe.

At our business premises in Stem Lane I built the new one ton Saracen IV Bruce Farr designed boat with a revolutionary drop keel. We made it quickly and very light with the same C-Flex system we had employed previously. I had designs on winning the One Ton Cup which was going to be held in Flensburg, Germany. If the new boat was going to race in the Onion Patch Series in the USA then time was very tight indeed.

The boat was launched six weeks from when we started to build it and the day after the launch we took it off to a race at the east end of Cowes. Despite having had the yacht measured, the handicap had not arrived. I hadn't sold the previous one which had been named as Yacht of the Year in 1976 and I'd put together a crew for that one in the same race. Bearing in mind that I had no official handicap I went up to the committee boat and asked them if I could join in the race after it had started to enable me to tune up. They gave me their permission as long as I didn't interfere with any other yachts.

The race started with my old boat getting clean away with Bill Dunstan at the helm. After a five minute pause we set off in the new boat. We overtook the whole fleet to leeward without interfering with any other yachts in the race. When we got to the finishing line we crossed it which, with the benefit of hindsight, was probably a mistake. We should have ducked out before crossing the line but at the time didn't give it a second thought. As we weren't flying a racing flag as one would if entered into a race officially, the rules didn't really apply. There had been some problems in the past with new yachts racing without having formally entered the race. One such had been Morning Cloud. Like us, they had no racing certificate and needed to tune the yacht as inevitably, due to changes of rules each year, the construction

Grandmother, left, and grandfather Sidney, right, with children Auntie Betty, Sidney (who died) and mum standing at the front. At the rear, grandmother's sister. (1922)

Left to right: Me, Carole, Dad, Mum, Vicky. (1945)

Our wooden store and home in Billericay. (1946)

Blue Cats Skiffle Group. Me in the middle at the microphone, and brother-in-law Brian Pink far right. (1958)

Johnny Mac Four: Johnny Reed rhythm, me, Joe Base on bass, and unknown rhythm. (1958)

Early tipper lorry and construction plant, McStone at Milford on Sea. (1964)

Diving for amphora off Croatia. *Right to left*: Captain Graham Pinch, me, Mark Gatehouse. (1987)

Racing *Saracen III* in the Worlds at Hanko, Norway. (1975)

Bill Stone and me at the launch of the two one-ton racing yachts I built – *Saracen IV*. (1976)

Opening of our first scheme away from our home town, in Bournemouth. *(Top) left to right*: Bill Stone, architect, Don Banks (buyer), finishing foreman, Harry Harrison, Fred Andress (surveyor), Simon Nunn (architectural assistant), Chris Powell (contracts manager), me. *(Bottom) left to right*: Evelyn (PA), John Gray (FD), Robert Young (chief architect), site manager.

My father's 70th birthday with his grandchildren at Westover House. (1978)

The boys – what a change. *(Top) left to right*: Clinton, Scott, Spencer. (1968) *(Bottom) left to right*: Clinton, Spencer, Scott. (1978)

Saracen in Hanko, Norway, winning the World and British Three Quarter Ton Cup. (1975)

Butler Verner sails, Solent Saracen 3/4 Ton British & World Champion.

The weather during the championship has been hard on boats and their gear. Solent Saracen, built in only six weeks prior to the British trials, was one of the few boats whose equipment did not fail.

The Daily Telegraph

Left to right: Tricia (Gwen's sister), me, Gwen, Mike (Gwen's brother); on our wedding day. (1982)

Gwen and me at Watton's Farm with my first Aston Martin. (1983)

Receiving my MBE. *Left to right*: Clinton, Gwen, me and Claire. (1984)

Tidworth Polo club success. *Left to right*: Spencer, me, Giles Omerod, Simon Kusyoe, with the best pony trained by Simon. (1985)

Aston Martin Volante 1986, and me on polo pony Crocket at Rhinefield in the New Forest. (1986)

was put off to the last minute. This would often coincide very closely with the timing of the main regattas. Obtaining a racing certificate would take some time as the yacht had to be measured on the water and it was quite a complicated formula that changed each year.

We returned to Lymington and put the boat on a low loader on the Sunday, bound for Liverpool docks to be loaded as deck cargo for America on the Monday. It had been launched on the Thursday, had performed extremely well in the trials on the Saturday, and was being shipped off to New York for the Onion Patch Series. It had been a rush to get the yacht ready in time but we had.

By the time the yacht arrived in New York I had the handicap certificate I anticipated. I arrived in the States with my navigator, David Worker, and we had to go to the World Trade Centre to get customs approval and clearance for the import of the boat from the dock at Queens. We arrived early one morning at the Twin Towers and eventually found our way to the right department in the vast complex. It was perhaps made to look even bigger because of the lack of people at that time of day. The reception area itself was the height of a three-storey building and the enquiry counter the length of several cricket pitches. We got into the wrong lift not realising that the "elevators" were floor specific and because of the height of the building an ascent might involve several changes as they carried passengers up in stages. We got to the 67th floor and found a lone supervisor who'd started work early that day. She ushered us to a desk in an open plan area the size of a small field. I remember asking her what she'd do if there was a fire in the place. She replied that she'd have to use the fire escape and that there were a number of empty floors left as such to act as fire breaks.

We got clearance and motored the boat with its mast flat on the deck up the Hudson River past the lofty gaze of the Statue of Liberty and right under the noisy flight path of the planes leaving LaGuardia airport. The panoramic and spectacular backdrop of Manhattan was an almost surreal setting for the two English yachtsmen and their vessel as the little engine barely coped with the strong American current. The river police wanted to know what the hell we were doing in those waters but once we'd satisfied them they wished us luck and sent us on our way.

Our first feeder race was to Rhode Island and I met Ted Turner, the renowned America's Cup skipper and owner of CNN. The sight of all the Maxis jostling for position at the start was quite something but we looked on rather than joined in with that particular mêlée.

The first race of the series we got clean away with a fast boat from Argentina in our class challenging us. We managed to get on the quarter wave of one of the Maxi boats and romped away from the opposition to win the first race. The second inshore race was a disaster and in the medium offshore race we came somewhere in the middle of the fleet and second to the Argentinians.

Before the Bermuda race and the finale, a contingent of American yacht officials came on board. They expressed their concern about the lightness of my boat and its ability to cope with the Atlantic Ocean. They had the cheek to call it "a Kleenex boat" and were threatening to ban us from the Bermuda race which they thought would be too dangerous for us to undertake. Chris Dunning, the captain of the British team, came to my rescue and he persuaded the officials that we were seaworthy. The Bermuda race partly crosses the Gulf Stream, the warm current of water that surges its way through the Atlantic and the Caribbean. Sailors can benefit from this current and enjoy an extra six knots of speed if they hit this strip of water correctly. It can work for you or against you depending on how you enter it. We had the charts and instruction from the Royal Navy to help us but the only way to tell when you've reached it is by the temperature of the water. We had a thermometer through the hull to give us constant temperature readings but we had to rely on our sound navigation, dead reckoning and a LORAN device. The race committee instructed us to have it with us. This gyro instrument was the rough forerunner of GPS and helped us to assess our position accurately and which way we were travelling in the helpful current.

We started the race with high enthusiasm and got away cleanly and ahead of the Argentinian boat. We hit the Gulf Stream and got the right side of it. Then the rain came. It fell with such force that it was like something out of the tropics. Our wet weather gear was no match and the water seeped into every possible wrinkle and crevice. Never had I been so wet. We looked like drowned rats.

The folklore surrounding the mysterious Bermuda Triangle overtook us and for a period of the race we became wrapped up in it and were quite concerned. It seemed as though we were sailing uphill and I have never ever experienced a sensation like it before or since. This extraordinary phenomenon lasted for two or three hours and all the crew experienced it. The feeling left us as suddenly as it had arrived and the horizon took on its former normal attitude and we sailed through the Triangle experience.

Sadly we came in second to the South American but the Royal Navy gave us a big welcome and took all our clothes and gear to their Chinese laundry and they returned it looking beautifully cleaned, pressed and dry.

Gwen arrived in Bermuda and we spent a week on holiday there before flying home. The boat followed us home via Queens for the One Ton Cup in Flensburg, sailing in the Baltic. The weather in Germany was just dreadful for sailing with gusts of seventy knots in the final race, and raising foam on the sea which kept it relatively flat and very difficult to sail. When the wind dropped to fifty knots it was a relief. One of the other English competitors unfortunately went aground and sank. Before the series I'd changed the drop keel to a fixed version. The yacht was unable to go upwind very well and its ability to point was insufficient to give it a real competitive edge. The boat that I'd taken to America never was really satisfactory and I sold it to a Welshman at a knockdown price.

I had taken part in three Fastnet races, which are run biannually, competing in both my one ton and three-quarter ton yachts with two races in very light weather. In our first race in 1973 we were doing fairly well and approaching the Lizard when we were engulfed in fog. While we were still sailing, albeit slowly, visibility was no more than twenty yards and eventually we heard water breaking on rocks. There was no option other than to start the motor, retrieve our course and go off south. We were disqualified after we reported the incident and it was held that we had sailed into the position even though it was unwittingly.

For the 1977 race it was reported in the press that we rounded the Fastnet Rock to go back home to Plymouth well in the lead. Unfortunately, by the time we reached Plymouth Sound the tide was against us and although we tacked in amongst the rocks, we had to anchor off for some twelve hours before the tide turned and wind increased sufficiently for us to continue. Needless to say we lost all we had gained.

After returning from America, Flensburg and attending Cowes Week, I only had three crew members who were able to take time off for the Fastnet Race in 1979. I decided that to attempt that six hundred mile race with just four of us was not safe. I watched from my house on the cliff in Milford on Sea as the fleet sailed past The Needles off the Isle of Wight on their first leg of the race, their spinnakers going before them. It wasn't until the next day that reports started to come in of problems. That was the year when the weather turned to killer proportions and twenty-three yachts were lost or disabled with fifteen fatalities. Among them was an American yachting friend, who I'd first met sailing in Norway. Another American, Ted Turner, skippered Tenacious and was the corrected-time winner of that ill-fated race. While watching television news of the race I saw David and Wendy Lewis, who I had known for many years, and their crew getting out of one of the air-sea rescue helicopters. They had to abandon their yacht when it filled with water and were winched up one by one by the overhead rescuers. Later their yacht was towed in by fishermen. It was ironic that, with all the sailing I had done that year in Bermuda, Flensburg and Cowes Week, the one race I wished to do was denied me. It was divine intervention or something as the race turned out to be one of Britain's most disastrous offshore yachting competitions ever.

My love affair with sailing in the '70s had the edge taken off it by the politics involved. There was the very unfair run in with Doug Peterson at the One Ton Series in Torquay in 1974 and the equally unfair business at the selection trials for the One Ton Cup with a boat called Winsome sailed by Daisy May of the Berthon Boat Company when he tried to barge in at a mark while on port, forcing me to tack away to avoid collision. That was the time when we ended up at the Royal Thames Yacht Club in Knightsbridge and, after hearing the protest appeal, I was told that May was a member of the Thames and as there was no collision I had no case. This was, of course, totally against the rules about having to alter course to avoid collision. I felt that I was up against "the old boys network". Actually it didn't do him much good as he wasn't selected for the UK.

At another protest meeting on a race, I appeared full of hope and, I thought, knowledge of the rules armed with a book showing quite clearly the rules, only to find that the person I was protesting against had written the book. I lost that one. However I did have one notable success against journalist and TV commentator, Bob Fisher, who arrived with his bulging briefcase under his arm for the appeal. It was quite clear-cut in that he tried to barge in at the starting mark when he had no right of way. It was similar to the incident that happened in Torquay with Doug Peterson. I called water, which is a term one has to use to notify the insurgent that he has no right of way. He did not respond and I therefore hit his yacht and protested him. With all his prevarication he still lost and he was disqualified.

You make friends and you can make enemies too. One such was the replacement navigator I took on when David Worker was unavailable. We were racing Saracen III at Burnham and were in the lead. I was sure we were going wrong as the rest of the fleet behind was sailing in a different direction but my navigator said we were not. When I asked what colour buoy we should be rounding he said red. We were heading for a green buoy. It suddenly dawned on me that he was colour blind. I suggested to him that his navigational ability was questionable and that there was no place on my boat for him anymore. I believe he must have taken my criticism rather too personally and he harboured a grudge, which as a member of some influence with the Royal Southern Yacht Club, was used against me.

The incident just prior to my American trip, when I crossed the finishing line with my un-handicapped boat, was probably the last straw. The Royal Southern Yacht Club tried to ban me from racing in the prestigious Solent Points Series. The club was only one of six involved with the series. After all the times I had raced for my country they didn't give their attempt at a ban a second thought. In fact they held the protest from the Southern without me being present and I was banned. Jack Knights, the yachting journalist, and Robin Ashier from the Royal Ocean Racing Club came out in my support and the rest of the clubs would not go along with the verdict, which effectively overruled the ban. But it was all too late. I'd had enough. I never could suffer fools gladly.

I never thought that I'd give up the competitive sailing I loved. There were so many wonderful and challenging moments. My emotions had run the scale from hysterical laughter to sheer terror. I guess that I had experienced something of the RAF fighter pilot's life after all. There is nothing finer than being at the helm of your own yacht early in the morning when you're on watch and the boat's gliding along with no sound other than just the whoosh of the water and the sun coming up over the horizon. I gave up ocean racing because I just couldn't stand the attitude of those that governed the sport. So-called professionals were gate-crashing the competitive side of sailing and the amateur was no longer the skipper of his own yacht. I would continue to sail for pleasure but never again for my country.

But I guess that the call of the sea is a hard one to ignore. My Farr boat Yacht of the Year from 1977 was converted into a cruiser and we took it to Majorca where we kept it for three years. My boys and I had great fun sailing around the waters there learning to spinnaker fly. The yacht by then was named Diversity and I gave it to the company. They had started a company sailing club which I wished to encourage as a team-building exercise.

I took up residency in Guernsey in 1996 and was invited to helm an American-designed Melges at the Guernsey Yacht Club. It was another world, a fantastic light day yacht with the hull, rudder, mast and keel constructed in carbon fibre and with a crew of four it was a very exhilarating and well-designed yacht. I bought one immediately. Racing in the Little Russell, the water on the south side of the island of Guernsey, was a great experience and with tides that can vary up to twelve feet it made for some great sailing with a fleet of other Melges. Later we went on to race in Lake Garda in Italy. The World Cup was held in Torquay in 1997 with over one hundred yachts on the start line from all over the world. The following year we did Spi West in France. I handed the helm to my son Clinton after a race. He involuntarily jibed and hit himself with the main boom, flew over the side and into the water, semi-conscious. He was picked up by a support boat and whisked ashore. His man overboard exploit appeared in the local rag the next day with a photograph of him cocooned in protective silver wrapping paper like an oven-ready Christmas turkey. We retired from the race.

We took a trip to La Rochelle but the French and their "knowledge" of port and starboard and their understanding of the racing rules was nil. We hit a buoy on rounding a weather mark and the penalty was two circles, which we did. Carrying on we picked up a wind shift which put us right back in contention and we ended up in third place. Unbeknown to us we were protested by the French who would not believe we had taken our penalty, but more than this they held a protest meeting without informing us and we were disqualified. We didn't hear anything about it until we got back to the UK. I then wrote a stinker of a letter to the race committee pointing out that they had not informed us of the protest, quoting the rules and suggesting that they were in the wrong. We had other yachts who had witnessed us taking the penalty and their skippers backed up my evidence. The French cancelled the disqualification and reinstated our position. This sort of knee-jerk, heavy-handed behaviour against foreigners was typical of the Gauls. Previous encounters in the '70s with their cheating by rowing at night and deliberately missing buoys didn't re-engage me with the sport I loved.

11. Planes, Planning and Pickets

Working hard and playing hard are of equal importance. Having spent time in Switzerland with a banking family, Gwen was a keen skier. Gwen's friend Jane Palmer was pretty competent and her boyfriend John Colwell and I were persuaded off to the snow in Obergurgl, Austria, in the 1970s. Our first lesson was with a seventy-year-old female ski instructor who seemed obsessed with getting us to master the snow plough and the ability to walk uphill on skis. It was bloody hard work and cold with it and not my idea of any fun at all. The following season it was Kitzbuhel in Austria and more beginners' classes of walking up the slope sideways on the cumbersome skis and snow ploughing down again. It wasn't until we discovered the French Ski School in Val d'Isère that the sport started to become fun when we were introduced to step turns. We had proper lessons, with races at the end of the week which gave an element of competition. John and I became proficient enough to ski with the girls and we started to enjoy the après ski.

On one occasion we had a short French ski instructor who, when he wasn't teaching skiing, was a baker. He asked the class to follow him one by one down a particular slope. He told us to stop and then instructed each of us to ski down so that he could see how well we were doing. He would go to the bottom first to watch our descent. Off he went at speed, zigzagging down the mountain, unaware that there was a road cut deep through the snow and invisible until it was too late. The poor skiing baker suddenly dropped out of sight down onto the frozen ice giving himself a nasty gash across his nose. At the end of that particular week his class turned up for the usual prize-giving farewell ceremony and we all put sticking plasters across our noses in tribute to his heroics. Sadly the École du Ski Français didn't see the funny side and the unfortunate baker had to go back to full-time baking.

In the 1980s we discovered Meribel in France and the Hotel le Grand Coeur. Skiing over to Courchevel and Les Trois Vallées was fantastic fun although Gwen had a nasty fall. To get her off the mountain we took down a sign and placed her on it like a stretcher and skied down to the mid-station. Gwen had snapped both cruciate ligaments in her knee, which caused her problems for years to come and she eventually had to have a new knee joint. The hotel offered some apartments that were linked to it for sale and I bought one of them for £50,000 on 9th September 1983. We still have it today.

The quickest way to get to the snow and around our different building sites wherever they were was by plane or helicopter. Trevor Foan, the guy we purchased the Peverel estate agency business from, had owned a single-engine two-seater and was a clear day flyer from Bournemouth Flying Club. In 1985, having travelled from Bournemouth to Eastbourne in his plane, we decided to buy a Cessna Golden Eagle twin with seven seats. We changed its registration number to G-RANY which raised the occasional chuckle. Well, we were in the elderly business. Our Irish pilot was called Brian McCann. He eventually took control of the Cessna 3 Citation jet we bought the following year for our international operations. That one crash-landed at Southampton but, I'm pleased to say, after we'd sold it in 1990. In 1987 we bought a Twin Squirrel six-seat helicopter. Dickey Bird was our pilot. He had flown for Robert Maxwell, owner of the *Daily Mirror* newspaper. We had approached him about landing on his building, the only approved rooftop in London, however he refused and we had to use the landing at Battersea, approached from the Thames.

The planes got us to our various European destinations and operations with our international business, Merlin in France, Duquesa in Spain and out to Norway. Flying down to Majorca in the Eagle meant we had to refuel in France. We could fly into Chambéry for the alpine skiing in Mirabel from our apartment. I would organise a long weekend skiing with business friends on the day the ski slopes opened. We sometimes stopped on the way to pick up Louis Adrey, the larger than life French dentist who I'd met through a Round Table visit. I was never a member of Round Table but met Louis through one of their networking visits. He was an extraordinary man who smoked all the time and had large sausage-shaped nicotine-covered fingers which can't have been that pleasant for his clients. He lived in a chateau in the middle of France with his wife Genevieve and drank wine like a fish. He taught me that a walnut eaten before a glass of wine helps the palate to appreciate the wine all the more. On one trip to his home I brought a sapling walnut tree back to England in the plane. I planted it at Watton's Farm but one of the boys sold the land with the house next door and the growing tree was promptly cut down.

The company plane was a real asset. Once I was flying up to Scotland to conclude a deal and we diverted to Manchester because I heard that a bankrupt site had come up on the outskirts. I signed the deal there and then for what turned out to be our regional office and works in Altrincham. Another time, again on the way to Scotland, I had a call saying a site we were wishing to purchase in Newcastle was being signed up that afternoon by Wimpey. We immediately diverted the plane. I marched into the lawyer's office, signed the contract and gave him a personal cheque to cover the deposit. But for being able to be in the right place at the right time because of the plane, I would probably not have acquired either. We must have flown about 1,000 hours a year and the majority of them trouble-free I'm pleased to say. John Gray, our financial director, suffered from vertigo and we had just persuaded him to use the plane when his condition wasn't made any better because one of the engines failed while he was flying to Ireland and the Channel Islands. Luckily the plane had two engines.

Our helicopter G-PAPA only let us down once. We were flying back from rather a good wine tasting session in London at Justerini & Brooks with their director William Glasson. I was a guest of Arthur

Griffiths and we'd been sampling some 1952 claret which I remember they had on their books at £1 and 10 shillings a bottle and some 1946 Armagnac. Gwen and I, Arthur and his wife were in the helicopter when Dickey woke me from my slumbers and said, "Would it be OK to land? A light for the rotor has come on."

My reply was something like, "Christ! You woke me up to ask me that. Get it down." So we put down at Popham next to the A303 and got a taxi home. There was nothing wrong with the chopper.

It was very useful in getting me around the country for site visits and in one day I could cover anything up to a dozen if they were properly set up with identified landing sites and waiting cars. We had a landing strip at home but the pilot wasn't best pleased when the ponies took an interest in the parked transport and started to chew it. It could take half an hour from my home to Battersea and another hour by car into the City. I used the helicopter too for flying to various polo matches. It certainly was the way to go and to arrive in style, and if needs be I could get back to the office in five minutes when landing in the grounds of the Royal Bath Hotel in Bournemouth after a game. In the gloom of 1989 and 1990 the company sold all our wings at a profit and we reverted to four wheels on the ground.

Back on the ground, Gwen and I lived at Hurst Barn, Milford on Sea from 1979 to 1991. I purchased a house at auction in the New Forest, just north of New Milton, which had about twelve acres of land with direct access onto the Forest. The hammer fell at £55,000. I completely gutted the house, removing all the plaster and the roof, and we rebuilt it after getting planning. I did a lot of the work myself. The location was fantastic and called Watton's Farm.

One Sunday morning Gwen and I were in bed and I was leafing through the latest copy of *Country Life* magazine. I saw a property advertised in a triple pullout called Squalls Estate near Tisbury in Wiltshire. I knew one of the acting partners in the estate agents handling the sale and made arrangements to view the property that afternoon. We were both bowled over by its location and four hundred acres including lakes, stables, barns, riding school and four-bedroom thatched house dating back in part to the 16th century.

We then left for our ski chalet in Meribel from where we made an offer of £900,000. On returning two weeks later we hadn't heard a thing so rang the agent. I was told that our offer was not sufficient and that they had somebody else viewing that afternoon who seemed willing to pay the asking price of just over £1 million. Gwen and I had fallen in love with the place and it seemed to have everything we wanted with potential to do so much more. I re-offered at £1.2 million on a Saturday and they came back and said that, provided we exchanged on the Monday morning at 9am in London, it was ours. I was aware that the owner was going through a divorce settlement but nevertheless we arrived in London at 9am on that Monday in 1986 with my lawyer, Steve White, and a cheque. They arrived at 11am. The vendor, however, could not exchange because he couldn't agree on terms with his wife who had joint ownership of the property. I said I'd give it until the Friday at midday. The sellers went to court and got approval for the sale and the deal was done. We bought Squalls. The other party who had wanted to do the deal came to see us afterwards and offered us an extra £500,000 which I turned down.

There was an issue over a right of way running through the middle of the grounds of the property but we felt confident that we could get this altered and did at a later date. We had to go to an appeals tribunal because of one objection from a local claiming that Cromwell and his armies had marched through the grounds to sack Wardour Castle behind. This proved to be a made up story and the right of way was changed.

The expanding business meant that there was a demand for expanding head office. We had outgrown our office in Lymington New Street and later Osborne House in New Milton High Street. In 1979 we purchased a site on an industrial estate in New Milton where I'd built one of my yachts. We bought two acres of land at Numbers 9 and 11 on the Stem Lane industrial estate, we then built new offices,

Queensway House and room for workshops and a storage yard. We later bought Numbers 1 and 3 when the owner, a boat building company, went bust and we did a deal with the liquidator Ernst & Young. It was from these two sets of buildings and offices that we started to develop our private sheltered housing schemes but it quickly became apparent that we didn't have enough space to cope with the new growing demand. We had already added on numerous prefab cabins but our projected growth meant we needed more office space.

One day I went to Arnett's showroom in Bournemouth to buy a Rolls-Royce. After meeting Mr Arnett I discovered that he had been given planning permission to develop his site into a four-storey office block. I went back to my architect team, looked at the scheme and it became apparent that we could get approval for an eleven-storey development. I went back to see Mr Arnett and did a deal with him for a new car and the site. I had to give him space in the building for his showrooms. He wasn't best pleased when he discovered that our planning application was for an eleven-storey building with underground parking. This was known as Homelife House and was completed by 1987.

The new Camargue two-door Rolls was delivered to my home. That same evening Gwen and I were going out to a party with two friends so we took the new vehicle. When we arrived the doors of the expensive new car wouldn't open, so in order for us to get out I had to lower the window and put the key in the outside lock to unlock the sealed door.

The next day I drove the new car on to the building site for our new head office and the same thing happened but this time the window would not lower either. I sat at the wheel while the workmen stared at the boss's arrival wondering what the hell he was doing. I pulled a sheaf of papers out and pretended that I was reading them while considering my next move. By luck I had one of the new "jumbo" mobile phones with me so I rang Arnett's and said in no uncertain terms that rather than going through the same palaver again I was going to leave the site and take the car home from where Arnett's could pick it up and sort it out. I certainly wasn't going to let the workmen on my building site have a laugh at my expense and show them that I couldn't get out of my new Roller. I wasn't best pleased.

On Sunday morning a week later I was washing the car. If one wants to inspect the bodywork for blemishes then washing the car is the way to do it. I noticed that the distinctive and famous radiator was about half an inch off centre. It genuinely was out of line with the bonnet and the bumper and, even though I did a double take, I could see that there was something wrong. I rang Mr Arnett.

"It is hand built," was his response. I can't remember mine exactly but it wasn't complimentary. There was no excuse whatsoever. I later used the example of the handmade expensive Rolls and the mass-produced Mini as an example of quality control when talking to the people who worked for me. I also used the fact that although the realignment was carried out, I didn't receive a letter or any sort of apology from Rolls-Royce about their sloppy workmanship. This was one of the worst examples of customer service or after sales care I had ever come across.

Homelife House was a new and prominent landmark for Bournemouth. We asked architects to tender for the design in a competition as we were looking for something that would really put our company boldly on the map. The winning design used lots of glass and was rather revolutionary and we awarded the contract to architects Headley Greentree of Southsea. It was likened to a 1930s radio with its retro style. The building won an award for its design and finish from the Bournemouth District Council.

The interior design was put together by Bill Bennette, a South African interior designer based in London, who I had used at home. We'd met him through Jane Colwell and he was very good and very camp. His designs included eight-foot high ash doors that looked very impressive.

I wanted a sculpture by Elisabeth Frink and went to visit her and her partner at her studio. We arrived and she opened the champagne almost immediately. My idea was for a piece to be placed outside the front of the new building that would reflect the business we were in and the people we were dealing with. I wanted a sculpture of a "mature" couple, male and female, in a Frink-like posture.

"I don't do women," was her answer to my request. We kept the £150,000 I had earmarked for the job.

A person of some standing was needed to open the new offices and we approached Margaret Thatcher. Sir Marcus Fox was on our board and his networking ability should have landed us the Iron Lady. She was too busy however and couldn't do the official opening for us in the time we had allotted. I was attending a luncheon in London with The Princess of Wales and happened to be sitting next to her Equerry, Lt Cdr Richard Aylard RN. It was a charity lunch and I got chatting to him about charitable subjects and mentioned that we had tried to get Mrs Thatcher to open our new head office for us. He remarked almost casually that had we thought about asking any of the Royal Family. I said that I hadn't. He said that if I gave him sufficient notice he could probably arrange for Princess Diana to come and do the opening especially with our connections in working for the elderly. I wrote a letter to Lt Cdr Aylard suggesting several dates and times for the ceremony. Eventually he came back to me with the acceptance which was a real coup.

My PA Lindsay Bryant worked out all the logistics and arrangements for the day. We had invited a number of elderly people to the building to meet Her Royal Highness and she chatted to them in her easy and natural manner about all sorts of things from knitting to flower arranging and bowling. It was as though she was an expert in all the topics she talked about. I was showing her around the building and I could not think of anybody in the world more perfect for the job. On the 7th floor we had a restaurant for employees managed by Compass and on the day of the opening my mother and father were there. Father was seventy-eight and not very fit. He had cancer and was sitting in the window with my mother. The Princess went over and sat down with them, leant over, and started chatting just as if they were old friends. It was a great moment of personal pride for me and quite something to see the three of them taking tea together and talking. My mother took the tea cup and saucer that Princess Di had been using home with her.

The publicity that surrounded the visit was the best possible and we gave a cheque for £2,000 to one of her charities.

The 8th floor of the building was mine. It housed offices for me, my assistant and my PA, the boardroom and a smaller meeting room, a dining area and a living suite with bedroom and shower. There was an atrium in the middle. The top floor was for the directors. Arnett's had their showroom on the ground floor but later went bust so we took the space back and turned it into more offices.

We had purchased some overspill offices as well, along the Bournemouth Road from a builder's merchants, Grays. These were used as a regional office but in the recession of the '90s we sold them and moved the South-West regional operation into the Head Office.

My son Spencer turned two of the floors into furnished lets. We had financed the property in the early '90s by charging it to Lloyds leasing. The small print wasn't studied in enough detail by our lawyers and accountants and we had a big tax problem which resulted in a cost of some £3 million over and above what we got on the lease after fifteen years.

Finding enough space to run the growing business from presented its own challenges but tussling with the planners for each new sheltered accommodation scheme was almost a daily occurrence.

I was used to planners. They were a particular breed, born and trained to say, "No".

In 1978 we had applied and been granted planning in New Milton High Street, having done a deal with the Co-op to take the supermarket space, with further shop units, offices and flats above. We'd deposited the building regulations with the council which meant that work could be started on the project immediately. We were under a time contract with the Co-op so I telephoned Mr King who was the chief building inspector for the New Forest region and based in Lyndhurst. His assistant, a reasonable fellow, rang back and said that Mr King wanted to see me so would I come to his office. When I arrived Mr King got up and locked the door behind me. He then turned on me saying that he'd had enough and that I was in for a serious bollocking. As quick as a flash I grabbed him by the tie and before a fight could start the assistant got between us to break things up. I told Mr King that I had come in to talk about the future and not the past. We had perhaps cut a few corners and argued forcibly in the past on the interpretation of the building regulations. It was an accepted practice that once the regulation documents had been deposited, we could start work on site. This had obviously put pressure on the Local Authority to check the application but we'd always sorted them out. The chief building inspector calmed down and I left with his blessing to start and his assurance that all was forgiven.

Some officials were just trying it on. At one site in Highcliffe we were putting in a thirty-six inch diameter surface water pipe. There was a phone call to the office at Osborne House from my site manager to say that the inspector said there was a kink in the pipe. Apparently we could buy him off for £2,000. "That's ridiculous," said I. I wanted to know his name so I could report him to the Local Authority. "Please don't do that," was the reply, together with the approval to proceed.

Educating the planners was an all-important task. This was not helped by journalists who described our schemes as "ghettos for old people". The *Daily Mail* ran with copy that implied too many old people living together wasn't right. We tried to point out that birds of a feather do flock together. When you are in your twenties you socialise and mix with those of a similar age and the same is true of the older generation. There was nothing unusual about what we were trying to foster. Nevertheless, two thirds of our plans for schemes were turned down and resulted in appeals.

One such was in Torquay. We bought two old hotels on the seafront in Babbacombe that really were past their sell-by date. We wanted to pull them down and build sheltered accommodation. The locals did not want to see hotels pulled down as they brought business into the town so the debate eventually led to a public enquiry. We brought in specialists, including barrister Jonathan Fulthorpe, to argue that tourism to the area had changed, that more people were taking their holidays in Spain and that the two old hotels in question could not survive. The planners brought up the issue of car parking and it was nearly always a major cause for the objection. We understood the issues and had of course got over that particular obstacle with our extensive and factual research. The elderly just don't use so many cars as the rest of the population so there is not the need for as many car parking spaces at homes for the elderly.

The appeal was expected to run for three days and halfway through day two the local council slapped a conservation order on the area we were talking about. Our barrister, Jonathan Fulthorpe, went mad and the inspectors turned on the planners and the whole appeal got rather heated. It lasted for five days and we won because they had shot themselves in the foot. The hotels were pulled down.

In Brighton we'd applied for a ten-storey building overlooking a park and after more than two years and an appeal we lost. We then applied for part of our costs that once again were over the car parking issue, which were granted. When you lose you nearly always get a blueprint of a plan that might be acceptable. We then went back to the council with the planners' approval and support. Still the council said, "No". We then went through a three-day public enquiry during which the car parking concerns were raised yet again even though they had already been overcome. The council didn't seem to mind spending its taxpayers' money and the inspector overturned the original decision and we built and sold for £8 million making a £3 million profit because the whole thing had dragged on for such a long time in a rising property market.

Each new scheme that we built sold well. There was a strong argument for bed space and in many cases we were encouraging movers to quit their three-bedroom properties for a one-bedroom flat. I attended the opening of the sales complex, of a scheme in Poole where we had a queue of potential buyers eager to put down deposits and on more than one occasion we drove the client, on their request, to their home to get their chequebook.

But despite the obvious demand, planners and councils still raised objections. At one meeting of the planning committee in Christchurch, the planning officers recommended the scheme. There were three planning officers, the committee, about eight members of the public, the local newspaper hack, Robert Young, my architect, and me. The committee voted and the result was a no.

"What shall I refuse it on?" asked one of the planning officers with obvious frustration. The reply came, "Just make up something." We appealed and after another eight months won with costs, changing the density of the plan. We reduced the number of units by converting a number of one-bedroom flats into two-bedroom flats. Three one-bed units would make two two-bed units, but the overall scheme was exactly the same size. We changed it back again before proceeding with the building. The planners agreed to the change although the committee wanted to refuse it. They were advised by the planners that there would be little chance of success at appeal as the bed spaces were no different and they would likely end up having to pay further costs of the appeal.

We learned to play the game. If we wanted a hundred units we asked for a hundred and twenty. Actually in Ferndown we asked for a hundred and twenty and got them so it didn't always go against us.

In Canterbury we put up a block with our uniform pre-made plastic windows only to be hauled up by the planners who told us that we had to use wooden frames. The building was in a conservation area and even though we did a survey of people passing by and 99% said they thought the window frames were made of wood, we lost and had to replace them with wooden ones.

In Cardiff we had bought the old council offices that were in a dreadful state of repair and had completed the purchase without any planning. We applied but meanwhile our regional office had decided to pull down the building. At 11am the same day as we had started demolition we were told that CADW (the Welsh equivalent of English Heritage) had imposed a spot listing status on the building, however a considerable amount of demolition had been completed. They had sent a fax to the council but not to us. We stopped work and CADW took us to court. Our London barrister informed us it was possible to list a building without telling the owners. It seemed that it was and there was no means of appeal against listed status. We had to plead guilty and he said that the fine would not exceed £50,000. We were fined £200,000. Meanwhile we received the planning permission on a listed building that had to come down and the council had sold it to us in good faith. I asked Gary Day, my town planner expert, to re-apply for another floor, to meet the council and make them aware of the misleading information they gave us on the purchase of the site. The extra floor with eleven flats was approved with the council's help. The extra floor we built paid for the £200,000 fine.

Planning is where the first profit is made. Without planning there's no profit. In Teignmouth, Devon we acquired an old hotel that had been very badly built. The centre part of the hotel was listed, the rest of it was a sham. The pretentious front columns were made out of bricks, the windows were steel and the render on the place looked like the batter on a piece of fish. It took eight years for planning approval and during the lengthy process the whole site was boarded up and became a playground for the local rats.

We had devised a roadshow with a video presentation that our architects could present to the planning departments to show them exactly what we were proposing in our niche market of private sheltered housing. It was important to educate and win hearts and minds so that the information could be disseminated to lay councillors to promote a positive attitude towards our proposals.

Some of our plans were a bit like climbing Everest. I did propose a scheme for elderly people at the Highcliffe Golf Club which was only nine holes. To do this we first had to persuade the members that we would replace their course and clubhouse on the site of the prestigious Chewton Glen Hotel, owned by Martin Skan. We had to convince him that this arrangement would enhance his hotel. We also had to get his neighbours on board and Oliver Nares and Hugh Stevenson had to be talked into approving the plans and into selling further land for the scheme. The Christchurch planning committee needed to be convinced for the change of the golf course to housing, and so we agreed to contribute to the restoration of the adjoining Highcliffe Castle, which was owned by the council and in bad state of repair. Further we needed to obtain planning from the New Forest Council for the new golf course and clubhouse, and from the highways department to widen the access road. We found ourselves negotiating at public meetings of members of the golf club and the eight parties all having a different axe to grind. We code-named the project "Patrick" and eventually everything began to fall into place. The market crashed and we tried to renegotiate terms but to no avail. We had spent well over £200,000 on the project so the decision to pull out was not taken lightly.

It wasn't only local difficulties we had to overcome, and central government too seemed to have it in for our plans. In the '90s they came up with their plan for affordable housing. I'd met Sir George Young when he was working with Michael Heseltine in 1977/78 on housing and the environment. He replaced Sir Marcus Fox who resigned in December 1999 as a non-executive director on our board. It was a mistake on my part to take him on as he had very little business sense whatsoever. Actually, he interviewed me for the job in Bournemouth and I appointed him to the board. He was a professional politician. He was instrumental in introducing the affordable homes plans in 1995/96 and when I saw the paper and realised what it meant, I was astonished and alarmed for the industry which seemed oblivious to the implications. He had omitted to tell me this at his interview.

Local government had no idea of the implications. We decided to raise the issue and assembled a group of influential journalists in London and explained the Government's plans for affordable housing to them over dinner. They didn't believe, or more likely were not willing to understand, what we were telling them. In effect the Government were demanding that 10 per cent of the land being built on, with in excess of forty homes, should be set aside for affordable housing. This later changed to 30 per cent and was up to 50 per cent in London. Once this was implemented it changed yet again to include the actual houses or the cost of them, and not just the land value, so it became a serious extra tax burden on house builders and land owners. The Home Builders' Federation seemed to have closed their eyes to the proposed new policy. We'd been through the act with a fine-tooth comb and couldn't see how this could be applied to developments for the elderly. You couldn't really have a happy or balanced mixture of the old and young living next to each other. Our sheltered accommodation schemes were very specific and you could not hive off 10 per cent of them as affordable homes for young families or single mums. It just wouldn't work, what with service charges and house managers and the whole way we had planned our schemes.

There was a public enquiry at Epsom for our four-storey sheltered scheme. We were surprised to see two further individuals from the Department of the Environment and a bunch of inspectors. We had been very successful at appeals in fighting the affordability issue and tearing the policy apart as far as sheltered housing was concerned. Very soon after the Epsom appeal amendments to the act were made to cover sheltered housing for the elderly but other builders and developers were expected to toe the line by providing affordable homes with up to 50 per cent on any schemes in London and in the rest of the UK on any development that was more than five houses. This plan stifled construction and was to my mind a dampener like the land tax of the 1970s. That had been repealed. Would they ever learn?

Sir George Young was pushing the Government's plan and I was fighting against it. It was a rocky working relationship. He queried my salary and my Aston Martin and the ground rent we charged on the house managers' flats we supplied for each scheme. He thought that we were making too much money. He just didn't understand the realities of the commercial world but I'd taken him on and I was stuck with him. There was a lesson to be learnt: Don't employ professional politicians and don't employ those who have very little or no knowledge of the commercial world.

The trade unions weren't as big a thorn in our side as Sir George. We crossed swords with them a few times. The Irish are a rebellious lot at the best of times and we couldn't take on any labour in Dublin unless they were a part of the union. It took us nine months to build a block and even though we had a very tough man in our HR department, Bob Sharpe, he couldn't stop some of the walkouts. We had a minor tussle with the unions or more probably the local mafia controlling the dockside workers in Jersey when they refused to unload a cargo of pre-stressed beams and other materials we had shipped out there, but the stand-off didn't last long once we agreed to use their transport.

We had our ugliest confrontation in London. The union had been speaking to our subcontractor bricklayers and were trying to sign them up as members and demand membership fees, which would in effect be paid to the union. In order for it not to spread like wildfire we had to take a stand. I rang Roger Humber at the Home Builders Federation and the National Federation of Building Trades Employers. His advice was that we should pay up.

"John," he said, "you're going to cause such an upset. Everybody else in the industry pays." It was common knowledge that some other house builders were paying wages to ghost workers, brickies and the like that didn't actually exist. The number of make-believe employees on builder's payroll would have populated a small town. The union got the money and the clout of course and the house builders didn't get any "trouble", or that was supposed to be how it worked.

"That's not the way I work," I replied to Mr Humber.

Bob Sharpe, himself an ex-trade union man, knew the workings behind the scenes. We arranged with all our subcontractors and the material suppliers of things like ready-mix and bricks that they would be available as normal and all of them agreed they would ignore any picket line. We knew the pickets would be out on Monday and we organised our people accordingly. The picket was ineffectual and our guys told their guys to basically take a hike.

The next day Paddy Matcham found that the crane on the site had been damaged. Someone had tampered with the cut outs for overloads. It would have toppled over had anyone tried to use it. Someone was playing dirty and surely not even the unions would muck about with health and safety. That night the site agent was followed home, his car was rammed and a brick thrown through the window of his home. There were threatening phone calls too and the scene was getting ugly. Our lawyers took out injunctions.

Another union picket mob turned up with a lot of blokes from Liverpool and we filmed them and went back to court. The injunction had been broken and the court duly fined the TGWU union. We never heard another word from them.

I rang Roger Humber and said, "We've won. They've gone and we ain't paying a penny." It was a lesson for the others in the industry but another that most of them had chosen to ignore.

12. Riding High, Diving Deep

I hate to come second at anything. Some might say that I'm competitive. It's just that I like to win. Coming second is not good enough. If I lost a sailing race it would play on my mind all week and if there was the chance to fight an appeal or protest, I would. The old adage "it's taking part and not winning that matters" is rubbish. It's winning that matters and it's winners who are remembered. I applied the same principles to horse riding and deep sea diving.

I'd watched and encouraged my daughter Claire to ride since she was four years old and first became interested in horses. Claire's first pony, Tony, gave her the basics of riding. Aged six she wanted to compete at showjumping on another pony called Black Pepper. Claire had a friend called Claire Chandler whose parents had bought her a pony. The Chandler pony was a good jumper and daughter Claire was impressed. She was giving lessons to her friend and wanted to see if she could find a similar pony. She contacted the breeder and discovered that there was another horse from the same strain so she rang the owner and Gwen bought the pony for £800. Claire went on to train it to showjump and eventually qualified it for the Horse of the Year Show at Wembley. She came second in her class and promptly sold it for £14,000. She was ten years old. She won the Young Rider of the Year award at Hickstead in 1994 with Zandor when she was nineteen and a Grand Prix at the Royal Bath Show on Capri. Claire has an eye for a good horse. When she left her private school, Wentworth in Bournemouth, she went into riding and breeding horses as a full-time business. Over the years she's had more than her fair share of spills and broken bones, including her foot and her back.

Not content with being an observer I wanted to have a go and in having a go I wanted to become good at it. I need to do the job and not watch it being done. Gwen bought me some lessons at the local riding school. The expression "fools and horses" could have been written for me because after just one lesson I was told that I was a natural. The owner Pat Pennington was also the principal instructor and she was a teacher in the true old-fashioned sense of the word. She was strict and quick to tell me what I was doing wrong.

"You've got a humpty back," she'd shout at me as I tried to work my way around the show jumps at the indoor school. That wasn't the last time I was to hear the word "humpty" in relation to me on horseback.

To get my posture in the saddle right she made me thread a broomstick from one elbow across my back to the other, pinning me in an upright position on my horse. There was no way I could slouch with that piece of wood forcing me to sit up as straight as a ramrod. If that wasn't a difficult enough task, I was then asked to jump without holding onto any reins. I fell off, of course I did, but Pat made me get right back up into the saddle again. Once again I fell off and broke the torturous broomstick.

"You'll jolly well have to pay for that," was Pat's response.

From 1980 to 1982 at least four times a week I'd go to the Burley Villa riding school run by the strict Pat Pennington. I'd be there at 7am most mornings then off for a shower and into the office by 8.30 at Stem Lane. At weekends we would compete in showjumping competitions across the South.

I bought a German-bred horse of over sixteen hands called Pootle. Pat found it for me and I paid £4,000. I persevered and we went showjumping to Gillingham, Hickstead and many other arenas. I bought another horse, Bubbles, who ended up with Harry Harrison, my construction director, who hunted with the New Forest Hounds. Sadly Bubbles was seriously wounded by an axe in one of those senseless and mysterious horse attacks. Another was an English thoroughbred called Miss Nova. I used to take her out into the New Forest and gallop her, and what a stupendous pace she had. I later gave her to Gwen. Unfortunately that horse cast in a stable and crossed a gut and died. Pootle was later ridden by Tim Davis and when he was nineteen he came second in his class at the Wembley Horse of the Year Show.

One morning I turned up at the riding school and Pat said that she had six different horses for me to ride. She was determined to get me to ride anything and not just something familiar and comfortable. I was beginning to understand the skill needed for showjumping. I thought that I could crack it, master the techniques but it was bloody difficult. I was also learning that the quality of the horse was a very important factor to success.

I went hunting, only twice, with the New Forest Hounds. I promptly jumped a five bar gate. The Master gave me a rollicking and told me that they didn't jump gates or anything else much but rather opened them or went around them. What a joke! Keith Lovelock, the guy I was grooming as CEO for the business, hunted too, and was a master at one time of the Portman Hunt. He invited me along with one hundred and fifty others in the field. I cleared a hedge rather than joining the queue of those trying to cross at a stile. Most ended up in an ignominious heap on the other side. As I cantered off in the clear I looked back over my shoulder at the confusion of horses and unseated riders, many of whom had broken bones. It was a pile-up of epic proportions. I had another outing with the South West Wilts and rode with a borrowed horse from Judge Royden Thomas's wife Caroline. He was a retired judge whose advice I sought when handling my time at the High Court under the cross examination of Lord Carman. Such was my hunting experience I only saw a fox once but plenty of protestors. The whole fox hunting arena wasn't for me.

There was always a lot of waiting around both with showjumping, hunting and cross-country eventing and I am always a much better participant than spectator. I was at a showjumping competition at the Hampshire Show one Sunday. Eventually my time came after hanging about for hours and my horse and I entered the ring. We had gone clear round with the last jump, a wall, between us and a place in the jump off. Right in front of the last jump the horse stopped dead in his tracks throwing me neatly over the wooden brick wall. I remounted and we tried it again. The same thing happened and when the horse refused I sailed over its head and over the jump once again. The third attempt was more earnest and I gave my mount some suitable encouragement. Again he wouldn't attempt the jump and this time I slid rather awkwardly over his head and shoulders and landed on top of the wooden brick wall. Three refusals and you're eliminated. That was the rule so we left the ring and the competition. Just as I was leaving there was some wag sitting on the side who'd been watching my efforts. As we went past him on our way out he couldn't wait to say as loud as he could,

"Humpty Dumpty sat on the wall!"

That was it for me. I had had enough of showjumping and much to Pat Pennington's annoyance, and probably the fact she was losing a good paying customer, I gave it up for good.

We had built stabling at Watton's Farm and we had fifteen acres for our horses. The local vet was "Jack" Broughton, a very good horse vet. He rang me at home on a Saturday morning and insisted that I go and visit the New Forest Polo Club at Lyndhurst that afternoon. I took an instant liking to the action I saw. There was no hanging about for your turn. It was fast, it needed individual skill as well as being a team game and it involved horses. I wanted a go. Jack let me have a ride on one of his ponies and for half an hour I had a go with a stick and a ball. The speed and dexterity of the smaller polo pony was remarkable. It would stop suddenly from going full tilt and turn on a sixpence. This was a different sort of discipline from the one Pat Pennington had been trying to drum into me, but her tuition really helped. Jack wanted his pony back to play and I'd nearly tired the poor thing out with my enthusiastic trial. I watched the match and was hooked and decided there and then that I would take up the sport.

After the game finished I was introduced to Giles Ormerod, whose son Maurice was later to marry my eldest granddaughter Laura. He encouraged me to get involved and with his help I bought my first two polo ponies. Later I employed him as my full-time polo professional. He had a handicap of plus two at the time but went up to three fairly quickly. The best in the world is handicapped at ten and in the UK we didn't have a player better than plus seven or eight. The handicap system starts at minus two. I joined the army club at Tidworth as well as the New Forest and it wasn't long before I had eight ponies.

Simon Kuseyo who was a Masai from Kenya had learnt to play the game while acting as a groom at the Nairobi Polo Club. He had come to England with Alan Kent, a professional player, and one day at Cowdray Polo Club he was asked to make up a team in practice chukkas as they were short of a player. He was so good that they gave him a handicap and soon he was playing off five. He joined my polo operation and team and I'd pay for him to come over from Africa to stay with me for the summer and train my horses and play. We played mainly low goal polo which is classed as four to eight. This is arrived at by adding up the handicaps of the four team players. Simon was a natural horseman and a good team player. He wasn't a prima donna like some of the Argentines. His biggest complaint was the elephants at home in his village rampaging through his allotments. He was one of the nicest of men I had ever met.

One day we played against the Prince of Wales team at the Guards Polo Club. Simon was very anxious when he heard we were up against His Royal Highness. He asked me what he should do if he came up against the Prince during the game and I told him to just give him hell like anybody else. We went on to win that game and proceeded up through the league in the Gerald Balding Cup. Sadly Simon died in a plane crash while leaving Nairobi on his way to a polo match. I donated a salver in his name to be played for at New Forest Polo Club.

Tidworth Polo Club was considering restricting non-army members from playing at their ground. I had bought some more land near Squalls Estate and decided to build my own polo ground. Ansty Polo Club was completed in 1988/89 and I did a lot of the work myself with refurbished stables and groom's quarters plus new barns and a portable clubhouse forty feet long by twelve feet wide which could be towed on and off the ground, therefore not needing planning consent. Because of the towing backwards and forwards and the hassle it caused I did apply for and won planning permission against much local opposition. The new clubhouse was a cedar-clad building with a thatched roof. We had a practice ground and the main polo ground on which the highlight of the year was the charity match in memory of Lord Romsey's daughter, Leonora, who died from leukaemia aged five in 1991. I approached Ronny Ferguson who I'd met at Windsor and asked him if Prince Charles would support our effort. He replied, "I doubt he will."

I asked him anyway. I was invited to his home with a few others in connection with raising funds for the repairs to the spire at Salisbury Cathedral. We had a common and sometimes controversial interest in buildings; mine with planners and his with architects such as those who'd designed "the carbuncle on the face of an old friend" at the National Gallery to which His Royal Highness had taken a dislike. We asked Prince Charles to come along and play in the charity match as he was Leonora's godfather. Over the next six years we raised about £230,000 net. The charity match was held at the end of July every year and a crowd of up to four thousand turned up as spectators to the event. It took a great deal of organising with hospitality, parking, ticket sales, police liaison, marching bands and the royal visitor. Lindsay my PA did a wonderful job with some very awkward people. The tight security even had lookouts for snipers in the surrounding hills to protect the Prince of Wales.

My team Squalls never beat my son Spencer's team Emlor which had His Royal Highness playing at the charity event. I believe that HRH was over-handicapped at plus three. He should have been, and was later, reduced to two.

I had an indoor riding school at Squalls in which we could play polo, particularly at the beginning of the season. On one occasion I played with my son Spencer, Claire my daughter and Laura my granddaughter. It was a wonderful family affair. I was breeding polo ponies and had about fifty by then. I'd been to Argentina on five occasions, both playing and looking for ponies. Spencer and I went to New Zealand as well, to look for new pony stock. We returned having purchased two. However the one I bought was very suspect and unplayable once we got it home. I was convinced that it had been doctored for our inspection. I had arrived at the farm unannounced but the owners kept me waiting for half an hour so they could presumably administer the enhancing drug to their duff pony. The expression "fools and horses" again rang in my ears.

Chimp was an Argentinian bred fifteen-hand pony and a favourite of mine. Unfortunately he died under me during a match, which seemed incredible. He suddenly slowed from a gallop to a trot and as he went down I walked off over his head to turn and look at him slumped on the pitch. He was dead twenty seconds later. I only ever played him once in a game for the seven minute stretch. He was so hard-working and I couldn't believe his demise like that. I never thought I could be upset over the death of a horse.

I had never broken a bone in my body until I started to ride. This was soon remedied with a broken collarbone on my left side while riding in the New Forest. In Argentina, just after the Falklands conflict, I was T-boned by one of my own Argentinian players which knocked me flat with a leg trapped under the horse and the right collarbone broken. My right leg was partially crushed and the horse lost an eye. I didn't discover this until the next day when I visited the yard. The poor horse had his head hanging down and when I asked the owner of the yard why he hadn't summoned a vet to put the animal down, he replied that it wasn't worth it. The horse died the following day. I'm afraid that the Argentines don't treat their horses with the respect we do in the UK. They do however know how to ride and play polo. They also know how to repair broken bones, especially broken collarbones. In the UK they gave you a sling to rest your arm in which didn't really help with the pain. In Argentina they took the pressure off the break with a cross bandage across your back and braced your arm accordingly, thus minimising the discomfort. I was coached by Alex Olmos at his estancia in Argentina and I sent Spencer out there for six months when he wanted to get serious about the sport. It was time and money well spent. He returned with all the skills and confidence of a good polo player.

My polo playing days came to an end when I was 59. It was May 1999 and my team was in a final at the Ansty Polo Club when one of my players suddenly changed direction and crossed in front of me without looking and his pony's hind leg caught the fore leg of my pony. My horse and I did a double flip and while I'd been unseated on several occasions this one was a disaster. The 400kg horse somersaulted over on top of me causing damage to my back. The pain was intense with multiple rib fractures one of which had punctured a lung; although my team thought I had winded myself I told them I could actually feel the bone in my lung. Painkillers didn't work and the on-site paramedic couldn't really do much for me. A helicopter flew me off to Salisbury and all the time everyone who bent over me kept asking me to tell them my name and address. They presumably wanted to make sure that I was still compos mentis. A local anaesthetic and a cut in my side for a tube were prescribed and all I wanted them to do was to get on with it, such was the pain. Four nurses had to hold me down when they tried to get the tube in through the incision. The anaesthetic hadn't taken effect but the tube did its job by draining the blood and air that had accumulated in my chest cavity and at last the pain left me. I spent five days in intensive care and a few days in Salisbury general hospital before being moved into a private one. I came to the conclusion that there were still other things that I wanted to do in this world and that if I carried on with polo there was the likelihood that I wouldn't succeed.

I was unable to play in our next charity match. Prince Charles sent me a personal note wishing me well and later I was able to introduce him to my surgeon just in case he had any more breaks. The Prince of Wales was very supportive of polo and Ansty, although I couldn't say the same about some of his minders. They seemed more concerned with corralling the media out of the Prince's way. I tried to persuade them one year that they could photograph the Prince during the prize-giving and then go away and leave him alone. This worked well but the following year there was a change of "guard". They reverted to their old ways and there were problems with, in particular, the *Daily Mail* and some adverse comments. It was obvious to me that if they are given proper access the media can behave. If they are held back and treated as the enemy then they will bite back. I believe that a lot of the bad press the Prince had was brought on by the poor handling of the press by his advisers and their overreaction.

I gave some of my ponies to my granddaughters and the rest were sold. The club at Ansty nearly fell into the hands of a scoundrel, another polo player, who wanted to take it on but didn't have the wherewithal to do it. I then did a deal with David Heaton-Ellis who took it on but the difficulty of getting teams together after the first season meant that it wasn't really viable. I had already asked the previous manager, George Smith, to resign as he wasn't really up to the job and eventually the club was shut down. The site is still there but the sound of pounding hooves and the bustle of the watching colourful crowd is a distant dream.

A further sport I took up was diving at sea and my first experience was in 1986 although I'd set out to have a go a lot earlier. When we bought Tim Ham's business in 1970 part of the acquisition was his old twenty-foot boat. It had an inboard engine and some diving equipment on board and that was about all. We took the thing out from its mooring at Keyhaven with Gwen, my boys and my brother-in-law,

Brian Pink, on board. We anchored off Hurst Spit with the idea of trying a bit of fishing and maybe some diving. A large liner came through and its wash caused us to drag our anchor which, in starting the engine, then got tied up around our propeller. We were ill-prepared with no flares, life jackets or radio and in the strong current we started to drift as the tide took us off towards The Needles rocks off the Isle of Wight. We waved for help at those that passed us and they waved back blissfully unaware of our plight. Finally I found a bucket and with some engine oil and a rag we lit our homemade distress signal and a passing helicopter called up some help to rescue us. A local with a motor cruiser took us in tow. The children were taken off safely and the boat was towed back to shore with me still on board. After tying the boat up alongside the quay we were invited aboard by the owner of the rescuing cruiser for a brandy to recover from our ordeal. Tim Ham turned up and came aboard to ask what had happened. He said, "You better come and see the results." When we returned to our stricken boat we found that it had sunk. The P-bracket had been pulled up through the bottom of the boat when the rope had entangled the propeller. We never got to use the diving gear.

Aguirre, which is Spanish for conquistador, was an 86-foot Italian built vessel. I bought it from a German on the recommendation of my yachting friend, George Stead. The whole family had gone down to our villa in Majorca for a holiday. My Farr yacht had been left at the boatyard for some running repairs over the winter. It hadn't been touched and I was furious. We met George at the airport and when I explained the problem with the yacht he invited us out on his 55ft cruiser. After a trip on his boat the boys lost interest in the Farr yacht which could only do six knots compared to twenty-five knots on George's cruiser and besides his had a barbeque deck. George's boat was moored alongside the German's in Majorca. My boys were very keen on the Italian vessel so we arranged the deal and for £1.5 million the boat was mine. The engines had only done about 50 hours so it was virtually new. It slept eight and Graham Pinch was its skipper, Zoe, his wife, the cook and a stewardess and deck hand made up the crew of four. The previous owner had been a diver and all the kit was included with the purchase. George was keen to show me how to use it and so in a bay off Majorca I had my first underwater experience and went down to ten metres. It was rather claustrophobic.

Our skipper, Graham, didn't know anything about the diving kit and so we ended up tying a balloon onto a thirty-foot length of string so we would know when we had got to that depth. We tied a plastic yellow milk bottle crate onto a further rope at six metres from the dinghy and that had two objectives; one to show us where the dinghy was from below the water and two to act as a safety stop point. In this way we could safely ascend and descend and get our first experience of the underwater world.

Never dive on your own and always, always with a buddy. It was a lesson I learnt early on. I was on holiday on board Aguirre. One day I had put a full 5mm wet suit on rather than a thin half suit and didn't check the weights so when I tried to descend I couldn't. I was trailing a balloon on the surface to show to those above that there was a diver below. I was having great difficulty in trying to descend and tried time after fruitless time. As I bobbed about in the bay I was concerned as the water skiers and speedboats flew around me at an alarming pace. When I realised my problem, I decided to swim back to Aguirre and was about to climb on board when the engines started up. The skipper had decided to move the boat as another boat moored close by was dragging its anchor towards us with no one on board. He had checked that my buoy, which had been blown on the surface, was well clear of Aguirre. The propellers driven by three 1,080 horse power engines would make mincemeat of anything they touched and a diver in a wet suit would be liquidised like a tomato in a Kenwood. As I clung onto the stern of the boat, thank God the skipper moved her forward. If he'd put her in reverse that would probably have been the end of me. I was blown off the rung of the ladder as the yacht pulled away. I was frightened and furious but lucky to be unhurt. I have never dived on my own since.

What I needed was a course of lessons. I enrolled on a BSAC course at Poole Dive Centre which took me through everything. I had ten lessons in a swimming pool, followed by exams. The lessons encouraged me to buy the right kit and throw the old gear away. Armed with renewed confidence we decided to take Aguirre to Turkey with a two-week break on the way in Malta. While in Malta Gwen and I obtained our PADI advanced open water certificates which included underwater navigation as well as diving at night. Graham with the boat and crew were to stay in Turkey for six years. The waters off Turkey are fantastic for sports sea diving and the water is as clear as gin. The wrecks are plentiful and the artefacts, such as amphorae and old cannon balls are preserved in their underwater grave. Diving is a remarkable experience with the feeling of weightlessness and the ability to glide along and to breathe in to ascend and out to drop down. You enter into another world. The sights you see make it almost addictive. The right gear is a must and with new computers you can tell at a glance the amount of oxygen you are using and how much you have left at that depth. Sports diving normally does not require a safety stop although we did so religiously. This was to ensure that the oxygen that is retained in the body is dissipated. If it wasn't then there was a likelihood of the bends when it expands in your joints as you surface. Another danger is coming up too fast. You have to make sure that the balance of the pressure in your ears is correct. Continuously breathing out is vital as the air in your lungs expands and can burst them if you hold your breath on the way up.

It was in Turkey that I met Tanner. He had retired from the army having bought himself out after being locked up in the glasshouse for three months or holiday camp as he called it. He was a Turkish national and the equivalent of an ex-SAS or SBS operator. He was a superb and supremely fit diver who knew his way around. He ran several miles every morning. His experience had included underwater work for his government with, in particular, the grisly task of retrieving dead bodies from sunken vessels and suicide jumpers from under the Bosporus Bridge. Tanner lived on the boat with us and was our invaluable guide both on land and under the sea. Tanner was an exceptionally good diver and he taught Scott, my youngest son, and Claire to dive.

One evening we were in a bar drinking until the early hours. We had been sitting cross-legged on the carpets consuming the local brew. Friend Ted Harber and his partner Caroline, Gwen and I and Tanner had left the bar and wandered back through the village to the pontoon to find our rib. Ted was bringing up the rear. The rest of us had clambered aboard the rib. There was a scream. Ted had decided to take a short-cut in the dark and walked straight off the end pontoon and into the sea. While we were considering what to do, quick as a flash Tanner ran and dived in after him. But for Tanner's lightning reaction, Ted might well have drowned in a drunken stupor.

In 1989 Tanner asked me if I would like to go for a deep dive on a single tank of air. We went down to 62 metres and although he wanted to go deeper, there was only one minute of air left at that depth. He kept his eyes glued to mine all the way down to see if there was any sign of panic or narcosis. There wasn't but I thought that it was more than enough and it was the deepest I've ever been.

Off Antalya in Turkey there is a First World War wreck that is off-limits to public divers. It had become too dangerous and unstable to explore. Tanner knew the commander of the port and so the three of us arranged a dive. We descended to nearly fifty metres and went right into the hold of the old French warship. I could see some of the cargo, the rusting old-fashioned half-track vehicles, corroded ammunition and the gaping holes where the explosive shells had ripped into the side of the ship bringing it down to the bottom. It was as though the sinking, the skirmish, had only just taken place and there we were in the midst of it all. Tanner and I visited the scene three or four times and once I did indeed get tangled up in some old wires. As soon as that happened I stopped and signalled to my buddy and, but for Tanner's help, I could still be there today.

I went diving in Croatia the year before the war out there. My brother-in-law, Mark Gatehouse, and I did a night dive into a cave at about twenty metres. We should have marked our way in with a line so that we could find our way out again, but foolishly we didn't. Panic uses up your air. Luckily we found our way out. There have been one or two other events I'd rather not have gone through. Clinton's wife Kathryn nearly came up too quickly on a dive in Turkey and hurt her ears. Luckily, with Tanner on hand, any serious harm that might have been done was avoided. On the same occasion I had to give Scott my air when his ran out.

Once in the Ionian Sea we dived from our rib and when we came up it was no longer there. The waves were quite rough and the skipper of the rib hadn't paid adequate attention and had lost us. We floundered about in the rough sea getting more and more anxious and tired until we attracted the attention of the people in another rib who alerted ours to come and rescue us. The skipper of the rib got a bollocking he wouldn't forget that day.

Most of my six hundred diving experiences have been ones of beauty. The longest I've been down is one and a half hours and the deepest is sixty-two meters. I've swum right alongside sharks at the gardens in Tobago Quays in the Caribbean and with manta rays at sixteen metres off the Maldives. I've dived down to wrecks galore in Turkey and retrieved parts of cannons as well as cannon balls. I've handfed giant guppies off Sardinia and seen two love-struck Americans propose and accept marriage to each other while diving off Palm Island.

Aguirre was sold to a Welsh car dealer for £800,000. I had the yacht for nearly fourteen years and several problems began to appear and in particular the three GM engines were causing big trouble. Within a year the Welshman went bust and the bank offered me the boat back at half the price. I said no thanks. My boys persuaded me to buy another "stink pot", saying that as children they had enjoyed Aguirre so much. The grandchildren were keen on a new boat too. I would have liked to have bought a serious sailing yacht again but instead I was talked into Dreamcatcher, a hundred-foot yacht built in Italy by the Ferretti Yachts Group. The grandchildren named it. I wanted Dream On but was outvoted. Launched in 2004, it was run by a New Zealand captain called Clint Burgess. I'd interviewed six others for the job and Clint stood out by far and he certainly knows what he is doing. We would take on a deck hand, a chef and a stewardess when the family were onboard. The yacht has three guest cabins and one for the owner and can sleep ten, plus crew accommodation. It is fully kitted out for diving with two sail boats in the stern garage. She is based in Puerto Portals in Majorca and normally kept there for the winter. Buying diesel fuel by the ton, we'd motor off in the summer to the South of France, Italy, Sardinia and the Greek islands. The two MTU 2,000 horsepower engines make it a thirsty beast. The boys agreed to pay for the running costs however while I forked out the initial capital expense. We had intended to only keep the boat for two years but here we are six years later still catching those dreams.

I guess if I had the time I would have liked to do some underwater treasure hunting and exploring. There was a friend of Mark Gatehouse, Gwen's brother-in-law, called Howard Curtis who worked on the oil rigs in the North Sea and other rigs around the world. He was a professional diver. He apparently knew the location of some treasure ships and had all the research material for locating them. We talked about diving and exploring for them. Sadly, though, Howard died and nothing more came of the idea. Mark is a bit of an adventurer and he and Mike Holmes, Gwen's brother who is an ex-naval commodore and who oversaw the supply and commissioning of Trident submarines, decided to sail together. He and Mark are both serious sailors and have raced across the Atlantic. On one trip in heavy seas at night Mike took over the helm from Mark and thought that Mark had gone below. There he was sailing along when all of a sudden he got a tap on the shoulder. What a shock. It was Mark who had gone up to the bow to adjust and check a foresail before going off watch. He had actually slipped and fallen over the side of the yacht. He had managed to grab the rope in the sea trailing behind for just such an emergency situation and had hauled himself back on to the yacht which is an amazing feat in itself. If you try it, you'll find that you are towed underwater and you'd have to summon all your strength to pull yourself back to the safety of the speeding yacht. The trimaran would have sailed on with its sole occupant completely oblivious to the fact that he was on his own with his mate lost in the Atlantic. What a close call.

Diving in the sea, it's like walking on the moon but a lot easier to get to. It's entering a different world, one that's a million miles away from the boardroom.

13. Good People, Bad People

I don't like cheats. I've come across them, be they French yachtsmen, dodgy car dealers, fouling Argentine polo players or thieves. I've come across a few of those, some clever and some not so. Some of them would never learn. One director of a finance company that went bust when we were starting out on the Buckland Park site contacted me years later and I met him in Almeria in Spain for lunch. He wanted to do business with us out there, but once bitten.

Then there was the guy we fired who was having an extension built on his house and the contractors would be awarded contracts with McCarthy & Stone on the basis that they would carry out work on his home. He was effectively charging the work to our business.

In the late 1970s I met a man who had a kitchen manufacturing business and a love for racehorses. He told me of the time in his early days when he made £20,000 profit and was advised by his accountant to roll it over by buying two horses for £5,000 each plus £10,000 to manage them. One of them went on to win everything and he sold the stallion to the National Stud for £1m. The other he sold for £25,000 having again been fairly successful. Success with horses compounded his tax "problem" rather than helping it. I was introduced to his CEO. We bought his kitchens for our sheltered schemes and once at a site in Yeovil his delivery truck turned up. The driver said that we could have the kitchens for nothing provided we tore up the delivery advice note. There was some scam on the go and we reported it back to their head office but heard nothing more. He sold out for £70 million to the management and retired to the Isle of Man.

Being informed is key to business success. There are some who have tried to bug meetings with me because they probably hadn't got the business confidence or had something to hide, or they believed something to gain surreptitiously. To my knowledge, I've been bugged at least three times in my working life and probably quite a lot more. I have only ever resorted to using a hidden listening device on two occasions and both of them when I knew that the other party was trying to cheat me. It was self-defence.

In 1986/87 John Gray and I were exploring a deal with a Scottish developer who wanted to negotiate a partnership with us. We were trying to get a foothold into the Scottish market. The amount of paperwork was becoming silly. The agreement between us was as thick as a Bible and when things get like that it's probably time to pull out. In my book, thick agreements equal doubt and thin agreements equal trust. The best deals I've done are probably the ones done with just a handshake. We had arranged a meeting in an Edinburgh hotel room and the negotiations were nearing their conclusion. They left John and me to talk through the proposition of percentage profits distribution and John and I agreed the range to offer them should be between 20 and 28 per cent. They came back into the room and after brief discussion they came up with the figure of 28 per cent. It soon became clear that they had been overhearing what we had been talking about in supposed privacy. We left.

We met up again because they had an interest on a site in Largs I thought was worth having. This time we'd bugged their room, or thought we had, to enable us to defend our position. The equipment either didn't work or they had installed an anti-bugging device. Either way we decided not to do anything in partnership with them. We did get hold of the Largs site though and went on to build a very profitable scheme.

Cheats don't prosper. It's hard, honest work that counts whether it's for profit or pleasure.

Good businesses are built by good people and early on I learnt that in order for us to grow I had to find good managers. It certainly isn't easy and there were some mistakes made on the way.

Getting it right was important. At the first company conference in Guernsey, held in 1980, we set out our five-year plan. Our first regional office opened in Eastbourne in 1981 with its regional manager Fred Andress from New Milton. The next was in Byfleet, south of London, with its manager Peter Askew and later Mike French. Altrincham was run by Alan Barton, Bedford by Tim Taylor and later Peter Cobb and the Glasgow office was managed by Jim Sharp. In 1983 the Halesowen office opened in the Midlands run by John Palmer. In each case the regional expansion was headed up by someone tried and tested from within the business and in this way promotion and a step up the ladder was visible to all.

I interviewed Keith Lovelock in 1986. I was looking for a house builder who could run an international division as I was thinking about diversifying into Europe. He was the same age as me and had a background working for Rush and Tomkins, Wimpey and Federated Homes. Because Keith had overseas experience and spoke fluent French I made him CEO. He was very amenable although rather aloof from his employees. Quiet-spoken, he would think things through and eventually persuade those around him to his way of thinking. He was what I'd call a common sense manager.

In 1987 we bought a failed French company called Merlin for its asset value from the banks. I believed that even though Europeans looked after their elderly in more traditional tight-knit family groups, there was still a need for the type of private sheltered accommodation that was taking off so well in the UK. With his previous knowledge Keith was against the acquisition but managed the business. Merlin built holiday homes in the Alps and the South of France. The idea was to use the company to obtain further access to sites across France for sheltered schemes and use the personnel to short-cut our way into the market. We were already building sites in Grasse, Juan-les-Pins and another in upmarket Antibes under the name of Homelife SA.

Merlin used to sponsor the Tour de France to the tune of £1 million. We sold the rights to Coca-Cola for £50,000 and maybe we could have got more. We had planned to develop some of the sites into homes for the elderly but the French red tape and the "legalese" and due diligence were to prove a minefield. I remember thinking don't ever buy another French business. I should have learnt from my sailing encounters with them. They were slippery customers. Almost the last straw came when the sales girl we were employing at the Paris office, in La Opera, was caught selling our sales leads to our competitor. She admitted the crime and we fired her. She took us to court and the French employment laws took us to the cleaners. She was awarded £50,000 in compensation because we hadn't given her a warning.

Our last attempt to make money with Merlin, renamed Quadrant SA, was an idea Keith had to build 130 apartments in Val Thorens just prior to the Winter Olympics held there in 1989. It turned into a flop and took years to sell. Keith bought a pair and knocked them into one for his family's private use. We made some money but couldn't get the margins we wanted and enjoyed back home. There was not enough to keep our interest over there viable. Keith didn't like Quadrant much and my view of sticking with what you know forced our decision to wind up the company.

In 1989 I asked Keith to join the main board. When the market downturn happened a year later we needed to shed all our development sites in Europe. At Duquesa in Spain we were going to build 150 villas right alongside the golf course and the sea. We had an offer which our board thought we should accept. Keith thought it was worth more and indeed got an offer from a developer in Gibraltar which made us an extra £1 million. The golf club was furious with us.

We had decided to build an hotel development in Santa Ponsa, Majorca. The idea seemed sound, offering a special holiday hotel in the sun for an elderly clientele, marketed via our own *Homelife* magazine to all our elderly clients in the UK, by that time some 35,000. This was a quarterly, put together by Kevin Holland, marketing, and Jane Kerr, PR, for all our customers and staff and had a print run of 15,000 copies. We were aiming to fill the rooms between October and April and we arranged flights and we were ABTA registered. An estate agent from New Milton, Richard Coope who had married an ex Miss UK, Marilyn Ward, was our man out there. He recruited a local called Sebastian Fray and the hotel, Casa Vida, was built. Our first guest was Len Squires, the purchaser we sold our first bungalow to in Lymington in 1963. He was the house painter who I worked with at FJ Pearce in 1959. The hotel was designed on the same principal as the schemes in the UK with small apartments, dining room, a resident house manager and a specially designed swimming pool. However I insisted that the design should give us the opportunity to sell the flats separately if it did not work out and this was fortuitous as many of the hotels on the island, instead of closing up for the winter, started to do exactly what we're doing. Our financial model for the hotel idea floundered. We decided to retreat in 1991 and sold the forty-six flats on a new timeshare concept based around six co-owners each owning two months revolving per annum. We did retain one two-bed flat as a free holiday incentive for employees who had well and truly exceeded their budgeted objectives. This useful incentive was later dropped, much against my better judgement.

Sebastian got hold of a block of land for us adjoining Casa Vida where originally the main power cable supplying electricity to the island ran ashore. We bought it for £20,000 but planning permission was granted then revoked in true Mediterranean political style. We doubled our money when we sold the site.

We had built a very successful scheme in Jersey notwithstanding the "mafia" who initially refused to transfer materials and equipment imported from the UK to the site. It was our wish to build further schemes on the island. We had found several sites for sheltered accommodation. When we took our proposed sketch schemes to the planners for their comments, the next thing we heard was that the Island States Authority had compulsorily purchased them. We suggested that we could act as their agent in exchange for keeping and running a scheme but nothing came of it and we pulled the pin on that potential enterprise as obviously the mafia was hard at work behind the scenes.

We also had to shelve our plans for Norway and Düsseldorf where the renting culture was stronger than the need to purchase. Our foray into the international market was short-lived and a distraction, especially in times of an economic slump.

From 1984 to 1990 John Begbie was my Financial Director. John came from the construction industry with John Laing. He was a very laid back individual whose mood swings did him no favours. It was to be shown that he really couldn't stand the heat in the kitchen. His replacement was Martin Towers. Even though he came highly recommended, it became clear that he too seemed more worried about the company's bankers than its shareholders. He too had to go.

Matthew Thorne had helped us with the flotation of the company in 1982. He'd been an accountant/director with County NatWest having qualified with Price Waterhouse and with some experience of working with the Beazer Group. He wore glasses that he'd remove at any and every photo call, which made the rest of us pull his leg. He presented himself very well, knew all about the City and came across as one of them. I never quite trusted him, feeling that he could be something of a plotter behind my back. We had several boardroom exchanges over strategy and he and I would end up arguing while all the others just looked on. He pushed for a pension policy based on two-thirds of pay at retirement which is something frowned upon today. I wouldn't agree to that. He tried to impose a ruling about the car I was allowed to have. He didn't win that one either. Terrier-like he wouldn't let go of the share options and the various permutations that this could bring to him and the board. I had to rein him in and so appointed Sir Marcus Fox as a non-executive director to chair the remuneration committee of which I and the CEO, Keith Lovelock, were also a part.

I was concerned at the amount of the provisions that Matthew was deducting from the profit and loss in the accounts. Not all of this was being agreed by the Inland Revenue. Three issues concerned me. The reported profits in the accounts were lower than they could have been and therefore the shares could have taken a knock. Secondly, the Inland Revenue were insisting on us paying tax on part of the deduction as they did not agree. Thirdly, these provisions were being written back in later years, inflating the profits and, in particular, the results of budgeted profits and thereby overachieving in bonus allocations. I believed this was misleading the public and shareholders as well as costing the company in cash flow and awarding bonuses by stealth. Matthew it seems had persuaded our accountants, Ernst & Young, to agree to his accounting methods. They wouldn't mind as this would cover them from any claim and acted as an insurance. It further concerned me just how much information was being divulged at the announcement of the group's results each half and full year. A lot of it was not in the public domain and therefore against stock market rules, and furthermore the information could have been used advantageously by our competitors. Matthew's explanation that all companies did this was not acceptable to me. We cut it back.

At a board meeting in July 1998 I brought up "City Representations" under item 6 on the agenda. It stated that either Keith or I would be solely responsible for representing the company in respect of "City Representations". This meant that all press releases or announcements to the City would be handled by either me or Keith Lovelock. Matthew ignored the new rule and went ahead with a photo shoot that appeared in the *FT* and *Times* in November. I wrote to him on November 12th giving him a written warning. It was quite obvious that Matthew had aspirations to be the company CEO and he wanted the City to see him as heir apparent. He responded to my warning letter and wanted it to be withdrawn. The board, and in particular Sir Marcus, agreed with me that Matthew was out of order and he gave him a public dressing down. I wanted Matthew to understand that he was a director of the company working for the good of the shareholders. He seemed hell-bent in feathering his own nest.

We argued too about the company IT and we spent about five years and hundreds of thousands of pounds trying to integrate the various construction systems that had evolved. We had a mainframe from Unisys and their man Paul Rutherford which needed scrapping. It would mean writing off about £1 million. I insisted on getting some outside help from NPC Consulting after spending £40,000 on analysing just what it was we needed. It was one of the best moves we made at that time and we appointed a new IT manager much to the disappointment of Matthew Thorne.

At a dinner that Matthew invited me to he vented his feelings. He felt he should have been appointed CEO and wanted to know why I hadn't put him up for the job. I told him that he wasn't up to it. That may be a problem of mine; I say it as I see it. He was never up to the job of chief executive and he should have spent less time scheming and more time concentrating on what he was undoubtedly good at.

Harry Harrison had worked with the business since 1972 as a surveyor from Drews in New Milton. He took over from my friend John Colwell and was our construction director. If anyone grew into a position of trust and respect, it was Harry. The trouble with Harry was that he, in turn, trusted everybody. He had an analytical mind and his ability to smooth out problems in an unflustered way was to be admired. His remarkable knowledge of the construction industry and the methods used were always put to effective use. His over-trusting nature, however, got him into trouble. The Midland Region was consistently turning in the best figures and I decided that I wanted to see why they were so much better than any other region with their construction budgets. Could their methods be used throughout the group I wondered? They never had any overspends on costs. We discovered that the surveyors were shifting costs around from one site to another, sometimes using phantom sites where work hadn't even started. The scam was so widespread we had to shut down the region and fire all the staff. Harry had too much faith in the individual. He was not ingenuous but very much believed in the employee's innocence. I did not.

In 1992 and after the Martin Towers policy of cutbacks I was put into the invidious position of making Harry Harrison and Kevin Holland redundant. It was a mistake. I was beginning to believe what I was being told by Towers and I regret having made such a drastic move. I went to Harry's home that same evening to try and explain the situation and offer him my help as a friend. It was Harry who had invented the DISH, the single piece of paper that covered all the key financial ingredients of a development from initial enquiry to buying the site right through to its completion and sale, a gestation period that could take anything up to five years. The system is still used today. Harry should never have gone. We have worked together on a few schemes since.

John Gray was commercial director from 1975 to 1993. He joined us as financial director in 1975 from our accountants, Watson's. He had a refreshing and common sense approach and was an extremely thorough accountant and a very good manager of people. He was a loyal company man and relished a challenge when it came to saving the business money on taxation. He wouldn't roll over to the taxman's requests. When we took over Peverel, initially for sales and marketing and later to implement estate management, it was John who set up the systems of control with the help of Nigel Bannister when we changed the course of Peverel to Property Management Co. John was always competitive whether in snooker, squash or business. It was him and I who established the ACOT meeting (arse on the corner of the table) that did so much to shape the way the company operated in the early days. He and I made some key decisions in this way with no minutes and plenty of good common sense.

Early in 1993 he and I started to implement the company survival strategy after a particularly lengthy ACOT session. One of our proposals was the sale of Peverel for £30 million, the company for which he was MD. Electra Investments who bought the business took John on as chairman at my suggestion. He had been one of many instrumental in growing and then saving the company.

David Giddings left the position he held in Bournemouth as loans manager for the NatWest Bank South West Region and asked to be made manager of the NatWest Christchurch branch. We moved our accounts from New Milton to Christchurch. He was responsible for introducing us to Lombard North Central for finance and later gave us an introduction to County Bank Ltd, who took on the sponsorship for the flotation of the company. When we did go public, our account at Christchurch was by far the largest and it enabled him to build up the branch to the largest in the district. David retired from NatWest and in 1986 I persuaded him to join McCarthy & Stone as a commercial director in charge of our nursing home division, which we had only just got off the ground. He had looked after us and it could be said that he was instrumental in the survival of the company in the days when we ditched Barclays. It was only fair that we should look after him and besides, he did have a lot of contacts. Later, in 1993, for various reasons, I had to ask David to resign and he became chief executive for a tin mining concern in Cornwall.

I appointed Keith Lovelock as the CEO for the group in 1993, at the time of the hiccup we were having with our bankers and brokers. I had fired the finance director, Martin Towers, and had sent Keith off on a public speaking course in Andover with Khalid Aziz Communications to brush up his presentation skills and these were put to good effect in persuading de Zoete & Bevan, a broking subsidiary of Barclays Bank, to stay with us.

I was grooming Keith for chairmanship for when I retired at the end of 2003. Out of the blue a bid to buy the company by 3i investments and take it back into private ownership floundered on his watch when he couldn't commit to the long-term management plan that they were seeking. I lost faith in him as being the safe pair of hands in which my investment would be best served. It became clear that his interests lay more with his own position and that of his fellow directors rather than the shareholders of the company. In the end Keith did rather well and as chairman oversaw the sale of the business to HBOS in 2006 for a greatly inflated sum at the height of the market, even though the company eventually collapsed under the burden of its debt.

Our public relations company, Andrew Marshal PR, suggested that we should take on an MP and sixty-year-old The Hon. Sir Marcus Fox MBE, who was the member for Shipley and Yorkshire, was appointed as a non-executive director in 1987. I'd been to a party in the House to celebrate his knighthood which he received on July 23rd 1986. He was later to become chairman of the influential 1922 Committee and served as Under-Secretary of State at the Department of the Environment and was Lord Commissioner of the Treasury. His knowledge of the building industry was considerable.

We immediately hit it off and he and his wife Lady Ann became very good friends. Marcus was a shrewd and hard-working man whose loyalty to me and the company was without question. It was good to see him in action and controlling the meetings with his strong Yorkshire manner; he would listen to an argument and then deliver his response in his forthright way. He was very good at mastering the sometimes petulant FD, Matthew Thorne.

His influence in Government circles was very useful. We had a problem with stamp duty on our flats. The Treasury had worked out that stamp duty to be paid by the purchaser exceeded the price of the flat that we were selling, which was a ridiculous situation. Over two hundred sales were being held up by lawyers as a result. Faced with a possible media backlash Marcus arranged a meeting with Angela Knight, a minister at the Treasury, to sort out the anomaly. Trevor Green, Company Secretary, and I met with her. It was obvious that she had been well briefed and she explained that the problem would be resolved by the end of that week.

"We know that we've made a mistake," she admitted. True to her word the problem was resolved by that weekend.

Marcus arranged dinners at the House to meet other MPs so that I could explain our plans for private sheltered accommodation and enlist their support for schemes on their patch. In 1997 he lost his seat at the General Election which hit him hard. He left us in December 1999 and after invaluable advice and direction it was a sad departure. Marcus died in 2002.

Marcus recommended his replacement as Sir George Young. George was the Member for North West Hampshire and he was Minister of State for the Environment between 1990 and 1994, responsible for housing and planning. When he interviewed me for the job, and that's what it felt like, he didn't reveal that he was the avid instigator of the Government's proposed affordable housing plan. Our relationship soured and on one occasion I wrote to him: "We don't wish to include politics within the company."

The search for a CEO for the time when Keith would take on my role as chairman was an important quest. In 2003 head hunters provided lists of suitable candidates and those on the shortlist were subjected to the psychometric testing that I thought really did sort out the wheat from the chaff. I was being driven home late one night after interviews and, on reading the results, the name Howard Phillips shone out like a beacon above the others. I rang Keith from the back of the car and said that we'd found our future CEO and Howard took on the role in 2005.

He had worked for the company as a surveyor in the Northern Region in the 1980s and was made MD of the Eastern Region when the incumbent left to work for a rival firm. In the year of the long knives of 1992 his position was made redundant with the closure of the region. In the meantime he took an MBA and in 1995 rejoined the company as MD for the Central Region. In 2000 he was appointed Operations Director North which covered all four UK northern regions.

Howard knew our business inside out. He knew the people and the product but to his disadvantage he enjoyed the good years when it's easy to do well in a rising property market. Real and effective managers are those that are successful when the market stalls.

Howard was a nice guy whose tenure under the new HBOS ownership was probably marred by a policy of land buying at reduced margins, to quickly increase unit numbers for the new owners. It was a double whammy when sales at any cost further eroded margins as a result of having to discount to encourage sales during the bottom of the cycle. The culture of the company under its new chairmanship, Geoff Ball from Cala Homes, was one of a more traditional house builder rather than an entrepreneurial provider to a niche market.

Mike Jennings had joined us in 1997. He had all the credentials for success with the company coming from Redrow Homes but he was too easily swayed by others and I felt he would take the soft option. He was Operations Director South and a main board director in charge of our Assisted Living Division. This was something that sprung from my solo visit to America in 1997. My visit was to look a lot more closely at the Assisted schemes, which were more care orientated and built by Holiday Retirement Incorporated, the company who later purchased Peverel. I was impressed. When I got back I instigated and was involved in all aspects of design, construction and sales. Of course, for these schemes the type of lease would be different and the ground rent would have to be more because of the extra risk and cost of management. Mike Jennings was against this increase but I made it clear that we required the increase and reluctantly he accepted. The first development went on to be a great success, and many more schemes have been very successful.

I had previously visited the US in 1985 with Trevor Foan to look at the way the Americans were developing their market for the elderly. It was incredible. Del Webb, the developers, had built an entire city just outside Phoenix in the desert of Arizona. It was called Sun City and could accommodate over 100,000 elderly. They had provided three hospitals and four golf courses. There were rubber walking tracks and bowling greens, workshops, swimming pools and the biggest theatre complex in the USA with the ability to push a wheelchair between the rows of seats. Frank Sinatra had performed there. They had spent over one million dollars on their sales show complex which was replaced each year. In America they had taken private sheltered accommodation to the next stage and beyond. I wanted to try a similar idea for the UK and so we planned something in Hartley Wintney with a block of fifty flats with terraces and about sixty houses and a large communal swimming pool designed by me. The planners, of course, said no but eventually said OK. Unfortunately, the market had turned down and it was slow to sell.

Simon Purser, who lived in Totnes, was a non-executive director between 1990 and 2006. He first came to look at what we were building in 1980 when County NatWest was thinking about helping the company to float on the Stock Exchange. He was a director and a typical matter-of-fact banker with a stiff upper lip and a corporate backbone to match. I don't think I ever saw him smile even when, with his help and against some serious odds, we persuaded our brokers that we were a worthy firm to be dealing with.

Trevor Green trained as a lawyer and was the dependable company secretary. In 1989 he joined us as Head of Legal Services from Tarmac after I had sacked his useless predecessor. He built up his department into a slick operation and managed the workload in conveyance of land purchase and sales as well as all the litigation and checking systems. He was a very able individual whose advice we continually sought.

Trevor Foan and I were friends, we still are, and he got me into flying, but we fell out in the late '80s because he didn't like what I was doing with my own private development company, McCarthy Homes Ltd. It was all above board and certainly not a conflict of interest with McCarthy & Stone. In 1980 I had met Brian Freeborne and he and I started to develop a few sites. Brian found the land and ran the operation from Christchurch. We had several schemes on the go including New Milton and Verwood. We sold one to Wimpey and developed another in New Milton with a dozen or so homes on it. We ran into planning problems with the Verwood site and ended up not making any money. Brian Freeborne went off and did other things. The company eventually stopped trading but not before I had asked Trevor to resign from McCarthy & Stone, which he did.

Supporting the key players at the head of the team were the rank and file employees. I took good care of them and spent much of my time looking at and listening to what was right and what was wrong with their jobs. The success of a company depends on its staff.

Some companies are run by fear and some by example. My intention was to run the business by example and I believe that this is the way to get the best out of people. Money is important but the workplace conditions have to be right as well. Communication in its broadest sense is a vital tool and employees need to see open communication within the business and outside to the customers. Motivation is a key driver to success and I tried to show employees that their future was assured and that there was scope for moving up the ladder. In the early years we would restructure the business quite regularly, using teams formed from the company to identify key areas for improvement. I would bring in Rowland Clifford as an independent chairman for such team building and he was instrumental in training managers and running motivational courses for directors. We always involved employees and their families where possible and in the search for senior managers it was a company rule that the final interview would include the candidate's partner. This would give us the opportunity to sell to the couple the importance and value of working for the company. This wasn't going to be just another nine to five job, this one was special. We held annual Christmas parties and there were company golf matches, cricket clubs and sailing activities, all of which were encouraged by the different regions.

The restructuring process was planned at away weekends, think tanks, involving senior management and often their other halves.

Numerous beneficial ideas sprung from these gatherings and were introduced into the business. The Colleague of the Year Award was one such. Ideas were put forward to enable the smooth running of the business such as the formation or buying of businesses to support the Group's future building programme. The think tank process encouraged the buying of both the lift manufacturing company and the uPVC window maker.

We introduced the Lou Tice system for motivation, inspiration and positive thinking. Lou Tice, an American motivational guru, worked out of the Pacific Institute. I had been to one of his meetings in London and came away very fired up. We arranged for two company gatherings in Manchester and Bournemouth with everybody attending. This was chaired by the TV presenter Cliff Michelmore. The representative from the Pacific Institute was recruited by Lou from a prison in the US where he was preaching his system. I must say he certainly had been indoctrinated into the Lou Tice way of thinking and was a highly motivated individual. We had about seven or eight hundred people at each presentation and everyone from the office cleaner to our top banker was encouraged to attend. It was 1988 and the company was valued at £500 million. We were aiming to be a £1 billion pound company and the motivational message supplied by the Lou Tice system helped to get this across. Attendance at these seminars encouraged a much higher level of self-esteem. Training was important and our niche market required a Henry Ford like approach to our business. We had laid down the parameters and we needed to make sure that all employees understood why and the importance of adhering to the plan.

Sales training was especially important. Product knowledge was vital. We'd thought the whole thing through from the level of the switches to the soundproofing and the service charges. The sales pitch for private sheltered accommodation was a very straightforward and compelling story. Most potential customers were female cash buyers and only 5 per cent required a mortgage as the majority were selling a bigger property. Good salespeople would be able to identify a need early on and either close the deal or invite the potential client back for a second look at the property. I'd go mad if, when visiting a site, I found the door to the show unit shut. There was no excuse. A shut door is not a sign of welcome. Doors had to be kept open. Likewise, when a customer walked into the show flat, the salesperson behind the desk should stand up immediately. Each salesperson was kitted out in the registered McCarthy & Stone blue-green tartan and I'd expect each sales presentation to last for forty-five minutes to an hour. We employed a company called Magpie who, like mystery shoppers, would call unannounced at various sites to see how the salespeople responded. This was very interesting and certainly sorted out those who were able to sell. The biggest problem was getting the salespeople to ask the question, "Would you like to buy?" It seemed that some salespeople knew all the patter but couldn't bring themselves to ask the all-important closing question.

There were regular sales training sessions and at one, with the agenda "First Impressions", my son Spencer and Kevin Holland moved all the signs in the hotel we were using so that on arrival all our employees had to work out for themselves where their rooms were and where they had to go for the various seminars. Their impression of the hotel was not what they expected and it was a great exercise in explaining the need for clear communication and understanding directions, and it showed up the doers from the ditherers.

Every year I'd take on one aspect of the company and go through it in detail. My middle name was "Trivia". When I got hold of the marketing department I was horrified to see just how much literature they were spewing out, with expensive documents going to every enquiry trying to list too much information and not clearly identifying the client's specific need. I got a copy of each printed piece of paper and stuck them up on my office wall. Spread in front of me was the classic case of well-intentioned information produced in an ad hoc way by different regions in the Group, without any thought given to the corporate message or brand identity. It was a bloody mess and I took it straight back to the basics. We had agreed and spent money on researching strap lines of copy, colours and logos but our "safe and secure retirement" message had become so confused I had to rein in the overenthusiastic marketing and design teams and their head, the man who liked to spend the money, Kevin Holland.

Another year I decided to tour all the developments under construction. Again, what I found was that the regions were deviating from the set-down policies and some of the quality was not up to standard. The problem was that new employees were not being inducted correctly. I set to with a video called "The McCarthy & Stone Way" which covered not just who we were but how we go about building our schemes and their role in selling the product.

Once a month I'd hold a lunch in my office at Bournemouth where I'd invite one employee of any persuasion from each region to join me for an informal discussion. We'd discuss any areas of concern. My PA Lindsay Bryant would attend and take private, confidential notes and the results provided a very useful understanding of the state of the business, particularly as far as human resource was concerned. Invariably those who attended passed the message on down in their respective regions and the message got through that the chairman was interested in all employees' observations.

Because we had sometimes over-promoted those that then couldn't handle the extra responsibility I introduced psychometric testing for new senior management. I tested it out on my son Spencer and Harry Harrison and was very impressed. This took away the risk of "good" interview technique and really showed up a person's capacity for best suiting the job description. Its use in the business spread and it lessened the risk of trying to place square pegs into round holes. The tests cut down on the time taken to recruit suitable candidates and minimised the risk of falling foul of employment laws given the amount of notice needed to remove an unsuitable employee from a position.

It did work. We took on an FD for the South East Region. I asked the FD, Matthew Thorne, at a board meeting if the candidate had been tested and was he satisfied. I was told that he had been. A year later the region had major problems at a site in Kent where costs had not been checked. The detailed accounts hadn't been done and the company had lost £850,000 on over runs and fraud. I asked for a copy of the regional FD's psychometric test and it was glaringly obvious that the man concerned was not interested in the detail but rather the bigger picture. Detail picks up over runs and fraud. It's bloody useless having a bigger picture if you can't get the detail right in the first place. In discussing this with Matthew I made it clear and in no uncertain terms that I thought that this was his responsibility because it was obvious that the regional FD he had appointed was not up to the job. He thought he knew better.

It is quite a responsibility employing anybody. Taking on your own family has its own special twists and turns.

My uncles had, of course, been a great help and Uncle Alex even spoke about work on his deathbed in 1998. I went to see him at the Spire hospital in Southampton. He was in the last throes of cancer and had an oxygen mask over his face. His concern was for the business and he talked about getting out and back to work. He died that night.

My father joined our sales team as a salesman at Leigh Park, Walkford. While there I do remember he reported to me one guy, the manager of a local supermarket, to whom we had sold a house on the estate, who was helping himself to the sand, cement and bricks as well as using our cement mixer from the site which was still under construction. Apparently our site agent had given him permission to take a wheelbarrow full of sand and the guy had overstepped the mark. Give an inch and they take a mile. Even though in my book he was stealing, the lawyers said that having given permission to help himself to some material on site, there wasn't anything we could do. There was. I sent him a bill.

After leaving school my sons joined the business when we were in Stem Lane. They had been to a state prep school in Lymington called Priestlands. It was bloody useless and the teachers really didn't want to know. I had met their master who said they should take up a trade. I don't think he had spoken to the boys until they were about to leave. Clinton was dyslexic and we sent him privately to Homefield School in Winkton near Christchurch. He was only there for a term when we pulled him out and he started at the business as an apprentice carpenter and joiner. Spencer joined as well, aged sixteen.

Spencer had been working for us at the weekends and he'd even been bloodied. While he was working at Homewood House he slipped and fell off the scaffolding, knocked himself out and ended up in Lymington Hospital.

The two eldest boys came to see me from time to time and on various occasions they wanted to leave. It can't have been easy for the boss's sons and they were both bullied in various ways. Spencer got it worst and was stripped and covered in shoe polish. Uncle Alex who ran the workshop knew what was going on but took the view that boys will be boys and that's what will happen to the sons of the boss. They should perhaps have worked elsewhere.

Clinton was on day release to college in Southampton and he really wanted to go it alone. He had a friend, Mark Snudden, and the two of them went off as self-employed building contractors, doing the sort of jobs that Bill Stone and I had done years before.

Spencer stayed on, attended Southampton College and obtained his Higher National Diploma in building. He was taken out of the workshops and put through various other departments in the business. He started in the buying department and after three months moved into surveying. He spent a year with the sales and marketing team and each time he moved he thought that this was the most important department in the business. He worked with the architects and land purchasing and ended up going out as a site agent. He learnt that if it isn't built right it won't work and he did well as a manager and was upgraded to assistant to CEO Keith Lovelock who obviously felt threatened when he confronted Spencer that he only got the job as my son. His attention to detail was notable. It was he who identified the fraud problem in Kent and did an audit report that found the fiddling and paying twice for work that was done once or paying for work that was never done at all. He found out what the regional FD could not. The regional FD had to find another job.

But Spencer too wanted to spread his wings and I didn't stand in his way, in fact I welcomed it. He went off to join his brother Clinton with a new building venture called Emlor Homes (named after Clinton's two daughters, Emma and Laura). I had bought a site in Tisbury at auction and applied for planning but was turned down. I gave it to them telling them not to mention anything about the McCarthy family but to use another name. They got planning permission for a detached house immediately, which got them up and running.

In 1995 they developed a site in Fontmell Magna in Dorset with fifteen homes and even though the timing wasn't perfect for the market, they did a great job by building an attractive development with a mix of Victorian and thatched and flint houses with a village green, mill and duck pond. I gave them some ducks. The development won them the What House Awards? UK House Builder of the Year award.

In 1996 while I was in Guernsey I sent them an e-mail suggesting that they get into the sheltered housing market. I shouldn't have sent it but I did. Their margins were not great for what they were doing.

They built their first dedicated sheltered scheme in 2001 in Romsey and another at Southbourne, near Bournemouth, with an office in Lymington. I advised them to take on a financial director and to get some bigger offices. They did both and built Mill Stream House in Ringwood with two floors and 10,000 square feet of space and Dean Marlow became their FD.

The boys' first scheme ran into some planning difficulties. Their site was right next door to one that McCarthy & Stone had put up. The planners argued about access but the boys wouldn't back down and they threatened a judicial review which resolved the problem. The local press had fun with the McCarthy name once again in the wicked property developer's spotlight. The boys won their appeal and discovered that it was all the fault of one disgruntled councillor who didn't like the McCarthy name. My own fault and the sins of the father I guess. It was history repeating itself and I told them that the sooner they got out of Lymington, the better. The bit of advice I gave them where there was no conflict of interest at all was, "Don't ever give personal guarantees to the bank."

My youngest son, Scott, had attended the same school as his brothers. Actually his education at Priestlands, if you could call it an education, was even worse. He too joined the company as an apprentice carpenter and joiner.

Harry Harrison came to see me one day and explained that Scott was not attending his day release programme.

"What shall we do?" asked Harry.

"What would you do?" I asked.

"Give him a warning and if he does it again fire him," was Harry's reply.

True to form and without any favouritism Harry issued the warning and nine months later he had to sack him. Scott came to see me in tears but there was nothing I could do. He was a strong-willed seventeen-year-old and he would just have to get on with his own life. He was living with his mother and I received several pleading phone calls asking for his job back.

He, helped by his brother Clinton, converted two flats in Bournemouth. They got into trouble with the bank and I had to step in. NatWest in Southampton were owed £70,000. I offered them £30,000 out of my own pocket and told them to call it a day. I took my lawyer Sally Norcross Webb to the meeting and she confirmed that it was thirty thousand or nothing. They accepted my offer.

Scott, aged twenty-one, married and built a house in Poole. He then embarked on three barn conversions near Shaftesbury, overspent on the job and his brothers had to finish the project. I'd warned him that any conversion will cost double what you think it will.

Scott's brothers were becoming frustrated with him. He just wouldn't listen to their, or my, advice. We sat him down and because he has a very good way with people we all decided that he would be good at going out and obtaining options on possible development sites, obtain the planning and then selling them on.

Scott then acquired a site in Lymington on the corner of Buckland Road and New Street and started to build fifteen houses. The latest recession kicked in and the whole scheme went badly wrong. He spent nearly five years in obtaining planning permission and his determination meant that in 2007 he could have sold it and made £1 million which his brothers and I strongly advised. What my youngest son sadly never learnt was the one thing I understood right from the start: Take the profit when you can and keep it simple.

My boys, all of them different, are chips off the old block. I remember that I did a SWOT analysis with them to determine the Strength, Weakness, Opportunities and Threats so we could best decide who did what at Churchill, the new name for Emlor Homes run by Clinton and Spencer. Clinton is good at construction and perhaps has a softer approach to people than I have. He's more like my father with his caring attitude and although he is not as ruthless at business as Spencer, he has learnt. Spencer is probably better than I was at his age and he gets on with things and makes things happen. He does not take the soft option and never leaves things in the air but he did have more training in business management. He, like Clinton, wants to win whether at business or sport. Scott is more sensitive and perhaps more creative than his brothers and he has the ability to get on with everybody. I sent him on a self-assertive course once but he knew the lot before he ever got there. Even though there has been a difference of opinions, the two eldest have great loyalty to their younger brother and have also taken him under the wing of Churchill.

It may sound corny but behind every good man there is nearly always an exceptionally good woman. Lindsay Bryant was the good woman behind me for most of my years at McCarthy & Stone. She transformed the way I worked. My first PA, or more properly bookkeeper and typist, was the girl we took on in Buckland Park who had to traipse through the mud to get to and from the little ten foot by twenty foot wooden shed we had as our first site office. Largely through her nagging we built our first office, Newcourt House in Lymington. She was followed by the extraordinary Evelyn who everyone, apart from me, thought was an ogre. She worked for me for thirteen years and made everyone's life hell. She was one of those that would count every pencil and paperclip. It came to the crunch and I really had to ask her to leave.

John Gray's secretary advertised for a new PA for me and Lindsay applied, got the job and started in 1983. I interviewed her. She had been working for a firm of accountants in Southampton and relished the opportunity of a job as personal secretary to the chairman of a public company. After two weeks she asked to speak to me and she suggested a different way of working. I would no longer run my own affairs or handle my own finances. She said it was her job to arrange everything thus leaving me to concentrate on the business. A bookkeeper called Margaret Willingham was taken on to look after the personal financial aspect of my life and handle the everyday payments, be it for housekeeping, sailing or polo. When Margaret left to retire to France, Pam Watson took over and she was followed by Daphne Dittrich who is still with me today. When I mention this to other CEOs they are aghast.

Lindsay insisted that we met first thing every morning when I was in the office to plan my diary and for her to give me an update. She brought order and a disciplined way of working into my life. She was protective and attentive and everything a CEO would wish for. She handled herself with calm assurance and worked on one hand with the press and organising our contact with royalty and on the other hand with fellow directors, employees and customers. She also arranged Gwen's birthday party in Venice. She had three pairs of hands. She was my eyes and ears for years. She heard and interpreted the jungle drums long before anyone else in the business.

Lindsay was so conscientious that she didn't tell me she was leaving her husband until I had returned from a holiday, by which time she had done the deed. She got together with Tom Edmond, a buyer and golfer, not sure in which order, at McCarthy & Stone, but didn't want her personal business upsetting her professional working life as far as I was concerned.

I owe a big debt of gratitude to Lindsay. She retired when I did in January 2003. Unfortunately the company was as mean as it could be considering the exceptional work that she so successfully undertook. It was left to me to show any gratitude. Lindsay is now retained by Churchill for a few mornings a week running my diary.

Peter Girling became my assistant for two years and helped with the Bobby Appeal set up, a charity I started to offer instant help to the elderly after their houses had been broken into. He left to start up a letting business based on tail-end properties that McCarthy & Stone couldn't sell and he did rather well at it.

Finding the right people was always the challenge. Once I was sitting in on an interview for a regional sales and marketing director. The candidate had come from another house builder, a public company called Bovis. I asked him how many designs of houses his company had. He replied that there were sixty-four different variations and that he'd got this number down from one hundred and ten. He was obviously proud of this achievement. I told him that we ran with two; a one-bedroom and a two-bedroom flat.

Needless to say the Bovis candidate was not employed.

14. Straight Shooting

There's a hunter-gatherer streak in all of us but not all of us pander to it. I did and have gone further than most in scratching that particular itch. A day out shooting is also a great way of meeting like-minded business types and the occasional scallywag.

My first shotgun was a Spanish side-by-side twelve-bore which I bought for £12 from a guy in North New Milton via an ad in the local rag. You didn't need a shotgun licence in those days. The barrels had a dent in them and the stock rattled like a loose tooth. I was twenty-four. Tim Ham had a gun and permission to shoot pigeons on eight hundred acres in Whiteparish. I hadn't got a clue and without any guidance didn't really understand the golden rules about gun safety. I blew a smoky hole in the ground once when the thing went off because I was walking with it loaded and unbroken. In hindsight I was bloody lucky I didn't blow my foot off or worse. I learnt my lesson and from then on safety became paramount.

After my marriage to my first wife, when we lived in our two-up-two-down with an outside loo, there was little money. Bill Stone and I were trying to build at Buckland Park and live on £8 a week. That first Christmas of married life, Tim Ham and I were on the banks of the Lymington River with our guns early one evening. There were two pheasants roosting in a tree and I shot them and one of them fell into the water below. I waded in up to my chest to retrieve the dead bird and proudly carried it home for our Christmas dinner.

I guess the wading episode persuaded me to get a dog. I'd grown up with dogs but nothing that would retrieve a dead bird without eating it. I had my first dog, Sandy, whilst still at school but he was run over. I ran home to find that my father had buried him. This was a great loss as he was only a puppy and my first real friend. I was distraught.

I recall that we had a mad female vet in Lymington. I was convinced she was a witch. She dressed in black and had a large protruding nose. I took our dog to see her for an injection against distemper and when I returned for the animal she said that the dog had broken a window and escaped. I found him and took him home. A few months later the dog contracted distemper and was in a sorry state. He hadn't been touched by the vet at all. One evening he became very ill and was not going to last the night so I decided that the best thing I could do was to put it out of its misery. I took him to Tim Ham's home where he was building a septic tank.

I wanted to shoot the dog and bury him in the hole.

"Would it be OK for me to bury him here?" I asked Tim. I returned to the car, intent on putting the poor thing out of its misery, and found the dog had died on the front seat of the car.

Bill Stone's wife Janet had a cat she absolutely doted on. The cat had a bad cough and I discovered that she had taken it to the same vet. She'd told Janet that the cat was very ill and was likely to die. On hearing the news I told Janet that we would take her cat for a second opinion after collecting it from the vet's house.

"What cat?" said the vet, only half opening the door. She denied she had the pet so I pushed past her and found the untouched feline.

"Oh that one's going to die," she cackled as we hurried off taking the cat with us. Apparently Janet's pet had nothing more serious than a cold. I don't know what happened to her but she certainly wasn't fit to be in charge of a broomstick, let alone animals.

The next dog we had was a mongrel when we were living in Orchard House. His name came from the boys who called it "Dedoor" when what they were trying to say was "doggie". He ran off and bit a policeman and had to be put down.

When we first moved to Watton's Farm we had a big brown bernese mountain dog, Gretel, which ran out into the road one day and hit a motorbike. It was normally the other way round with vehicles running over dogs but our dog broke his jaw and had to have it wired up after the incident. In 1985 I bought my first black labrador, Turk.

I didn't shoot for some years and it wasn't until I had moved into Hurst Barn with Gwen that I went to a charity do at Lockerly Hall near Romsey in 1984. Ted Heath was there waving his baton about conducting an orchestra. When it came to the auction I bid for and won a day out for one gun at Lockerly. I bought myself a Henry Atkin twelve-bore from Greenfields in Salisbury together with all the brand new shooting kit and turned up for my day looking something like the new boy at his new school. I shot at the sort of birds I wouldn't bother lifting my gun up to now. The owner of the shoot was the flamboyant Roger Croft and he invited me to join him on several other shooting occasions. He was keen to do business with me and I put him in touch with a couple of schemes in Eastleigh and Romsey. They both went wrong. He sued his lawyers, Turners from Bournemouth, over their poor advice and won and promised me a commission from the favourable outcome, but nothing ever materialised. He then suggested another venture between me and him and another shooting man, Roger Gilley, who had a very large leisure company but none of the potential money appeared from either of the other two so I didn't step up with mine. Nothing happened.

He was certainly a colourful character as many in the shooting world are. He became short of money and sold Lockerly Hall where he had fancied himself as Lord of the Manor. He bought a house in the Close of Salisbury Cathedral not far from where Ted Heath had his and he used to throw rather lavish parties. At Christmas time I remember he insisted on old-fashioned silver sixpences being put into the Christmas pudding. He commissioned a bronze sculpted bust of himself but eventually he lost the lot and really went bust, and last I heard he had ended up living in a caravan in France and writing a book about Salisbury.

In 1986 the move to Squalls, set in four hundred acres, opened up the opportunity for some more regular game shooting. My neighbour Graham Fry had five hundred acres and we agreed a deal to add my four hundred to his. I therefore had a regular slot for two guns every fortnight and really started to get into the swing of things.

Graham used to put down the birds and he'd keeper the shoot himself with some local help. The "local help" was probably responsible for the poaching that went on. We'd also find dead poults on the ground shot by an air gun which was pretty senseless.

One of my earliest guests was Philip Peak. He was a professional fundraiser and someone always on the move. He'd worked for Help the Aged amongst others and later I engaged his services for my charity. I introduced £100,000 into the McCarthy Foundation, part of which was used to finance the building and fitting out of a scheme for elderly battered women in Liverpool. I was invited to open McCarthy Lodge on 31st June 1991 and met some of the residents. They were delightful and the salt of the earth. One of them had been robbed five times and beaten up as well if you can believe it. She was eighty-five years old. Our idea was to provide a temporary home for the women to get themselves back on their feet before finding them more suitable places to live. The foundation went on to raise significant funds and distributed them to worthy causes directly related to the elderly. I was concerned, however, that the direction of the foundation was too indiscriminate and I suggested that we carry out some research. We came up with the Bobby Appeal.

The Bobby Appeal would raise funds for a kitted-out van, liveried as a police vehicle, and a driver to visit the home of any elderly person who had been broken into. The handyman driver with the tools in his van would make sure that all the locks were replaced and that any broken windows or doors were made good. Elderly victims of a break-in would at least be left with a secure property to sleep in. After an incident, instead of the police just taking statements, they would be able to call up the Bobby Van who would respond by making the victim's home safe once again. They would also put in the window a sign stating that the building was under surveillance. The elderly are vulnerable and prone to repeated attacks. The idea was that the Bobby Vans would eventually operate nationwide with the police's full cooperation and management. I had sold the idea to three Chief Constables and the scheme had received a blessing from on high at the Home Office. The Prince of Wales became Patron and we had a launch at St James's Palace. We had five vans on parade liveried and kitted out ready to go. These were the first of twenty-five supplied by Vauxhall at half-price for the charity. Sir Marcus Fox was the chairman. We were going to raise £10 million.

After all the good intention, Sir Marcus resigned and I persuaded Khalid Aziz, an ex Southern TV presenter and motivational speaker, to join the charity and he became chairman. He fell out with Philip Peak and when the Hampshire police started to question my integrity, I was devastated. It seemed that a woman on the Hampshire police commission had got a bee in her bonnet over the idea of charging anyone under fifty-five for the service to cover the costs and she started to lobby other police forces over her concern. My idea was to make the scheme financially self-sufficient and I certainly wasn't going to spend my time in furthering the argument, especially as at that time the housing market and our company, in particular, were in difficulties. I needed to concentrate on the main business. I had set the boat sailing and would leave it up to others to take the helm. It was probably a question of too many cooks and committees spoiling the broth and not pursuing the scheme with the vigour that was required. I resigned. The scheme is still going to a greater or lesser extent. I believe it was a good idea then and remains so.

Philip Peak was a friend of Mike Dawson who ran Tunstall Telecom, the business we eventually used as the main monitor for all our sheltered accommodation schemes. We thought about buying his business but he took the company public. Like some others he was not pleased with the City and bought the company back into private ownership and eventually sold out for £70 million. Mike invited me shooting at Reiveaux in Helmsley, Yorkshire. It was dreadful when in the late 1990s Mike got shot. I remember being told about the accident. He was standing on number seven peg and his friend, a very experienced gun, was walking on the flank and had two barrels at a low bird between him and the end of the line. Mike was hit hard in the face. He lost one eye and forty per cent vision in the other. His hand was mutilated too. The friend who shot him had been shooting for thirty years. It just goes to show how dangerous a lapse of concentration can be and how even the most experienced and safest of guns can sometimes in the heat of the moment do something reckless. Philip Peak brought Mike out on a day after the accident but poor Mike just couldn't see. I too had first-hand experience of the dangers of shooting, but luckily not to anything like that degree. Once in Spain I'd shot a partridge that hit Bill Riddle and knocked him to the ground. His ear defenders probably took most of the impact but he could not continue that day. The very next day I was hit by a pheasant but luckily it hit a tree before landing on me.

Withyslade and Haredene Farm, which joined my neighbour Fry's land, added another four hundred acres to our shoot and greatly improved our sport every two weeks in the South Wiltshire countryside until it ended in 2007. Fry wanted to commercialise the shoot and increase the price substantially. I was of the opinion that the shoot was not up to the quality that would be required so I then withdrew my support. I did have some coaching and I enjoyed shooting but I wasn't satisfied with my ability and perhaps never will be. My first attempt at clays was at Roundwood, on Charles Church's estate where the A303 meets the M3 motorway. Desmond Sturgess was my first shooting coach there.

Philip Peak introduced me to The Gaggle of Geezers. This was the name of the group of guns who formed the syndicate at Alton Pancras in Dorset. Its members were Martin Lewis who had a joinery company near Sturminster Newton. He was, and still is, the organiser. There were three BMW dealers; Malcolm Clarke from London, David Burton who was CEO of Woods and Mike Evans who sold the German marque in Cornwall. John Puddepha owned the Pines Hotel in Swanage and some homes for the elderly. Bill Riddle owned a golf course or two and a waste management company. Michael and Sally Cannon had made money in pubs and breweries. There was Ken Hesketh, an orthopaedic surgeon, and his wife Monique. Simon Pollock was the owner of caravan parks later to be known as "leisure parks". Donnie Nesbit was into private number plates, Keith and Tricia Trussler were farmers, Paul Stalker was a motivational speaker and Malcolm Barnes was a Dorset farmer and jolly local council chairman with an aversion to political correctness. David Mulcahy was a surveyor and Tony Pool, an entrepreneur.

We'd meet at The Gaggle of Geese in the village, hence our team name. The keeper at Alton Pancras was Ray Goddard and he held the licence to shoot on the land for three days a week. I was in the Tuesday team of eight guns and for £19 a bird we enjoyed our sport. Malcolm Clarke would always grumble about the cost and the quality of the shooting. Malcolm did like to shoot more than his fair share and if you were unlucky enough to be a back gun to him, you wouldn't get a lot to have a go at. On the last day of the season in 1998 Ray the keeper suddenly announced that we wouldn't be shooting there anymore. We met in the pub and decided to form a roving syndicate which, as it turned out, was the best thing we could have done.

As a roving team of guns we found good and bad places. Armswell had been the best drive out of the Alton Pancras, one hundred and fifty bird days if we were lucky, and although it was good it wasn't that good. However, since then Paul Yates has taken over and greatly improved the shoot. Marty Lewis found us shoots by word of mouth and through his shooting contacts and other members of our team. He organised the days and charged us a fee for his trouble. Cheltenham was a disaster with just a cheese roll for lunch, no coffee or drink breaks, nothing afterwards and one hundred and fifty mediocre birds for £23 a pop.

"What the hell are we doing here?" was the cry from The Gaggle.

Prescombe was a different kettle of fish, or covey of partridge, and Steve Thomas knew how to put on a good show. We went more upmarket and shot at Rupert Scott's Encombe Estate and at the Earl of Sandwich's Beaminster shoot. Members dropped out and new ones came on board including my two boys. Clinton had been shooting since he was a teenager and had befriended A.J. "Smoker" Smith's son as a shooting companion. Peter Dunford joined the group. I have known Peter for over forty years and he is married to Jenny. He was the son of George Dunford, the builder I used to work for in the evenings when I was an apprentice carpenter. He took over his father's business when George died and now he has relinquished the reins to his son Oliver. I introduced Peter to The Gaggle and Brian Wiggins, a dealer in "posh" cars, joined as well as Arthur Wardman who was into property and engineering in the Midlands. Jolly John Yeoman had quarries and was into shipping and cows. Suzie Lever from Iwerne Minster, whose husband Philip was a partner in Sage Software, joined us. Gradually Marty began to get a stream of good shoots and each year some twenty-five venues were analysed and changed if they were not up to expectations. Likewise, the guns became more selective and skilled with their shooting.

On 7th December 2000 Steve Thomas organised a day for the company at Beaminster so that I could invite some of my business contacts. We included Keith Lovelock and Matthew Thorn as well as some brokers and bankers. I was being driven to the hotel the night before the shoot to have supper with all the guests and it was chucking it down. It had been pouring with rain all day. Barry Lake, my chauffeur, was at the wheel of the new Rolls while I worked away in the back on my laptop. I had returned from a meeting in London. We had turned off the road from Bournemouth to Dorchester where the

GPS system told the chauffeur to take the left fork in the road at the bottom of the hill, I thought we should have gone right. At a dip in the road the lights just caught sight of what looked like a big, dark puddle and as the car entered it, it very quickly became clear that Barry Lake had driven us into one. The Rolls stopped dead in the middle of the water. All the electrics started to short out and go berserk with the windows opening, the car seats moving and the radio going on and off as the water started to leak into the car.

"Abandon ship!" I shouted as the water came up to the top of the seats. I rolled up my pinstriped trouser legs and set off in the dark for dry land. Barry retrieved my guns and muttering something about how we couldn't really leave the Rolls-Royce parked where it was, he too waded out of the water.

We walked, or rather squelched, our way to a farmhouse whose lights we could see through the rain. We knocked on the door and when it opened the farmer said he couldn't and wouldn't help us. He was perhaps a bit surprised by the sight of two wet men on his doorstep, one in a soggy pinstriped suit and the other quite obviously armed to the teeth with shotguns. We found a phone box and rang the hotel. Gwen came to our eventual rescue in the Range Rover and when we reached the hotel we found that they had suffered a power cut in the heavy rainfall.

The Rolls had done 12,000 miles. The £112,000 car was a write-off and all we got from the insurance was £40,000. It was an expensive "puddle". Sometime later somebody at work gave me a framed cartoon of our exploit which summed up the incident rather well. The words "walking on water" were mentioned in the caption.

I'd seen Will Thatcher shooting at home. He is an extremely good shot and an excellent gun coach. He'd won the World Championship at FITASC and obviously sees the pattern of the shot. He offered to help me and I took him up on it. I went along and shot a few clays on the Downs at Chilmark shooting ground and Will suggested that I try an over-and-under gun. I had previously borrowed one from Malcolm

Clarke who had an extensive gun collection. I didn't get on with it at all well. Will was insistent I should persevere so I had a go with his gun. He suggested that I tried six clays with my old Atkin side-by-side and six with his over-and-under. I hit a third more targets with Will's gun. I did it once more with the same result. So I took myself off to Greenfields in Salisbury to order a Perazzi over-and-under twelve-bore.

Will has been invaluable in coaching as well as driving and loading at the numerous shoots around the country. He is certainly a good friend and a person who I respect for his undeniable calm ability to shoot well, whether it's clays or game birds.

I'd always promised myself a pair of Purdeys and had ordered them just prior to my retirement. The twelve-bore side-by-sides were to be engraved by a twenty-six year old master of the art called Max Gobbi, an Italian, who I'd met at the Game Fair. I had originally asked Purdey to engrave the guns with the designs I wanted including my dogs with some gold inlays. They had quoted an extra £36,000 for the engraving. The Italian had quoted £12,000 so not surprisingly he got the job. His excellent engraving on my guns was featured in an Italian magazine. Purdey still charged over £105,000 for the pair of twelve-bores and it took four years for them to deliver the guns. They were not at all helpful and probably didn't like the idea of someone else doing the engraving on their guns.

While I was waiting for the pair of Purdeys I went to the West London Shooting School on the insistence of Purdey and had the dimensions of my Atkin checked out. After trying out a test gun with variable stocks and casts, I came away with what I believed were the correct dimensions for a gun that would fit me correctly. Apparently I had been prone to shooting to the left with my old Atkin. Armed with the new information and while waiting for the new guns, I bought another Purdey with thirty-inch barrels and gave Alan Pike at Greenfields all the dimensions from West London, so that he could adjust the stock. I took the new thirty-inch Purdey off for a session with Dave Olive, a well-known shooting coach at his ground near Andover.

I took four shots and Dave could see that my gun didn't fit me and told me so. He told me to go away and have the gun altered and then come back for a lesson. I wasn't best pleased. Apparently it was three-quarters of an inch too long in the stock and needed to be shortened and there was too much cast, which had been put on to correct the length of the stock. I took the gun back to Greenfields who said that they were not surprised.

"Why didn't you say something?" said I. It seemed that Greenfields were adopting a policy of the customer is always right.

I rang Purdey who were making the new pair to the wrong measurements. They wanted £4,000 to change the stock dimensions even though at the time they had not started making the guns let alone the stocks. I told them what they could do with their guns. It was, after all, their insistences of the involvement of the West London Shooting School and the wrong measurements that were to blame. If they didn't do it and if the guns I was paying over £100,000 for didn't fit me then they could cancel the order. Purdey it seemed were behaving like Rolls-Royce when it came to customer relations. Both firms have great brand names but in my case both failed significantly to live up to their reputation for quality and service.

The pair of Purdeys eventually turned up complete with Max Gobbi's engraving and a leather and oak case for an extra £5,000. My sons Spencer and Clinton bought it for me. It was a beautiful retirement present, marred only by Purdey's high-handed unhelpfulness.

Even then I had problems with them and while shooting on a Saturday at Rushmore one gun wouldn't eject. During the shoot one of the pickers up, Aubrey, took the gun to Alan Pike at Greenfields who worked on it that day so I could pick it up on Sunday before taking it off shooting in Spain on the Monday. Now that is service for you.

I prefer the side-by-sides on grouse because they are lighter and therefore move more quickly than the heavier over-and-unders. The pair of Perazzi guns, also beautifully engraved by Max Gobbi, arrived in time for the 2010 season. I bought another second-hand Perazzi after my first and so have four Perazzis and three Purdeys in the gun safe as well as my old Henry Atkin which was completely refurbished after the stock was broken shooting grouse.

Angus Barnes is the owner of the lease of the Combe Sydenham shoot at Exmoor and I met him when I was invited to join his syndicate by Steve Smith, one of the top ten shots in the country. I saw Steve bring down the best left and right at pheasant on a drive called Isengard. This syndicate consisted of Jonathan Bennett, Bill Riddle, John Puddepha and Bill Joyce, another consistently recognised top shot and Land Rover dealer from Trowbridge. It is said that his son Adrian is a better shot than his father but the high curling pheasants that Bill can bring down does it for me. Unfortunately some City whiz kids bought into the Exmoor shoot and we were dispensed with. The shoot has been expanded with extra shoots such as Edgcott being added on to it.

The Gaggle syndicate shot in Wales at Lake Vyrnwy for six seasons as my guests. Brian Bisaca who owned the shoot and the Lake Vyrnwy hotel was a nice enough fellow. One year his young keeper who was a hundred birds light on the three hundred I'd paid for said that he'd make it up to us the following season. When the time came he gave us an extra fifty but I deducted the hundred we were due. They also insisted that if we wished to shoot there the following year we had to stay in the hotel which we didn't want to do. The wine was not up to our standard. We didn't shoot again at Lake Vyrnwy.

I'd got to know Lady Linlithgow at Bryngwyn, near Llanfyllin. She used to be a director with Sotheby's and was a useful contact to have on the local shoots. She is a delightful person and runs a very tight ship. Her Georgian house has enough beautiful rooms for eight guns and the wives love to accept invitations to enjoy the sumptuous candlelit shooting party dinners. We stayed with her at least five or six nights of the year. We shot at the Three Valleys near Welshpool run by Robert Jones and at Brigands, a real quality shoot owned by Gwyn Evans, where I have seen and killed the highest birds ever on the Marsh drive.

Vaynor Park offered great and consistent quality as did the Llanarmon estate owned by Bobby McAlpine. Bill Riddle, John Yeoman and I would take a day's shooting and some of us would fly up to Welshpool where the Range Rovers would pick us up and transfer us to Bryngwyn.

I think the biggest day I ever had in the UK was with Duncan Davidson, the founder and main shareholder in Persimmon Homes. He invited me up to shoot in Yorkshire and I flew up to Liverpool in our company plane. He'd said to me in his invitation letter that I should bring double guns but I thought I'd be fine with just my Atkin and a loader.

"How big a day are we expecting?" I asked on the car journey to my host's house.

"I'm not allowed to say," was the reply from the driver. "But we do sometimes have one thousand bird days."

The house, it was a hall, was enormous and a valet met me and showed me to my quarters and unpacked my kit. At the black tie pre-shoot dinner half the building industry seemed to be guests.

The chairman of Wimpey was there and Lawrie Barratt and the plumber, Kevin McDonald, who owned the Polypipe business. I think we were all surprised to see each other. I remember the enormous oak dining table and hanging on the wall at one end a large oil painting about nine by six foot of a swan being attacked by a lurcher as another flies off. There's a man with his gun looking on at the scene.

On the morning of the shoot, we were loaded into a row of eight new dark blue Range Rovers and driven to our pegs. There were five gamekeepers in attendance and we shot 780 birds. I saw some being hit above the power lines that ran through one of the drives so the pheasants weren't low.

The Brixton Deverill shoot in Wiltshire run by Kim Beddall can present some wonderful birds and the keeper, Sean, certainly knows what he's doing. The hidden "extras" can become as challenging as the birds, for example, to charge for your wife's lunch is nearly an insult when you are already paying top dollar. However it is fun to shoot there and everybody is dedicated to the guns having a wonderful day's sport.

John Puddepha introduced me to Rushmore, the renowned partridge shoot in Dorset run by Jamie Lee. Jamie is very good company, easy-going, with a warm and lively personality while at the same time running a seriously good shoot. He can be heard on the radio deploying his beaters with extraordinary skill to ensure that the ten guns all have shooting. I have never come away without having a stupendous day even if my shooting had waned. On top of this he is a renowned and brilliant shot with both shotgun for birds and rifle for game, as are many others in the syndicate. He asked me to be a part of the shoot syndicate and I was delighted to accept. Jamie and his beautiful wife Lydia have become good friends. He is also a very good cook and generous host at his home in Wiltshire. I enjoy shooting at Rushmore, sometimes with a younger and more colourful crowd of celebrities on about twelve days a season. On my days, the shoot chef, Paul, cooks the most beautiful stuffed partridge that I've ever had. A larger than life Scotsman, Charles McQueen, has been expertly shooting at Rushmore since Jamie's father started the shoot over 40 years ago. This is also about the date of the Scotsman's Range Rover. Jamie now runs the shoot and often shoots with his neighbour, Guy Ritchie, and rubs shoulders with the great and the good as well as other "shooting stars" one of whom is Eric Clapton. Eric and I compared notes, literally, about the Two Eyes cafe in Soho where I had my audition with my group back in the '60s. Eric had done the same but the outcome of his session had done far more for his music than it had for mine.

There is a lake on the Squalls Estate that is hidden away behind the house and the buildings. On one of its banks there is a row of rough wooden crosses with the name of a dog carved onto each. Some belonged to Claire and some to Gwen but three of them were my gun dogs. Turk was the first black labrador I took on in 1986. He was trained by Jill Gill but I buggered him up because I didn't have the knowledge that's needed to properly run a good peg gun dog. My second, Raja, was trained by a Dorset man called Major Morty Turner-Cook and I'd learnt to not let him off after a "runner" while the shoot was underway. I was better with my third, Fergus, again trained by Jill Gill. He was the most laid-back dog ever. I can now control my fourth, Oak, bred and trained by Robin Watson. He is the fastest retriever ever and as well as his jumping ability he demonstrates remarkable control in the field and is steady at my side while on the shooting peg.

Not far from where the dogs are buried I had built a two-storey log cabin with a mezzanine inside and counter levered outside with a balcony. The logs are local cedar, some weighing over a ton. Two brothers made it to my design, built it in Wales and then shipped it to Squalls and re-erected it by the lake. This is my trophy room and the place where I can entertain friends and family surrounded by the memories of those exciting trips to Scotland and Africa.

Once again it was thanks to John Puddepha who introduced me to red stag deer stalking in Scotland. It was when I was sixty-two and Gwen and I were invited to the Puddepha's Scottish home, Mount Blair, near Blairgowrie. John and Rosemary, his wife, are very dear friends and exceedingly good hosts. I went up the hill with the stalker Graham Kerr and my Sauer .234 rifle with Swarovski sights after having proved that I could hit a steel outline of a deer as a test target at 150 yards.

We climbed up the hill with Gwen in our footsteps and quite near the top saw a herd of red deer. It was a magnificent sight. We walked around to come upwind of them. Gwen was asked to stay where she was while the stalker and I crawled forward and then onto our bellies with me following a few inches behind his boots. We wormed our way like snakes for about one hundred yards until we could clearly see our target. The animal the stalker wanted me to shoot was lying down about 140 yards away and was rather difficult to identify among the herd and after toing and froing I eventually spotted the beast. I had to wait for him to stand up which was just as well as by this time my neck was aching like hell. He was a ten-pointer and as I waited for the chance my adrenalin pumped and I tried to focus on the job in hand. The stag got up and on turning broadside I fired my Sauer .234 hundred gram bullet as instructed. The rifle's recoil forced the telescopic sights back above my eye and cut me so that I couldn't tell whether I'd hit the deer or not. I had, with a clean shot, and the animal was dead.

Graham said that the stag was an old one and was pleased that we had taken him off the hill. He then got out his marigolds and carried out the grollocking of the dead animal and, as if there wasn't enough blood on my face from the cut above my eye, he then bloodied me with the warm blood of the deer I had dispatched. It was time for our "piece" and coffee. The gillie was called up on the radio and arrived with a quad bike. The beast was strapped on and I felt elated and we started back for home off the hill with the sounds and smells of that wonderful countryside making us drunk. It was a really hot walk home and I must have looked a sight with my glowing face smothered in blood, my own and the deer's mingling. What a reception we had from John and Rosemary Puddepha as we came triumphant off the hill.

I have had some really good stalking as a guest of Jamie Lee in Rushmore with Dave Brown, the keeper, and have shot Roebuck, Muntjac and a specimen Fallow buck which took three days of crawling on our stomachs. I was lucky enough to stalk a Sika buck in Swanage with Morgan Andrews which turned out to be of gold medal standard.

In 1999 I shot a Royal stag twelve pointer on the Inverness beat at Invercauld on the land owned by Herbert Cuthbertson and achieved the record in that year of 19.4 stone with the help of stalker Liam Donald. We'd stalked up a burn and crawled our way through the water. The stag we were after was again lying down chewing the cud and surrounded by hinds. We waited. The stalker wasn't comfortable with the situation after lying in running water for three-quarters of an hour. The stag got up. I fired and shot it cleanly. At the same time I should think about one thousand deer appeared and gathered together before taking off across the hillside.

The same year as my first deer stalking experience John Puddepha asked me to accompany him to South Africa, for hunting at Ant's Nest.

We flew to Johannesburg and then went by car for three hours north west to Waterberg in the Limpopo province. Ant's Nest is a stone and wooden built thatched lodge with a pool and all the mod cons of a safari hotel run by Ant and Tessa Baber.

It sits in a fenced reserve to keep all the game in and leases concessions for hunting. Lapalala Wilderness is an hour's drive from Ant's Nest and we had five days with a personal hunter (PH) who was Ant himself, taking us through the generally flat and dry bush with trees and occasional waterholes. I borrowed a .375 rifle and was after kudu, a big antelope with handsome spiralling horns. I hoped to get within a hundred yards of an animal to take the shot.

You know when you've hit your target because you can hear the sound of the bullet and a thud as it connects with its quarry. I hit the kudu at about one hundred yards and he fell with all four legs in the air. Ant shook my hand and said well shot and with that the kudu bull got up and ran off into some rocks. Ant grabbed my rifle and took a shot and missed. He then went back to the truck to get his black labrador who followed the spoor for about seventy yards. The antelope was dead, lying in amongst the rocks. I had shot my first African trophy. That same trip I had a warthog, a zebra, a red hartebeest and a wildebeest.

Hunting for big game is a dangerous business. You can never outrun any game and elephants, who you may think of as slow and lumbering animals, are very fast on their feet. You need a good PH with you and he'll make all the difference. In 2005 I was on my first hunt in Zimbabwe and lucky to have Butch Croaton, a white Zimbabwean, in his late thirties with me when I shot my first Cape buffalo. We flew to Harare, the capital of Zimbabwe, and then took a smaller plane to the outfitter at Ingwe which was situated in one million acres of unfenced bush. We arrived at midday and immediately zeroed our hired .375 rifles with 300 grain Barnes X soft point. It was too hot to do much before three in the afternoon and the animals were resting, so we had lunch and a siesta before moving off at 4pm in the Toyota Land Cruiser, that rugged steel-framed workhorse so favoured by those on safari. We perched on top of the open bed of the truck. Butch saw in the distance an old dagger boy, the nickname for the old Cape buffalo. Hearing the tap on the tin roof the driver stopped. After glassing with his binoculars Butch confirmed that this animal was worth going for. We drove on past the old bull Cape buffalo for two miles and then stalked back upwind. John Puddepha and I tossed a coin to see who'd be taking the shot and I won. John was given the cine-camera to record the hunt.

It took ages to spot the animal as it was lying down. We crept in to within forty yards. After a twenty-minute wait it stood up but only after Butch had thrown some rocks to get it moving.

"Take a shot!" he said. I refused as he was walking away and I did not want to take a raking shot down its back. The old bull headed off and turned to stop behind a bush. I could plainly see the head and the tail about one hundred and thirty yards away. Suddenly the buffalo came out and the PH whistled and the animal stopped broadside on and I fired. Thump. I heard the bullet hit its mark. The bull ran off. It was the perfect shot in the right place. We waited and listened and suddenly heard the crash as it went down in the bush. The PH always carries his own rifle for dangerous game. He led the way with me behind. This was always the dangerous time as a wounded buffalo will start to stalk you. There it was laid out. He suggested that I put in a safety shot which I did but the bull was already dead. By this time it was beginning to grow dark and they decided to leave the bull there for the night and come back in the morning to retrieve it. One of the trackers then took off his boiler suit, spread-eagled it on a branch they'd cut down and planted it alongside the carcass. The idea was that the smell would keep the lions and hyenas away acting like an overnight scarecrow. The following morning after the photo shoot they winched the body, which could have weighed anything up to a ton, onto the Land Cruiser and took it back to the camp to skin and butcher it. My ten-day hunt was over on the same day that I arrived. It was all too easy I thought. Pity that John had forgotten to turn the camera on.

It's easy to go out and not shoot anything but it's always an expensive business. You've got the PH and two black trackers in their regulation boiler suits and a government official from CITES. The Convention on International Trade in Endangered Species controls all big game shooting worldwide and gives approval to shoot specific animals as a part of a cull. The number of CITES certificates is rigorously controlled and they are allocated each year for each region and for each animal. The trophy can then be transported back home with official sanction. The cost of an expedition can easily be $1,000 a day. Then you have to pay outfitters' tips for the house boys and the cook, the skinner, the trackers at say, sixty dollars each, and the government rep and the PH at not less than one thousand dollars. Then there is the trophy fee for each animal. To shoot an impala will cost $500 and if you want to shoot a black rhino there is CITES approval for three hundred thousand dollars each. I don't want to shoot rhino. They are too scarce. The income from the trophy fee goes 50 per cent to the local village and the rest to the government. After taking some meat for the camp, the remainder goes to the local village. The only meat they don't want is lion.

I have shot four out of the "Big Five": Leopard, Lion, Buffalo, Elephant and Rhino. My lion was a fifteen-day hunt in Zimbabwe with a trophy fee of $12,000. This included shooting the bait, a cow Cape buffalo which was cut in half keeping all the "goodies" as bait for the lion. One half of the dead buffalo was hung up with chains from a tree so that a big cat can just reach it. It's important to establish the size and gender of the cat, and the hair on the bait and the footprints around it were the guide and showed if it was worth pursuing with further bait and erecting a blind or hide. There is little doubt that there are a considerable number of lions and lionesses in Zimbabwe and in less than an hour we had seen three prides totalling twenty-one lions. My first buffalo had claw marks down its back where it had been attacked. I remember on one occasion tracking buffalo only to find that in front of us there were lions following the same herd. Who was going to get there first I thought?

There were plenty of signs of lionesses around our bait and after three days the signs showed a lion but it wasn't an MGM specimen. The mane hair was not dark or thick enough to make him a really good lion but we were going to wait and see anyhow.

We built a blind in a tree not far from where we'd put the original bait and we staked the other half of the dead buffalo on the ground with a chain. We didn't want them to take the bait off into the bush. We took the bench seat out of the Toyota and put it in the hide and returned at dusk with our rifles and infrared spot lamps. Expecting to be there until the early morning, there were three of us up the tree, myself, the PH and his trainee. At 5pm, just as it was getting dark, I woke the PH because I'd seen two vultures come in but not going for the bait. They were holding back for some reason. Sure enough a lioness sauntered up to the bait followed by another and after a brief fight they settled down to eat opposite each other. We then heard a mighty roar. It was a lion. He bounded in scattering the lionesses. Both females ran and one of them rolled over in submission as the lion descended on the bait. I asked the PH to mark him out of five for me. He gave it a three.

"Let's take him," I said.

The heart of a lion is further back from the front leg compared to a stag and I aimed at the spot and pulled the trigger. The lion leapt two metres into the air and four metres to the side before falling dead on the spot. Both females walked up to him as he lay there and both touched him. It was either out of respect or to check to see if he was dead. A third lioness came along with her cubs and all of them touched the dead lion too before tucking in to the buffalo bait. If I had my time again with that lion I would have shot him but not from a blind. I can understand the reluctance of the PH and his responsibility for the client's welfare, but a proper stalk would have been a more mind-blowing experience.

I've been on a fourteen-day elephant hunt from an outfitter in Maura camp with Butch. We didn't shoot a bull elephant but we walked over one hundred miles tracking a particular elephant from his spoor which was marked very differently from other elephant tracks through forest, bush, rock and sand from dried up water beds. We came across a big tree he'd uprooted as though it was a toy. Its diameter was two feet and six inches. You could see the deep marks which were easily recognisable from his spoor where his back legs had driven into the ground as he pushed against the tree. Elephants are very powerful creatures and Butch and I nearly got caught out. We'd heard elephants breaking off branches. When we approached the noise there were bundles of leaves on the track where they had shredded them. All of a sudden there they were, a calf and its mother who scurried off as soon as they saw us. Then from behind a bush the matriarch appeared. She charged, trumpeting loudly. Butch tried shouting down the cow but from forty yards away there was little time. She came on. Butch shouted to me to get behind him and no sooner had I done so and let off the safety of my double rifle, a Krieghoff .470, than she was on us. Butch lifted his rifle and not having time to put it to his shoulder he let loose a round that hit her in the front of the brain. She collapsed in front of us finishing just three yards from his feet. Meanwhile his trackers and the government man had run. I have often been asked was I scared and the answer is no. There was just no time to be scared.

Some of the stories told around the campfire were straight from the pages of *Boy's Own* and the bravado and derring-do of the Great White Hunter are as strong as they have ever been. Englishmen like Jamie Lee, he of Rushmore fame and someone who has been as close to a charging rogue bull elephant as anyone would wish to be, and his hunting, shooting and fishing friend, Scott Luard, keep the legend alive. Jamie has been instrumental in helping to organise some of my most successful and exciting hunting expeditions. On some occasions he has also encouraged perhaps a little too much Irish coffee of an evening around that friendly campfire, to such an extent that my ability to hunt the next day has been a little impaired to say the least. But that's Jamie and as host he would expect you to enjoy yourself and would go to great lengths to ensure you'd have a good night, if not a sore head in the morning.

I got a phone call at home asking me if I wanted to shoot a rogue elephant in Mozambique. It would cost me $20,000 all in with no CITES and I'd have to leave England straightaway and there was no time to get visas for my rifle. It was April and I'd normally travel to Africa in either May, September or October. I flew to the country and met up with the PH, a South African called Ivan Bezuidenhout, and then chartered a small plane to take me and him to the tented bush campsite and an airstrip that had not been used for years. Bull elephants are more prone to raiding plantations and destroying the canopy of the forest and in this case the elephant had been trampling melons. Not that he was eating them all; he just liked stamping on them as elephants do when they push trees down. It is as much as a show of their strength as it is about eating the leaves and stripping the bark.

We had to track the rogue elephant at night and even with a full moon, sleeping out under the trees in the bush was quite a scary thing to do. After standing listening all night with his hands behind his ears, at 3am one of the trackers heard the elephant. I was tapped on the shoulder and as wide awake as I'd ever been. Off we went stopping and listening. We didn't see him but we could hear him sucking up water from the nearby waterhole. Then we could hear the branches breaking about thirty yards away as the elephant got our wind and went away from us. Days went by and we tracked his progress through the bush.

One evening at dusk we reached a waterhole and dug in for the night inside a bush right next to the water's edge and we set the sticks up, so we had a clear sight for firing. There were five of us, me, the PH, his assistant and two local trackers. Because of the short notice, I couldn't take my own gun on this trip so I was using the PH's .470 side-by-side rifle hammer gun loaded with self-load bullets. It had a ring peep sight. There was no scope, I didn't really need one at such close range but I had never shot the gun before and Ivan didn't want me to waste ammunition. He said it was zeroed but I never got to try it out and it was a strange fit.

Sitting as I was with an unusual rifle on the side of a waterhole at night in a bush I was suddenly aware that a whole herd of elephants had just arrived. I didn't hear them until they were there. None of us could move. We dared not and both our rifles were out of reach. I could just make out the dark shapes, great black beasts as they loomed in the waterhole right in front of our tiny bush, no more than six yards away. Had they chosen to they could have walked straight through the bush we were hiding in and trampled us to a pulp. It was probably the longest fifteen minutes of my life. Even the PH was frightened. Thank God they left the same way they had arrived. The PH felt sure that the rogue bull hadn't been with the herd. About an hour later he indicated to get ready and he grabbed the flashlight and turned it on and there was a female and her calf illuminated and the two of them took off. They had circled us and were coming up at us from behind. The trackers were thinking about running off and doing a double take. Ivan kept flashing the light on and off which frightened the elephants away. We relaxed once more but cuddled our rifles rather too closely in our sweaty hands.

An hour passed. We heard the sound of something opposite us once more and the PH was sure this was our bull. We got ready. He switched his torch on at the same time as I cocked the gun. There was our elephant but his flashlight put a shadow over the peephole so I couldn't get a proper sight.

"Fire!" shouted Ivan. I brought the gun up to where I thought the aiming point was and fired. I hit the elephant who went down on his knees. He then got up. Again I fired and he turned and again went down on his knees. He managed to regain his feet and ambled off as I reloaded and shot at the rear hip. An elephant can't walk on three legs. The bull disappeared into the night. I certainly wasn't going to hunt for a wounded rogue elephant at night. The next morning there was a clear spoor trail but that was the end of my time. I had to fly home. Later Ivan sent me a photo when they retrieved the elephant two days later. While both shots had hit the head, neither had found the brain but it was fatally hit. I would never hunt elephant at night shooting with somebody else's rifle ever again.

My next chance for an elephant came with a twenty-one day hunt in Botswana for a $72,000 trophy fee. Elephants in Botswana are renowned for being plentiful with over seventy thousand and some with very large tusks. The damage they do is quite phenomenal. Trees are uprooted, making a wooded area look like a bombsite. Bushes and undergrowth are broken off and this is the catalyst for starting a desert and the wind spreads the unhindered sand. It's a vicious circle as the reduction in supply of their natural food leads to the death of the calves and eventually others in the herd. Big herds of elephant have become their own worst enemies and apparently every ten years their numbers can double. The habitat destruction has to be seen to be believed and anyone who objects to the shooting of an elephant probably doesn't understand the full picture. Such is the case with most "antis".

The American outfitters were Rann Safaris and although they were well organised the oldest PH, Cecil Riggs, was terrible to his black staff and it was obvious they had no respect for him. The hunt for an elephant was more like a quick drive down the road then a three-hundred yard leisurely stroll followed by a pot shot in the ear at a rather sleepy big bull. I killed him by hitting him in the brain and he dropped on the spot but it was hardly a hunt. The tusks weighed 57 and 54 lbs respectively and I took the shot with my German Krieghoff side-by-side .470 rifle with a Kynoch 500grn nitro express bullet I'd bought from Manningham Buller in Wareham. It was on day three and I felt a bit cheated. Cecil obviously didn't want to get out of his Toyota. There were far better elephants about that we could have hunted in a more traditional way. Once I'd had mine I was encouraged to spend money on other game. I felt as though I was being ripped off. I overheard the two-way conversation on the radio when Cecil was told to get on with it.

"What else is he going to shoot?" was the unnecessary question.

Over the remaining eleven days I shot a zebra, a tsessebe which is a savannah and floodplain antelope with my Blaser R93. 7mm

Remington H&H 150 gram and a duiker, a medium-sized antelope, with the twelve-bore over-and-under with BB and that was it. I was pushed to go for more but declined. Rather than a serious fourteen-day elephant hunt, that particular trip should have been sold as an expensive three-day event. Even though Arthur went there the following year for an elephant, I wouldn't recommend it and, in particular, the old PH who should perhaps be put out to elephant grass.

I hunted leopard with Butch from a blind/hide on the ground. If one shoots a female there is a fine of $5,000, therefore you need to positively identify that you are lined up on a tom so a clear view of his testicles is the only sure way, the bait therefore needs to be in a tree at a height that gives you a clear view. We used an impala and put half a kudu cow up in the branches of a tree. After three visits from females the much more careful male cat crawled slowly along the branch to the bait. Butch knew that this was the male we could take. He held an infrared night light in whose eerie glow I could see the cat and his glistening eyes. "Take him now!" said Butch. I fired my Sauer .375 with its soft nosed Barnes X bullet and there was a flash that temporarily blinded me. I didn't see the leopard as he jumped off the branch. He jumped and didn't fall. Butch told me to go and get into the Toyota truck immediately. I said that I'd go with him to look for the leopard.

"No," he said, "you go and sit in the truck with the government man."

I did as I was told. I was devastated that I had put him into the position of hunting a wounded leopard at night. Butch fetched a twelve-bore shotgun with BB gauge shot and a flashlight taped to the barrel. I sat there feeling very concerned. I need not have been. The leopard was dead and shot through the heart with an exit hole on his offside of three inches. He'd still run twenty metres or so with his adrenalin rush and I felt upset that I might not have killed him cleanly. I had and was reassured by Butch who said it was a great shot.

The crocodile has a brain the size of a golf ball. In 2010 I shot one and a hippo both on the Zambezi. I was with Butch and shot the crocodile at sixty yards as he sunned himself on the river bank after gorging himself on one of my $25 village goats as bait. We were in a blind on the opposite sandbank. We hadn't been in the blind for more than an hour when he slithered up onto the sandbank. Butch told me to shoot him in the brain which is between the ear and the eye, an inch down, and then immediately to fire a backup shot into the neck to break his spine in case I'd missed with the first shot. It wasn't necessary as the first was smack on but I did as I was told and took a second shot in case he was just knocked out. If he slides into the water it is probably the last you would see of him, not knowing whether you have shot him or not. Once having shot you are up for the trophy fee irrespective.

"Again," said Butch, "that was the heart." I guess I was too quick, probably too cocky, as I was convinced I'd got him with the first shot and once again got a bang above my eye from the scope as the rifle recoiled from the third shot. I had not mounted the gun properly into my shoulder.

We had an aluminium punt with an engine with four of us on board. The PH, me, a tracker and the CITES man. We'd spent an evening and a morning looking for hippos on the land but a herd of buffalo and then some elephants had got in the way so we had been in the punt on the river for six and a half hours that morning, waiting for an appropriate opportunity. We were in a backwater with lots of weed and about to give up for the day when we saw a pod of some twenty hippos. It's important to see the animal's tusks to assess the age and sex of the hippo. All you see in the water most of the time are the ears, the eyes and the nostrils. They then drop under the water and reappear for a breath every five minutes or so. Hippos like to yawn and when doing so raise themselves, open their mouths to about three feet wide and that is when you can see the length of their tusks giving a guide to their age.

Suddenly one came up and opened his mouth. Butch identified him. He had a black spot on one ear. "He's the one," said Butch. I was lying prone in the front of the boat with my .375 Sauer and a solid bullet. Up he came again.

"Yes that's him!" the PH said. As he went down the PH said no. I fired my Sauer .375 H&H with a Kynoch 300 grain solid bullet. The hippo's brain is the size of a cricket ball and the shot has to be between the ear and the eye. It was a seventy-five yard shot.

"Good shot!" shouted Butch and he went to shake my hand.

"No," said I, "I haven't seen him."

"Don't worry," said Butch, "I did."

The recoil from the rifle when you're looking down a scope is such that you don't see what's happened. You only get one shot at a hippo or crocodile. If you miss or it disappears, you still have to pay.

The animal I'd shot sank. Even with other hippos about, Butch stripped off and jumped into the water after locating the beast by prodding the depths with a stick. He stood on top of the submerged animal up to his neck. It was dead so I shook his hand. The water was very muddy and so he had to dive under and feel his way in order to get the ropes around its head so that we could tow it to the bank. It's amazing how many local village helpers appeared and we soon had the two ton weight rolled up the bank onto dry land. It was skinned there and then and once we had taken what we had wanted from the dead animal the locals went at the remains like a swarm of furious carnivores hacking off the meat with knives and machetes. It was a feeding frenzy for the natives who carried the fresh hippo meat away to their homes in woven straw containers. It really is a different world. They cut down and use the overhead electric cables for snaring buffalo. I saw the mosquito nets that some charity or other had sent out as well-meaning aid. They were being well used as fishing nets. It was ironic that as we were hunting the hippo we heard a child in distress crying loudly not too far away. We learnt later he had died that afternoon from malaria. He was the son of the local tracker we had been using. I must say I felt guilty that here we were paying a substantial amount of money for a hunt and it's ironic that a few pounds would have given the lad a serum that might have saved his life.

Fishing is not my thing but we did have a spare day after our hippo hunt so we went tiger fish fishing on the Zambezi. That was something else. We would catch some small bream, cut them up for bait and wait. When the tiger fish bite they run off with the reel burning until you strike and then the fight starts for the retrieve. You do not want to get your fingers anywhere near a 12lb tiger's teeth. They are up to half an inch long and overlap outside their jaw. The wire trace has to be removed with care.

I love showing people that are interested around my lakeside trophy lodge. On the walls is the proof of my African exploits. Among them are the mounted heads of Cape buffalo, kudu, red hartebeest, sable and many other antelope and the head and hide of the lion. The leopard is a disappointment. The African taxidermists haven't captured the sleek cat as I wanted it. He was intended to crouch on a beam looking down and snarling at visitors. He ended up as if he is out for a stroll in the lodge with all the nonchalance of a big domestic cat in a zoo when he should at least be there as he was when I last had my sights on him, a hunting cat in the wild. I've found someone in the UK, William Mathews, who was working, before he retired, for the renowned taxidermist company in Africa, Rowland Ward. He will do proper justice to future trophies. In taking a life the least I can do is preserve its memory for future generations in as noble and beautiful a form as is possible.

The best shot I have ever taken was a Sable at 230 yards. The worst, one I still regret, was a 420 yard shot at a roan antelope. I knew at the time that I was probably being too ambitious with the 7mm Magnum Blaser 93 rifle I was using off sticks, but I still took the shot. I hit it and we tracked it for over three hours. We went back the next day but due to the very heavy dew, the tracks and blood had disappeared. We couldn't see any vultures either. We never found the result. That cost me $5,000.

I guess you always want to test yourself, prove to yourself that it can be done even when you think that it can't.

15. Critics, Concerns and Crisis Management

When you have done well there are those who seek to do you down. Successful business ventures often provide the stalking ground for those seeking out bad news. Bad news sells more newspapers and one particular stalker was a journalist called Ian Cowie and his boss Max Hastings. Cowie joined *The Daily Telegraph* team in 1986 and was hungry for an early scalp on his financial journalistic belt. My relationship with the press wasn't bad. In fact with most of them I made determined efforts to appeal to their better natures. I spoke fairly regularly to Fred Wellings and David Hoppit of *The Telegraph*. In 2006 Fred wrote a book 'British Housebuilders' in which I featured on several pages. The two *Telegraph* journalists, Diana Wildman a freelance for the *Daily Mail* and Jeremy Gates at the *Express* all came out to Majorca and stayed at our Casa Vida property. I picked up their bills, of course. I dealt with Alexandra Jackson and Chris Warman at *The Times*, Michael Furnell of *The Sunday Telegraph* and Caroline McGhie of *The Sunday Times*.

I guess that we should have seen it coming. A very profitable private sheltered accommodation provider and the elderly people it dealt with could form an interesting cocktail. Ian Cowie contacted our PR company to say that he was about to release a candid report on McCarthy & Stone and would we like to comment. While he gave a brief outline that it was to do with service charges and their increase, it was all very nebulous. We arranged a telephone call on the same day, a

Friday. We agreed that Nigel Bannister of Peverel should speak to him. After all it was Peverel that operated the service arm of our group and who had supplied the budgets. Several of us gathered in the office to listen to the questions and hear the response. Nigel did rather well. He suggested that Ian should come down and see us so that the full details of the accounts could be explained to him by representatives of Ernst & Young, the group's accountants. There were several complications to the questions that a face-to-face meeting with a few financial spreadsheets would perhaps iron out. Time didn't allow for a visit and he informed us that the story was going to press in a matter of hours because the deadline was that evening.

The article appeared that weekend and it was damning to say the least, with comments from residents and misleading figures on the service charges. It didn't show us up in a very good light at all. I read the half-page article the following morning at Watton's Farm and got on the phone to John Gray at his Lymington home. We agreed to hold a crisis management meeting on the Monday. I could see that this was going to have a big impact on sales and we needed to put an action plan together. I had earlier introduced into the company a crisis management procedure and policy, a part of which was to put a management team together to try and minimise the effect on the business of any adverse public criticism. The team was made up of me, John Gray, Nigel Bannister, Kevin Holland, Lindsay Bryant and the PR consultants. We had prepared for such an event with a dedicated room, phone and fax lines and each of the team was given a particular role. Apparently the whole episode started because someone complained to Age Concern that we were ripping their granny off over the service charges paid to Peverel. I made an immediate appointment for the next day to meet Lady Sally Greengross who was President of Age Concern. I had had a lot of contact with Sally and we sponsored her organisation. She helped me to network with many other influential people including John Yates of Help the Aged. The complaint against us was that service charges were higher than our clients had been originally told and this was the main point that Ian Cowie was concerned about. In his article he quoted increased charges of between 16 and 50 per cent.

What no one had appreciated was that budgets for the service charge were prepared well before the release of the flats for sale and therefore often well before all the relevant and detailed information was to hand. Each scheme would vary due to the finished design, be it face brickwork or painted render, number of flats, the height of the building which may require scaffolding for decoration, length of corridors, heating and lighting, and so on. Even though we prided ourselves in uniformity of construction technique, each development would have variations that would have impact on the service charges levied.

The fact that our service charges had to be based on an estimate at a particular time with often unforeseen costs and before a scheme was finished was a major consideration. Another was the effect on billing of the staggered financial years. For example, a scheme might take two years or more to sell out and it might be a further year before the financial year end and for the accounts to be finalised and for an annual meeting of the residents to be called.

Another factor for consideration was that elements of the service charge included the cost of things like water rates. We had found that if we installed a single water meter for the whole scheme, the savings to the resident were significant and costs were cheaper than if each resident paid direct to the water board on an individual meter. We had taken this decision as soon as we realised the benefit to the residents, however it did increase their service charge. Nobody liked paying taxes or council rates and if there was no charge as far as the resident was concerned then all well and good but it was impractical.

Some of our residents' children were quick to point the accusing finger. We had by then many thousands of very happy customers but as happens when the press gets hold of a story, the flames were fanned and what started as a local flare up became an inferno.

On 23rd March 1989 the Labour MP for Edinburgh South, Nigel Griffiths, stood up in the House and spoke.

"I thank you, Mr Deputy Speaker, on behalf of thousands of retired people, for giving me an opportunity in this adjournment debate to raise the problems facing them in retirement flats with unresponsive managers. Over 20,000 new flats and houses for retired people have been built in this decade, yet their residents have minimal rights. Elderly people have been lured in their thousands into purchasing retirement homes only to find that they have no control over the accounts or the managers. Many of them are having to suffer incompetent management and soaring costs. There is ample evidence of firms profiteering at the expense of the frail and elderly.

People responded in their thousands to advertisements such as that from McCarthy & Stone which said: "You are free of future worries of running a large property. Our friendly management support team, Peverel Management Services now offers you the perfect retirement home in Homeroyal House." Once residents move into such homes they often find that the management prices soar. The developers are either luring people in with artificial prices or imposing large increases to swell their profits. At present, it appears that management agencies of retirement properties allow developers to write themselves blank cheques at the expense of tenants and residents. Complaints are dismissed out of hand. I shall read some of the letters I have received.

At Fleetwood Farm in Southport, the managers, Northern County Homes, took exception to a committee being formed. An elderly resident writes: "Now they have sent their bully boy with a stick. We all fought in the last war and won — but not for this kind of treatment." McCarthy & Stone wrote to residents in Scotland's largest retirement complex in Edinburgh saying: "We do not recognise any committee or other group as representing the views or interests of residents as a whole." Yet Mr McCarthy, with an eye on public relations, claims publicly to encourage residents' associations. At High Wycombe, the Warden Housing Association has not produced properly audited accounts after 22 months. In Crowborough, a resident of Martlet's Court wrote to me saying: "The elderly are being conned and it is time the Government should bring in laws to protect us." In Upminster, retired people who are not satisfied with management are forced to sell at two-thirds of the market price. In Homeabbey House in Cheltenham, one resident writes of McCarthy & Stone: "Their replies have been totally unsatisfactory and often unrelated to the issues I raised. I have been disgusted with their attitude towards elderly people." It is a scandal that retired people who have reached the pinnacle of their professions in the services during and after the war, in churches, public administration, commerce, business and industry should be treated as if they are doddery old fools. If I were ever to hold the Minister's position, I could wish for no better or more competent advisers than the residents who have briefed me in Homecross House in Edinburgh or the retired people who have written so lucidly from Torquay to Tunbridge Wells, from Harrow to Hove and from many other parts of the United Kingdom. It is an insult to those retired people who have served this country so well that developers like McCarthy & Stone often refuse even to acknowledge their letters.

In Homeroyal House in Edinburgh, residents were issued in 1987 with a brochure from McCarthy & Stone which said: "Management charges rise at a rate either slightly below or at the level of inflation." The sales staff repeated that assurance, yet in the 18 months since one of my constituents purchased a flat there, the management charge has risen by over 16 per cent, twice the then rate of inflation.

McCarthy & Stone has done nothing to honour its promise to keep charges down. The charge for the son of one of my constituents staying overnight in the guest room rose by 60 per cent in the five months between April and September, although each resident had already contributed £250 to furnish the guest room — a total of well over £8,000. I wonder how much of that went to equip one bedroom and how much went to McCarthy & Stone's profits. As one resident said to me: "The strategy is to lure retired people in. They become trapped in the vice with no escape." In many cases, the management agency is a subsidiary of the developer. Peverel Management Services serves McCarthy & Stone, not the residents. Their interests are all too often neglected.

When I first wrote to McCarthy & Stone about these rocketing costs, John McCarthy wrote back saying that that was a ludicrous claim. I gave him the figures, and he wrote back saying that his present costs were unrealistically low. The McCarthy & Stone residents do not believe that those costs are unrealistically low. In Homeross House about £20,000 is spent on staffing, £20,000 on service provision and a further £20,000 — one third of the total — goes on management charges for which only minimal management services are given.

From Homedrive House in Hove, the residents committee has written to me saying: "We do not wish to line the pockets of Peverel Management Services." Such letters are all too familiar to Ian Cowie and The Daily Telegraph. I pay tribute to them, to Allison Clements of The Scotsman and to the Edinburgh Evening News for alerting Parliament and the public to the pitfalls of retirement homes. My hon. Friend the Member for Edinburgh, Central (Mr Darling) has also been pressing for retired people to be given justice by McCarthy & Stone.

Colonel Scott, the residents association convener at McCarthy & Stone's Homeross House, wrote to me: "Our main difficulty is that we cannot get replies to our letters." People have written to me from Bournemouth to Blackpool saying the same. At Homeabbey House, a resident wrote complaining to McCarthy & Stone and enclosed a cheque to settle an account. McCarthy & Stone replied saying that the original letter had got lost. Surprisingly, the cheque in the same envelope had been cashed.

Years go by, yet McCarthy & Stone still fails to produce proper accounts. The pattern is the same in Edinburgh, Bournemouth, Torbay and Torquay. Residents are promised the accounts next week, then next month, then next year and then they are told that the accounts are in the post. At Homeroyal House, only one set of accounts has been finalised in two years. At a meeting minuted in April last year, the McCarthy & Stone manager agreed to produce audited accounts in October; that was not done. In November, he told the residents that the accounts were ready; none appeared. In February this year, he informed residents that the accounts would be produced the following week. A month later, they still have not been produced.

Throughout the country, millions of pounds are unaccounted for. The money has not vanished; it sits in the bank accounts of McCarthy & Stone and Peverel Management. When the residents write to John McCarthy about that, they receive no answer. Arthur Young, the accountants for McCarthy & Stone, present accounts for charges that have not been incurred. It sends bills to residents such as one for £3,000 that was sent to one of my constituents and it then issues a correction saying that McCarthy & Stone owes the residents £2,000.

Mr McCarthy spoke out in an article called: "The truth behind the gossip". It was so full of inaccuracies that it was really the gossip behind the truth. It was a half-fictional account of the workings of McCarthy & Stone that many of the residents found hard to credit.

People should think carefully before purchasing retirement homes. I would not urge anybody to buy from McCarthy & Stone. Indeed, I would urge them to boycott McCarthy & Stone until another piece of valuable work has been carried out in this House. The hon. Member for Fylde (Mr Jack) has done invaluable work on a voluntary code of practice for the retirement homes industry. I very much welcome that. But the House has heard me detail the problems facing retired people.

Mr McCarthy wrote to me on 20th February: "We are already implementing the code of practice." Does a 69 per cent increase in management bureaucracy charges comply with that code of practice? Is it part of his code not to carry out repairs, not to reply to letters, to charge people £100 for parking their cars, to charge them for selling their own houses or to dictate to them who their managers and accountants will be? He has brought the code of practice into disrepute even before the ink has dried."

The Parliamentary Under-Secretary of State for Social Security, Peter Lloyd, then replied.

"There is no doubt that the concept of sheltered housing for the elderly is an excellent one. In most cases, those elderly people who opt to move into sheltered accommodation are happy, both with the standard of the accommodation and with the way in which their homes are managed.

The amount of sheltered housing has increased significantly over the past decade and there are now more than 20,000 homes nationwide. The industry is to be congratulated on its efforts to meet a real and growing demand. Typically, sheltered housing consists of a cluster of purpose-built flats, with some communal facilities and a resident warden. The vast bulk of such properties are owner-occupied, usually bought outright on a long lease with the proceeds from the sale of a previous home. I understand that in Scotland the homes are likely to be freehold rather than leasehold, due to differences in property law.

The attraction of such housing for the relatively fit elderly is obvious when the home in which they have lived, perhaps for many years, becomes too large and difficult to maintain. Sheltered housing combines the dignity and independence of a home of one's own with the convenience of modern purpose-built housing, the security of knowing that a warden is at hand should help be needed, the congenial company of like-minded neighbours and freedom from the need to worry about organising and paying for maintaining and repairing one's home.

It is that last consideration — the freedom from worry about the possibility of large unbudgeted bills for unexpected repairs or improvements, that concerned the hon. Member for Edinburgh, South in his detailed and copiously documented speech. As I said, most residents of sheltered housing are very happy with their decision. But some are undoubtedly finding their retirement years fraught with unexpected anxieties caused by large bills for service charges of which, they say, the glossy brochures published by the builder or management company completely failed to warn them. In some other cases their invoices have been incorrect or misleading.

I know that the hon. Member for Edinburgh, South is not alone in his concern about this problem. As he rightly said, my hon. Friend the Member for Fylde (Mr Jack) has been addressing this very subject through a joint working party with some of the organisations most concerned, and I am grateful for his generous recognition of my hon. Friend's efforts. Those represented on the joint working party include Age Concern, the National Consumer Council, the National

Homelife
House, head
office of
McCarthy &
Stone Plc.
(1986)

Princess of Wales, Lord Lieutenant of Dorset and me
at the official opening of Homelife House.
(4 December, 1987)

Company helicopter
G-PAPA at Watton's
Farm. (1988)

Me and Terry
Wogan with
draft ads for
Telegraph
campaign.
(1989)

Cartoon in the *Daily
Mail* on the flotation
of the company.
(1982)

Meeting John Major
at 10 Downing
Street. (1992)

Spencer being
presented the Royal
Windsor Cup by Her
Majesty the Queen.
(2007)

Me and Prince
Charles after a
charity match at
Ansty Polo Club.
(1993)

HIGHGROVE HOUSE

14th September, 1998

Dear John,

I am afraid this is a very overdue note to thank you and all those involved for staging such a successful day on Sunday 2nd August at Ansty, in aid of The Leonora Children's Cancer Fund. I gather you achieved a record this year of around £50,000, which is a magnificent achievement and I really do congratulate you.

I am deeply grateful for the immense effort you have put into building up this event and it is marvellous to feel that the charity should have benefitted so handsomely.

I was horrified to hear of your accident earlier this year and can only trust that you make a full and complete recovery. You have certainly made great progress so far!

Yours most sincerely

Charles

Letter from Prince Charles wishing me well after my accident playing polo. (1998)

70th birthday shoot with Will Thatcher coaching, and Oak my gun dog. (2009)

DreamCatcher with garage door open, store for two sailing Toppers and diving gear. (2005)

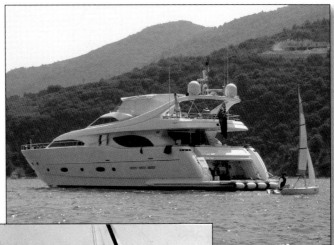

Saracen IV racing in Marseilles, powering through the Belgium yacht to leeward. (1976)

Spencer and Clinton announcing record results for the year. (2006)

Spencer, Clinton
and me at
Brigands estate.
(2007)

My second elephant – 57lb and 54lb tusks – in Botswana. (2008)

Gwen and me
at Brigands
estate. (2007)

70th birthday, Grenada. *(Top) left to right*: Maurice Omerod; Clinton; Peter Woods, Emma's boyfriend; Aston Mc; me; James Mc; Spencer; Cody Scholes; Duncan Scholes; Claire's partner, Scott. *(Sitting) left to right*: Laura and Rosie Omerod; Lisa; Bridget Mc; Emma Mc; Ellie Mc; Kathryn Mc; Claire Mc. *(Sitting on sand) left to right*: Grace Mc, Molly Ormerod, Hugo Ormerod, Max Mc. (2009)

13 foot 6 inch croc on the Zambezi, Africa. (2010)

Left to right: Arthur Wardman, Jamie Lee, John Puddepha, me, Clinton, Bill Riddle, Spencer, Simon Pollock, Brian Wiggins. My birthday shoot at the Brigands estate. (2010)

Federation of Housing Associations and the National Housebuilders Federation. The aim of the working party was to draw up a voluntary code of practice with the builders and managers of sheltered accommodation, which will ensure that the good management practices of the best-run sheltered housing are adopted by them all.

The code will focus on four main principles: first, how to develop a soundly planned housing scheme; secondly, deciding what estate management services to provide; thirdly, calculating the service charges to pay for those services; and fourthly, customer information, complaints procedures and arbitration to deal with some of the problems that the hon. Member for Edinburgh, South rightly highlights.

The code will stress the need for adequate pre-purchase information and include model guidance — for example, a model leaflet on consumers' legal rights. It will ensure that developers do not hand schemes over, once sold, to inexperienced management agencies. The latter must be reputable and developers will have to sign a standard agreement with them to ensure they inherit the original obligations that the developer entered into with his buyers. The draft code has gone out for consultation and the final version should be published later in the year.

Tenants paying management fees and for services that are recoverable as a variable service charge have statutory protection under the Landlord and Tenant Act 1985. That includes a right to be consulted about major works, a right to information about costs, an opportunity to inspect the supporting documents on which the service charges were based, and a right to challenge unreasonable demands. Those protections were originally for tenants of flats, but they were strengthened and extended to other dwellings by the Landlord and Tenant Act 1987.

That act gives further protection to tenants. For example, when the landlord or his agent is failing in his duties to the tenants, they now have a right to apply to the county court for the appointment of a manager to take over the running of the block; when leases do not provide for the satisfactory management of a block, any party to the lease can apply to the court to vary the terms of the lease; and recognised tenants associations are now entitled to ask landlords to consult them on the appointment of managing agents. Also, from 1st April 1989, under section 42 of the Act, all service charge contributions, including contributions to sinking funds, will have to be held in trust for the benefit of the tenants. The same applies to any income accruing from the investment of such money. That change will be very welcome for some residents particularly those in some of the categories to which the hon. Gentleman referred.

I have listened carefully to the hon. Gentleman's argument for further legislative action, but I do not feel that there is a case for additional coercive action at this stage. I would like first to have an opportunity to test the effect of the voluntary approach. I hope that the code of conduct which I have outlined will be adopted and that it will substantially strengthen the position of residents of sheltered housing.

That will benefit all residents of sheltered accommodation, not merely those who are able and willing to spend their retirement monitoring the performance of their landlords and going through some complex prescribed procedure when they wish to sack or replace an unsatisfactory management company. I do not think that it would be justifiable to treat the owners of sheltered housing differently from the owners of ordinary service flats. However, I and my colleagues in the Department of the Environment will watch this issue with close attention. We shall expect to see a reduction in the complaints received from residents of sheltered housing as the voluntary code of conduct is adopted. If that does not occur, no doubt my colleagues at the Department of the Environment will wish to look at this matter again to see what might be done.

In most cases, sheltered housing is owned outright by the occupants. Housing benefit would not be payable except to meet up to 80 per cent of the occupant's rates or community charge if his financial circumstances justified it. If the owner is entitled to income support, some help may be available with that part of the service charge that relates just to the accommodation. This would include the cost of heating, lighting and cleaning the communal area of the accommodation. If the owner is buying the sheltered accommodation on a mortgage, income support would be available to help with the cost of the mortgage interest payments, but not with the capital element.

I hope that the hon. Gentleman will realise from what I have said that the Government shares his concern for the predicament of elderly people who find that the cost of their retirement homes is greater than they anticipated. Although we may differ about the best solution at this stage, I am grateful for his views. I hope that he will continue to monitor the position, in his constituency and more widely. I know that my colleagues in the Department of the Environment will be ready to consider any further representations that he wishes to make. Finally, I congratulate him on securing the time to raise this important issue today."

There were so many misleading inaccuracies in Griffiths's speech and of course no right of reply, so we decided to put a paper together covering every one of his allegations. We were right there in the glaring spotlight of adverse publicity and had to do something about it. Within forty-eight hours John Gray and I had prepared a document which we sent out to every Member of Parliament. There were six hundred envelopes posted. My PA Lindsay Bryant with the help of Sir Marcus Fox and our PR company, Michael Saunders, and our litigation lawyers, Carter Ruck, arranged for us to go to the House of Commons and present our side of the story to MPs. We turned up to the large committee room at the House and presented our case to only about fifteen members. There were six of us, me and John Gray and his number two Steve Secker, two from our accountants Ernst & Young and Nigel Bannister from Peverel.

I opened the meeting and off we went with our campaign of enlightenment. We may as well have been preaching to a bunch of dummies. The questions they asked were ridiculous. Not one of them could understand basic accounts such as accruals, carry forward and provisions. They didn't even understand budgets versus actuals and the whole exercise was a complete waste of our management time and money. This has been borne out by their own expenses claims fiasco.

What Griffiths had omitted to say was that the management charge by Peverel was lower than that charged by the Registered Housing Associations.

Peverel had instigated the voluntary code referred to by Peter Lloyd MP. McCarthy & Stone had paid their share of service charges for unsold units at the same rate. Scotland had a different system with no lease but freehold sale and did have the right to change management if they had so wished.

The next string to our fight back bow was Terry Wogan. We'd used him the year before, in June 1988, at a ceremony to give a new flat as a competition prize to Mr and Mrs Adlam from Worthing. I met him in London for a photo shoot. He wanted £5,000 appearance money which did seem rather a lot. Nevertheless, our PR people thought that Terry was the right man for our fight back message. We had our pictures taken for a campaign that appeared in full pages of *The Daily Telegraph*. It took the form of questions and answers appearing in speech bubbles over the two of us trying to answer a number of the issues and innuendos that we had been tarred with. You can never be sure of the exact power of advertising but the campaign may have helped to reassure the doubters. We eventually got Ian Cowie to come and see us in Bournemouth but the result was another half page of rubbish in *The Telegraph* which added more fuel to his fire. One of his claims was that our service charges had increased by 30 per cent. He totally misconstrued how they were calculated but actually a 30 per cent increase over a period of three years and the extra net savings we had created by moving some of the utility costs into the service charge wasn't that bad given the state of the economy at that time and the rampant inflation. One area that seemed to have been conveniently forgotten was the considerable cost increases brought on by the Government such as water and electricity. At the time they were responsible as well for rates and taxes and the very high inflation of which they had lost control.

We saw the Scottish MP Mr Griffiths, who was taken aback by our circular to all his compatriots. He came to visit the Peverel office in Stem Lane. He did modify his stance somewhat when we led him through the files, however he wasn't going to be appeased and apart from satisfaction of the bollocking we gave him, the visit was another waste of time.

In February 2010 the *Scottish Daily Record* reported that the Edinburgh South MP said then that his behaviour had "fallen below acceptable standards" and he expressed his "shame" after it was claimed he had a tryst with a woman in his Commons office on Remembrance Day 2008. It was reported he had tried to defend a £3,600 claim for a television, DVD player and digital radio in his London home by saying he had to listen to "Scottish radio" and watch "Scottish TV". The former minister was said to have told the Commons fees office that a flat-screen television was the "sensible option" in a cramped flat. The fees office wrote back days later to tell him that while the explanation was understandable, the "level of purchases" remained under question, and Mr Griffiths did not pursue the claim.

He announced his resignation.

The Telegraph contacted us and we met their editor at the offices of our financial PR company, Michael Saunders. I knew that Max Hastings was involved and despite my request for an article setting the facts straight and an apology, he wouldn't agree to anything other than a worthless claim that in future if they wrote about us again it would be with glowing reference. We went to the High Court in 1991. George Carman was acting for *The Daily Telegraph* and Lord Williams was our brief. We were suing the paper for libel and claiming £800,000 in damages. Carman said the claim was too high and besides there was no valid claim.

It was pure theatre from start to finish. I had spoken to a local judge, Royden Thomas, who knew Carman. His advice was very welcomed and he told me to watch Carman like a hawk.

He would start off slowly, smiling, talking to you with a practised charm and friendly manner calculated to obtain your confidence. Then he would lob in a verbal hand grenade designed to blow away your confidence and he'd follow it up sternly by ignoring you and looking all the time at the jurors who, of course, were the decisive audience.

In replying I took my time. I did not reply immediately and I always looked at the judge or the jurors, never into Carman's eyes. It was important not to be flustered.

He would always try and take statements out of context, so in replying it was important to cover the whole point from beginning to end and not just the snippet he was trying to focus attention on.

He loved painting mental pictures and he was very good at taking things out of context. He asked me to read out to the jury a quote from a specific paragraph in one of our brochures. I said: "Certainly, but I would need to read the proceeding and following paragraphs which would put the piece in context." He very reluctantly agreed. After I read out the whole thing I awaited in anticipation for the cross-examination. He looked at the jury and said:

"I will come back to that."

I knew then that we would hear nothing further on that particular subject.

In connection with our claim for damages, Carman was trying to say we had over-cooked the costs which I denied.

"Mr McCarthy," asked Lord Williams, "have you ever put in an insurance claim? We all do and we all inflate them don't we?"

After a pause I replied:

"No. That's illegal. You can't do that."

"You're not a crook are you Mr McCarthy?"

"No," I replied with conviction. Our brief was wonderful at picking out all the salient points and getting the jury to understand them simply.

The case was due to be heard over four or five days. Kevin Holland, our Sales and Marketing Director, was very good in the witness box. He developed an argument using the Homepride advertisement and the fact that the Homepride men as depicted in their bowler hats were not actually real. He was trying to convey to the court that in advertising there will always be a degree of interpretation, a slant of creative license. George Carman was stumped by the argument and when he declared in his way, "We'll come back to that," we knew we had tripped him up once again.

Things were, we felt, going our way and over the first two days I was enjoying the experience.

At the end of the third day, halfway through the proceedings, we were undone. We'd had a case against us in Dorchester brought by the Office of Fair Trading over some wrong marketing information supplied via sales literature to customers. A recent piece of new legislation had come in to protect consumers from misleading information in connection with finance and mortgages. It was a requirement that a warning had to be incorporated into literature: "If you don't keep up your payments you could lose your home." Another was that signs shall carry the full address of the company, and that all promotional material must have the date of incorporation. We had devised a loan of 10 per cent of the purchase price to the resident where there was no repayment in any form until either the death of the owner or the sale. In the circumstances, we were of the opinion that the legislation did not apply to us. Our in-house lawyer suggested that we should plead guilty with a small fine of £2,000 which would be very much cheaper than going through a whole court action. Because the material hadn't been dated or addressed and didn't contain such lines as required, he was of the opinion we were technically in breach.

A resident of the scheme in Dorchester had informed *The Daily Telegraph* of the outcome. The judge was approached by Carman and he asked if the latest revelation on the Dorchester decision could be included as a part of their evidence against us. The judge adjourned to consider and said that he'd rule on the point the following morning.

Williams was of the opinion that the judge would not allow the new evidence in at this late stage and in any case he felt that he could defend it. I was not so sure. That night I went back to the Waldorf Hotel and pondered our predicament over a bottle of Chablis.

The following morning *The Telegraph* asked if we wanted to settle. I was concerned that the jurors may well construe the previous action as culpable on that particular detail and the judge might agree. We concluded a deal with the other side. We each agreed to pay our own costs of £200,000 and the wording of a statement for the press. We later learnt that the judge had decided that he would not allow the evidence in. We would have won. Given the uncertainty at the time I still felt that we had done the right thing. The problem with litigation is that you never know what might come out of the woodwork.

The whole exercise had been an expensive and time-consuming affair. We'd certainly lost sales. We'd learnt the hard way about crisis management. We, with the Home Builders Federation, had already introduced a code for management of sheltered housing in the private sector which was chaired by Nigel Bannister. Most importantly we had defended our reputation. There is little doubt that before any other media was to publish anything libellous about us they were now aware we would not lie down. While we still had to estimate the costs before sales release we set up procedures in detail that were then presented as part of the pack to would-be purchasers and made sure that the lawyer for the purchaser had copies. There was to be none of this, "I did not appreciate the costs." The most important change was that we introduced a budget meeting with the residents at which they could have their say on what would be included. This solved a lot of problems.

We were already monitoring "concerns" as we called them, which had to have a reply within twenty-four to forty-eight hours and any concerns not resolved after thirty days were to be reported to the main board. Needless to say, not many reached us. We already had a service department solely for acting and remedying any concerns. All company sales literature was dated with the correct address and had to be legally-approved copy that would avoid any misunderstandings. There was new legislation approved giving the right for owners to sack the management company if 70 per cent of the tenants voted to replace them. Not one of the hundreds of schemes that were managed by Peverel, including the ones referred to by Griffiths, was voted off. It had been a witch-hunt without a witch.

One area of criticism was that there was a perceived conflict of interest between McCarthy & Stone and Peverel. In 1993 we sold Peverel for £30 million to its management through Electra Investments. Interestingly, in the formative days of us moving into the provision of sheltered housing in the private sector, a number of institutions including Housing Associations were not interested in taking on the management. They seemed to have missed out.

Our critics tried to shoot us down in flames but they weren't using the right ammunition and they weren't very good shots either.

16. What Goes Up Must Come Down

I have seen five recessions during my time in the building industry: 1967, 1974, 1980, 1989 to 1993 and 2007 to 2010. All of them were inflamed by the governments at hand and more particularly by the banks whose lending criteria just went out of the window.

1977 saw the first block of sheltered housing completed at the Waverley House scheme. The next scheme was built right opposite in 1978 at the doctor's ex-surgery. The next development, Homegrange House, was at the back of Westover Hall, the old place we bought from the unsure Mr Knowleson. Another scheme was built in Lymington at Homewood next door to the house I'd bought for Eileen to live in as a part of my divorce settlement with her. There was one in Highcliffe and we spread our wings to Bournemouth and Winchester.

Each scheme brought substantial profit growth. In 1977 we made £49,000 profit before tax, in 1978 £199,000, in 1979 £607,000, in 1980 £924,000 and in 1981 £1,433,000.

Right from day one I have always been very wary of the City. Their so-called professionalism with fees to match, the Chinese Walls and a culture of short-term gain and the inside information network turned me off their methods.

Nevertheless, the decision to go public was made in 1980. My first dealing with County Bank was when we met in Old Broad Street. That name alone should have been enough of a warning. I met Matthew

Thorne and Simon Purser who were directors. Simon came down and looked us over thoroughly, did his homework and helped us through the lengthy due diligence and we put together a prospectus for potential investors. The whole process took two years.

I was asked to present our proposition to a gathering of City salesmen and brokers whose initial reaction was here comes another house builder. When I got onto the product we were offering, I could see that it struck a chord with many in the room as most had parents or relatives who would probably need the sort of private sheltered accommodation that we were producing. In entering our scheme most occupants would be trading down and selling their bigger homes to take up residence in our smaller flats. I sensed that the renewed interest in the room from my audience could have something to do with the fact that selling relatives might have spare funds and I could see several making the calculations and counting their chickens before they had hatched.

Going public was seen as the most effective way of cornering the significant market share for our specialist sector in the UK. At the same time we wanted to create a brand image for McCarthy & Stone. We decided to enter the unlisted securities market because we only needed to dispose of ten per cent of our shares to the market to obtain a Stock Exchange listing. A full listing would have meant offering twenty-five per cent of the shares. The due diligence process was not as stringent as that required for a full listing, at least that was what was implied. The amount of information required still proved to be significant. I was convinced that the City was out to make money out of the whole process of going public, not just with fees, but by undervaluing the flotation so that their mates could make a quick killing. It is common that the sponsoring bank would tout the market before the price of the shares is set. To talk up the company virtually guarantees success of the flotation and as the bank would be underwriting the share price there was always lots of talking up. As it was, the shares were oversubscribed by over 200 per cent which gives some idea of the undervaluation. I could almost hear them saying, "Ha, but our sales team did such a good job!" They would say that wouldn't they?

By the time of the flotation we were building, or had completed, twenty-seven schemes and the company had made in six months £1,030,000 and had forecast £2,000,000 by August 1982. At the date of flotation in June 1982 the company was valued at a placing price of 137p per share. The market capitalisation was £11.4 million. The brokers we appointed were de Zoete & Bevan Limited, a subsidiary of Barclays Bank. The solicitors were Travers Smith Braithwaite and the auditors Arthur Young (later to be Ernst & Young). In February 1982 we acquired Peverel and Co. Limited, the estate agency, owned by Trevor Foan who we subsequently appointed to our board as Sales and Land Director. Bill Stone was aged 44; Rodney Harrison was 33 and appointed as Construction Director. He had been with the company for eleven years overseeing the surveying and estimating functions. John Gray was 34 and the Finance Director. We employed 206 managers and staff. My salary was £43,500 and Bill Stone was on £30,000.

We had raised £1,000,000 at the flotation for extra working capital. Bill had sold £300,000 worth of his shares and I'd sold £100,000 worth. In all, the company had sold off 15 per cent of its shares for the flotation on the unlisted market. At 31st August 1982, the end of our financial year, we made £2,155,000 and declared our first dividend of £53,000. Bill and I waived our dividend of just over £280,000 that year. For a new company brought to the unlisted securities market the figures were very impressive. We'd sold two hundred and thirty units that year. Importantly we had doubled our net asset value from £2.98 million to £5.43 million. Right from the start we wrote off any interest accrued in the year. Our competitors, such as they were when they eventually appeared, put that interest to work in progress which caused them serious problems when the market turned down by artificially inflating their values. Of the nine and a half million new shares created, the McCarthy family owned five million, one hundred thousand and Bill Stone owned two million.

The City wanted and expected us to perform. We were certainly in the spotlight and we had to achieve our figures and the sales targets that were expected of us. On occasions this led to some creative accounting with sales. We only normally counted sales when the cash came in but in some regions this practice was bent to massage the figures so as to hit sales targets. This was frowned on and later caused us serious headaches so we banned the practice of counting sales before the cash was in the account for that year.

We were courted and wined and dined by bankers and brokers, lawyers, PR and advertising executives. Besides excellent wine and a good meal there was nearly always the opportunity to meet others associated with our industry. We had two PR companies on board, one for general company PR and one to promote our City and financial interests run by Michael Sandler. He introduced me to Sir Philip Harris of the Queensway Group and I did a useful deal with him for furniture and carpets for all our show flats in sheltered schemes. I also met Mike Dawson of Tunstall Telecom whose equipment we used for monitoring security and communications in all the flats. His company was later floated too.

The fees charged by these "London Boys" were astronomical but we paid them telling ourselves they were good value for money. We needed to be seen networking in all the right places and our PR people acted as the expensive lubrication for those particular City cogs. We had arrived and we were running with the hare and hunting with the hounds.

In the 1982 annual report I wrote the following about our prospects:

"Our aim is to consolidate and build on the strength of the business we understand by a progressive extension of our geographical coverage, and advantage will be taken of suitable opportunities as they arise. We consider that, with the expected increase in the number of over-seventies during the next 13 years, the demand for our type of accommodation is ensured."

By 1983 profits were £3.684 million from sales of completed units, which had increased from 230 in the previous year to 492 and we had established regional offices in New Milton, Eastbourne, Halesowen, Bedford, Altrincham and Glasgow. We were already recognised as the market leader. Our objectives were well in hand.

In December 1983 we had a rights issue of one new share for every four held. I and Bill Stone took up our rights, increasing our shareholding respectively to 9,000 and 4,000. This raised a further £12.1 million of working capital.

Following the rights issue, in February 1984 the company applied for an official listing as a public company. This meant having 25 per cent of its shares on the market. In July 1984 this was achieved by increasing the number of shares in the company and the money introduced to the company as further working capital was £5 million. This then gave Bill and me a shareholding of 6.8 million and 20.1 million. The directors waived their dividend for 1984.

In January 1985, to increase the capital yet further, a convertible unsecured loan stock was issued giving a dividend of 7 per cent to 2004 and raising a further £16.3 million. Bill did not take up the offer but sold the rights. I took up the offer, selling some of the rights and with the residue buying the stock on offer.

In August 1988 a further 20 million redeemable preference shares at 8.75 per cent were issued and raised a further £22 million for working capital.

A further rights issue in 1992 raised £13.3 million to reduce borrowings. I sold my rights.

The profits before tax for the following years were 1984 £6.8 million, 1985 £9.5 million, 1986 £16.1 million, 1987 £24.9 million and 1988 £34.1 million.

Each time there was a new issue of shares I would parade myself off round the various institutions to encourage their investment. I was always concerned that the amount of information we were being encouraged to divulge to the press and potential investors and brokers was giving away too much. The detail we gave was always far more than that usually fed to the general public. We were encouraged to and indeed felt obliged to give so much information. Forecasts were not written in stone but a good indication of anticipated results was always expected and our brokers would handle the information accordingly. Pre-tax profits were disclosed, net borrowings, stock amounts, sales performance details, margins, future cash flows, work in progress, land stock, gearing of the company, build costs, average sale prices, interest payment detail, marketing campaigns, details of any part exchange, planning and the appeals won, lost and pursued, site purchases and the areas of proposed development. In fact, all sorts of information was made available and picked over by the inquisitors. In fact, all sorts of information was made available and picked over by the inquisitors. I always thought that it was being used by the favoured few. I thought, and said as much to our brokers and lawyers, that all such meetings should be regulated and formalised with the information circulated to everybody.

We continued to open up further regional offices in Exeter, Cardiff, York and Jersey. Towards the end of 1988 I became concerned because the Government's budget in April of that year declared the intention of removing the joint tax allowances for home ownership between husband and wife. This could have a bad effect on our sales. I sent the secondary board away on a two-day think tank to come up with a plan should the company lose 30 per cent of its business. They came back with a plan and sure enough by October business started to wind down. Visitor flows to our new sites diminished and sales dropped. We made 175 people redundant in January 1989 and we closed down our regional office in Eastbourne.

On 1st May 1989 I announced our interim figures for trading up to 28th February which showed a record profit of £11 million for the first half of the year. It was, however, pretty obvious that the market was turning down more quickly and deeply than we had anticipated. By July 1989 we closed down more regional offices in Peter Cobb's Bedford region, York, Exeter and Halesowen and we consolidated the South West regional office into the head office in Bournemouth. Because

I had insisted as a policy that all offices were purchased as freeholds, the values had increased and we were able to sell them at a profit. We made over 600 redundancies during 1989. Some of our land stock was sold and by the end of 1989 we'd shed £21 million worth of land at a profit of over £3 million. Later we were able to buy some of them back for a third of the price from those developers who got into trouble.

These fundamental decisions were taken by John Gray and me sitting on the corner of a desk at nine o'clock one evening after seeing the reports from the regions. Interestingly, other house builders did nothing in taking any steps to shore up their positions until late in 1990. The press took us to task for making so many people redundant and our brokers became concerned and came to see us. They wanted to know our intentions. We left them with a clear picture as we saw it. By December 1989 we announced a much lower profit for year ending 31st August of £7.1 million. At the press conference to announce the poor results I painted a concerned picture for the immediate future and our share price took a hammering accordingly.

I said, "The current financial year is going to be difficult for the Group. We have continued to experience depressed trading conditions since the year end."

My comments of difficult years ahead were borne out and in 1990 we reported a loss of £10.8 million. Because we had been proactive rather than reactive to the economic downturn, unlike our competitors, we weathered the recession. During 1990 and 1991 those competitors who hadn't read the signs went bust including the largest, Anglia Secure Homes Plc, who had been trying to emulate our business. They were registered as a public company and even had an MP, Steve Norris, on their board as we had on ours. He contacted me for a meeting. He wanted to know whether we would be interested in buying the company but my answer was an emphatic no.

I personally had a small company called McCarthy Homes and during the late '80s early '90s the company had run up debts of some £2 million with NatWest Bank. In 1991 the bank asked for its money back but under the terms of the agreement with them, their charge became worthless. At a meeting in London in consideration of McCarthy & Stone arrangements, a separate meeting was held on the same day when the question of the debt was discussed. I told them that if they had read the terms in detail then there was no valid claim by the bank. After some discussion they agreed that they would write the debt off. I was astounded. I came away from that meeting feeling very pleased indeed. This was another example of the banks' inconsistency with their documentation. Many of the managers we were dealing with for loans had no understanding of the property business. Banks seemed keen to lend money at the best rate possible, imposing the highest charges and they didn't always look at the detail of what they were lending for. A site will be worthless if there are hiccups with planning or covenants and even though lawyers are supposed to look at the small print, banks used to only really consider the bigger picture. This got me off the hook on several occasions.

McCarthy & Stone continued to struggle and made losses in 1991 of £16.9 million, including a provision of £5.8 million against land. However we had a tax credit of £6.5 million and we had reduced borrowings from £118.8 million to £58.1 million.

In 1992 losses were £20.2 million, including an increased provision of £10.3 million on land and buildings which we later wrote back in the accounts.

In 1989 we had already set about reducing debt and gave our banks some comfort that we were acting responsibly. We had not requested further funds and we paid our interest on time. We leased our head office premises in Bournemouth for £10 million with Lloyds Leasing. We sold and leased back our office in Byfleet for £2 million. We sold our York office for £700,000 and the London office at 10 Mount Row, just off Berkeley Square, went for £1.6 million. We bought the lease in 1986 for £450,000 and at a drinks party at Claridges in October 1988 I asked the Duke of Westminster if he'd extend our lease from thirty to fifty years. He said he would and it only cost us an extra £45,000. We sold our nursing home company with its five sites to BUPA for £9.2 million. We had accumulated significant freeholds and ground rent from the flats we had built. I had insisted from the start that the ground rent should be more than the norm for the industry and these would be reviewed only upwards every seven years geared to the retail price index. We sold the first tranche of these (FRIs) for £21 million and every two years after we sold similar lots for between £20 million and £30 million to the Roche Group. There was other income from these ground rents, such as when owners came to sell their flats they would have to pay a 1 per cent transfer fee to the freeholder who would ensure that the flats were occupied by an elderly resident. All the properties had to be insured and the commission from the premiums was substantial and on top of the annual management charge. The ground rents were valued at twelve times and later to an increase of over twenty times. Sales dropped to 1,576 units when in 1988 we had achieved 2,596 units. This was to drop further in 1990 to 1,002 units. We introduced several incentives to try and encourage sales and one of these was free service charges for a limited period. Another was delaying anything up to 25 per cent of the sale price which would be paid on death or sale of the flat. We'd charge interest of 10 per cent on the money, which was very reasonable at the time. These schemes seemed to work but they were not without their problems given the decrease in value of some of the units and the fact that interest rates came down so that 10 per cent became a rate to be grumbled about. The whole "discount for business" idea cost the company about £18 million and took several years to be repaid.

We renegotiated our loans in 1989 with our eleven banks after breaking some of the covenants. Our covenants with our banks meant that the interest we had to pay for loans should be covered by up to four times by the profits we made. £1 million of interest repayment therefore would mean £4 million of profit. Such was not the case. Our FD on the board at the time was John Begbie. Unfortunately he was running scared and wasn't one of the strongest of characters to have around when times got tough. I went to the meeting in London and explained the position, but meanwhile Begbie had disappeared. I said that even though we had acted appropriately having recognised the downturn we still needed to amend our agreements with our bankers. This was agreed and at very little cost with just the legal fees involved. We had to give regular updates on our cash position and sales progress and we formed a committee to monitor and report on the position every week. Meanwhile John Begbie had a mental breakdown and left the company. My previous FD who was looking after one of the divisions returned to caretake the role while we looked for a replacement. After a strong recommendation from County NatWest, I interviewed a candidate called Martin Towers who'd just lost his job as a result of a takeover at Boots. Even though he was wearing loafer shoes when he came for the interview we appointed him. He got to grips with our position. With Kevin Holland, our Sales and Marketing Director, a presentation was prepared for the banks as in 1991, and in 1992 it was obvious that we were going to make losses. The loans were getting close to being reviewed by the eleven bank syndicate.

I had to apologise to the shareholders at the AGM, something I'd never had to do before. I said, "The costs of our renegotiations with the banks were over £1.5 million and they had ripped us off but that was what we were forced to pay for renewal of the loans."

Unfortunately, I was not aware that the leading bank, NatWest, had a representative at the meeting, Graham Bentley, and that he was not amused at my remarks. So what? It was the truth. We didn't have to ask for any further funds and we managed to pay all the interest due. Dividends however were cut right back and I waived my 1991 dividend of £100,000 as a gesture. The preference share dividend was also dropped but this was to prove a problem later when I once again had to refinance.

By the end of 1992 I could see that the recession was coming to an end and that we would need funds for the purchase of sites. Meanwhile the financial director was encouraging a spiral of sales which was winding the company down even further. This was much against my better judgement. Unbeknown to me he went to a meeting of the banks who had agreed loans of up to a maximum £120 million with a further £46 million in reserve if required. We were running on borrowings of £70 million so there was plenty of headroom. We had sold off a number of our operating arms such as the lift company and the window manufacturing company.

I had learnt that during his meeting with the banks the FD, Martin Towers, had been derogatory about the board's handling of the business and had cast doubt over its future. I was aghast. I asked him to come and see me and fired him on the spot.

The day after Towers' toppling I had a meeting with the head of the bank consortium, Bentley, who said that he couldn't believe what I had done. He told me that the rest of the banks had gone "ape shit". I knew he was being serious because he'd never used bad language before. He was the typical tall, lean and hungry-looking, clean-cut corporate lending director. As we met in his office fairly high up in the NatWest tower I told him that there was no alternative and that he shouldn't be concerned. When I got back to my office our brokers had left a phone message. Leslie Johnson, the director looking after our account, wanted me to call him. He told me that they had heard what I'd done and they felt they could no longer act for us. This would have been disastrous. I called in our non-executive director, Simon Purser, who was an ex-banker and asked him to persuade the brokers to give us two weeks grace before acting, in which time we'd come up with our next-step recommendations. He spoke to Leslie Johnson and bought us some time. We contacted one of the directors of County NatWest Bank, the bank who had helped us in the flotation and offered him the position of FD on our board. Matthew Thorne joined us and we put a plan together. Keith Lovelock, who I'd appointed as CEO to give more confidence to our backers, the new FD and I presented our plans to the brokers. At the end they left the room to consider their verdict and returned to say that they would continue to act for the company. It was a defining moment because had de Zoete & Bevan resigned the City would have deserted us like rats off a sinking ship.

During this difficult time the banks didn't exactly bend over backwards to help. Apart from the extortionate fees and interest rates they charged, one of them, the Midland, wanted out. They were in difficulty and wouldn't agree to the changes. They couldn't get out though because they were a part of the consortium. If any one of them quit, this would lead to the others having to take up the slack between them. Other foreign banks who had helped us were trying to get out because of difficult trading conditions in Australia, Canada and France.

At one meeting I attended with the Midland Bank I remember that they had just been to a board meeting with the Bank of England. One of their directors said to me that I shouldn't really worry about things. They were obviously distraught and told me that changes were being planned. They were. They were taken over by HSBC.

At another meeting with Crédit Lyonnais, the woman running the account took me to task and lectured me about good marketing practice. She said she knew all about our business because she had been speaking to Wimpey, the house builders. She obviously had no bloody idea at all and we ended up having one hell of a row in her offices. Not the entente cordiale at all. They too wanted out.

Crédit Agricole, another French bank and part of the eleven, were talking about charging us £34,000 as a fixing fee to sign up to the new agreement which would mean I would have to pay the same to each of the eleven. I couldn't believe this and in my frustration suggested to Bentley that I take a suitcase with the cash in it around to the Crédit Agricole HQ. Mr Bentley calmed me down and persuaded me that perhaps my idea was not one of the best I'd had. We ended up paying them all their blood money. There was a Japanese bank involved as well but they toed the line and were less vociferous than their French counterparts.

I managed to conquer all these fears. Over the previous six years or so I had been having regular meetings with the representatives from the Bank of England in Winchester. The meetings occurred about once or twice a year and we used to exchange information about the market and how things were going. There was one very good contact I made so I got in touch with him and explained the problem we were having particularly with the foreign banks and I asked him what could be done. He said that "we could lean on them" and that was all I would hear. Sure enough in the end all of them came around to our way of thinking and they all stepped into line and agreed terms.

One part of the refinancing jigsaw involved the preference shares for which we had not paid the dividend. One investor held a significant amount of those shares and he lived in Berkshire in a grand house right opposite the Royal Berkshire Golf Club as it was then called. Luckily our brokers acted for him as well and one of Leslie Johnson's sidekicks knew him particularly well as his broker. We needed him to agree to the terms of issuing more preference shares in lieu of the dividend payment. I asked our brokers if they'd set up a meeting with the individual concerned as the amendment required seemed to be a sticking point. The investor's secretary refused point blank to arrange an appointment for us. I found out where he lived and the broker who knew him well said that we should just turn up unannounced. We cold called on him at 10am the following day. Four of us turned up unannounced, two from the brokers and me and my financial director, and were ushered in by his housekeeper. Rather than flinging us all out on our ears he was delightful. He and I talked about everything under the sun rather than the point of the visit. He explained how he'd made his money and expanded his preference share portfolio from £2 million to £21 million. I explained how I had built up a company from nothing and how the current choppy financial waters were in danger of upsetting the boat. I turned up the McCarthy charm and we agreed to give him extra shares in lieu of the money due. His help would assist us and to my great relief he said he'd help and we left the meeting knowing that we had secured the refinancing deal with no barriers in the way. The boys from de Zoete & Bevan had cut the cake both ways. They'd managed to keep both of their clients happy. When we got back to the office there was a call from the Berkshire gentleman's secretary to say that it was disgraceful that we had gone behind her back and that we should be ashamed of ourselves. It was just as well we had. The investor kept to his word and we agreed terms which was to increase his preference shares by the amount that we had withheld as dividend payment to him.

Not long after the deal with the eleven banks had been secured, our brokers de Zoete & Bevan and their director Leslie Johnson asked for a lunch meeting and we went to the Terrace Room at The Savoy. Leslie was in his late thirties or early forties and the typical City type. He was also about the same height as me but I was about to cut him down a peg or two.

In the middle of lunch he said that he wished to apologise for their threat to resign the account. He told us that we had proved our case and knew the business better than they did. He congratulated us. Talk about shutting the stable door after the horse has bolted. I wasn't having any of it. We fired our fair-weather friends and they were eventually incorporated into Barclays and wound up. Unquestionable loyalty at all times, rough and smooth, is an absolute prerequisite for me. I appointed UBS Warburg.

In March 1993 we restructured the company once again. Bill Stone stepped down as non-executive director. John Gray, who'd been a director since 1973 and joint CEO with me, stepped down. Keith Lovelock was Chief Executive and I retained the position of Executive Chairman. Matthew Thorne was FD and Simon Purser remained a non-executive director. In the same year we made a loss of £11.2 million.

We were hell-bent on reducing our borrowing which stood at £60 million, down from £118.8 million. We sold Peverel and Co. for £30 million with the proviso that if it was sold for anything above that in the next five years we would receive twenty per cent. Peverel was sold to Electra and they retained the original management team. John Gray left McCarthy & Stone to become chairman of Peverel while Nigel Bannister continued as Chief Executive Director. We pulled out of our French operation and wound that business up. I was still hands-on and oversaw the planning, architects and marketing departments. In 1994 economic fortunes turned and increased sales saw a return to profit.

I had been determined to get into a cash positive position and even though 1995 saw another small dip in the market we expanded our business once again. By 1997 we were cash positive and remained there until I retired at the end of December in 2003 with about £86 million in the bank. During this time I was under pressure from my FD, Matthew Thorne, to arrange loans with the banks even though cash flow projections and budgets showed no requirement for borrowing. I agreed to some arrangements in the end, much against my better judgement, especially as we were paying a non-utilisation fee for the loans. They were all agreed without any charges being taken on the company. This confirmed to me that we didn't need the loans at all and demonstrated how banks fell over themselves in the rush to lend us money we didn't really want, without much security at all.

I had led the business through what I regarded then as the most difficult time for UK house builders. In 1995 to 2000 I persuaded the board that we should re-open several regional offices in North London, York and others. There was a second dip in the economy in 1995 but there was no serious adverse effect on the company and we continued to progress our profits each year: 1994 £4.7 million, 1995 £9.2 million, 1996 £11 million, 1997 £20.5 million, 1998 £28.5 million and 1999 £39.6 million.

On 4th April 1996 I moved to Guernsey and bought a house there and became a non-resident of the UK. I could catch the 7am flight from Guernsey to Southampton arriving at 7.30am. The car would pick me up and get me to the Bournemouth office by 8.15am. I could also fly into London if needs be, by 8am. While I was only allowed 90 days in the UK, travelling days did not count at the time as long as they were at varied dates.

Also in 1996 I began to take a close interest in IT and had installed in Guernsey a computer system with email and fax machines so I could, in effect, do a lot of work from home. I encouraged all board members to do the same and arranged for personal installations in their homes and offices. Laptops became a common feature without too many complaints. Even the CEO, Keith Lovelock, learnt to master the keyboard and was soon typing his own communications to the rest of us. This wasn't to be for the Finance Director, Matthew Thorne, who continued to dictate everything to his secretary including his emails. Even with all the leg-pulling he was not prepared to embrace the new technology.

My employment contract was amended on 21st February 1996, widening my brief to Overseas Director as well as Executive Chairman. The objective was to broaden the business opportunities in other English-speaking countries with specific direction to look for other avenues within our knowledge of the elderly. I spent some time looking at the market and researching in America and what was happening over there. Meanwhile Peverel had been bought by an American firm called Holiday Incorporated, which under their CEO Patrick Kennedy was building assisted living schemes throughout the USA. I flew to their HQ in Seattle, California to meet Bill Colson and his team. I was very impressed with their set-up and saw that they too had employed my idea of standardisation. Wherever we went in his Hawker 145 to places like Phoenix and Houston, there were prefabricated timber buildings made in Canada and transported down in twenty extremely large lorries to be put up within two months. All their schemes were the same wherever they were in the USA. I travelled across the country with Bill and saw the ideas they were implementing. They had taken our idea a stage further, providing restaurant facilities and cleaning for flats with, in some cases, more on-call nursing care even offering Alzheimer's facilities. I was very impressed with the staff care and consideration for the residents. They were called "Assisted Living" rather than just sheltered accommodation. In the States renting was the order of the day rather than the purchasing ethos seen in the UK. I returned to the UK fired up with the assisted living idea and we set up a subsidiary company offering leased units with a much higher service charge element for extra care and restaurant facilities. The first scheme was completed in 2000 in Bicester.

From 1998, when we were in credit with about £24 million in the bank and we had more cash than we were using, we would lend it to the banks. I made a policy based on past experience and in particular the collapse of BCCI that we would never lend more than £6 million to any one bank at any one time on deposit. This seemed a prudent move and the old adage, as safe as the bank, was sadly to be proved one of hollow words. We didn't get our fingers burnt.

Profits in 2000 were £53.5 million and in 2001 £60.5 million.

On 7th April 2001 I returned to the UK having spent four years in the Channel Islands as Overseas Director. The company continued to show growth and we were opening more regional offices. I gave notice that I would become non-executive chairman, reducing my time in the office and gradually winding down. My intention was to retire at the end of 2003.

Profits for 2002 were £75.4 million and for 2003 £116 million.

However the share price wasn't moving in line with the profits that the company was reporting and this concerned me for some time. I thought about selling a chunk of the company which might push the share price up. The share price had dropped back from over 500p to 125p. By 2001 the price was about 260p and I had suggested to the board that we should try and test the market. In 1998 we approached a new company, Hawkpoint, and Luke Withnell their founding director we knew from NatWest Markets. Luke felt that they could sell the company. We had previously been approached by 3i Investment who were interested and whose offer was more than the quoted share price.

Keith Lovelock couldn't agree with the 3i proposition on his and the other directors' positions and the potential deal was scuppered. Hawkpoint thought that they could do a deal with either another developer or house builder, known as a trade sale, or to another investment company. I asked if they could also approach American investors because I'd seen that there was already some US interest in some UK building companies. The board were concerned about what would happen to their own positions if the company was sold or taken over. It was eventually agreed to revise the terms of their employment and in the event of a sale they would receive two times their salary and bonuses based on the past year if they were relieved of the position or retired within three months of the sale. The proposed sale was launched in the City by Hawkpoint under the code name Senator. Nobody came forward with a cast-iron offer. I was most disappointed. I could not fathom why, when the company had a fantastic niche, with a high brand image and was a very profitable business. However, with the offer to sell, the share price improved to 330p.

My two sons, Clinton and Spencer, were doing well with their business. They had, like McCarthy & Stone, changed direction from a general house builder to building sheltered units. Churchill Retirement Living was born. It seemed to me that the rest of the board had gone cold on the company sale. I suggested to my sons that together we should put in a bid to buy McCarthy & Stone and take it back into private ownership. Between us we had about £150 million and there would be a need to raise further funds from the banks to make a sensible bid. At the same time I was negotiating with the remuneration committee my revised salary and proposed sale of my shareholding to see me to the end of 2003 and retirement. We approached and appointed PricewaterhouseCoopers to act as our brokers in a proposal. Simon Boadle took the lead, he was already known to me from advice on the previous aborted sale of the company. We spent about three months putting plans together to merge the two companies. I asked for a meeting at UBS, who were the brokers for McCarthy & Stone, to discuss my departure from the firm and in particular my shareholding.

By this time we had a letter of commitment from NatWest Bank to finance our takeover. We'd also approached HBOS who had been recommended by PwC as a company which was investing significantly in property. Armed with the NatWest letter of commitment the meeting took place at the UBS offices in the City with me and Spencer, guys from PwC and from the other side Michael Mead from UBS and Simon Purser, a non-executive director from McCarthy & Stone. I'd given the impression that the meeting was to do with my shareholding and the others were therefore surprised when we arrived with our accountants to make an indicative offer of 505p per share for the company. It was obvious that our offer was serious. I told them that we would be changing management at McCarthy & Stone and that my son Spencer would be appointed as Chief Executive and I would become the Chairman once again. This hit them like a bombshell.

It was our intention that, firstly, we would amalgamate Churchill into the Group, secondly, we would run down McCarthy & Stone's land bank and finished stock, and we would not buy more land or build further units for a year. We would then be able to repay a significant amount of the proposed borrowings making it very much more manageable when the inevitable downturn in the market arrived.

It was June 2003 and the meeting broke up with our family offer under consideration. The next day I went to see Keith Lovelock, CEO of McCarthy & Stone, who'd sent me an email previously after the 3i offer, expressing his concerns about continuing with the business as a number of his friends had died. I was concerned about how the business would be run while I still had a significant shareholding in it. Keith denied the inference he had made although his email was quite clear. The board later convened and turned down our offer. I, of course, was still a member of that board but felt I had no alternative other than to act in the way I had. Firstly, there was the concerning inference of Keith's email, secondly, the fact that the share price was well undervalued, and thirdly I was about to retire and required assurance on my investment. There seemed to be no appetite from the board to do a deal. The board was not acting in the best interest of the shareholders and I was a major shareholder.

We had another meeting with PwC and Simon Boadle who suggested that we increase our offer. We had, of course, not gone in with our highest. Simon thought that we would need to increase our offer to something near the 700p mark. I said I was not prepared to pay that and that it was an overvalued price for a company operating in a market that was already overheated. The last thing I wanted was to be beholden to the banks once again for something that wasn't worth the risk, notwithstanding that in the year I left McCarthy & Stone had made £147.8 million before tax and would have over £80 million in the bank. HBOS had asked to be present at the meeting and Peter Cummings their Chief Executive arrived. All along I'd made it very clear from the start that any purchase would be conditional on the family owning 100 per cent of the equity. Peter Cummings started off the meeting by asking how much equity HBOS would be getting in the deal. I was completely taken aback. I said none. He said they would not consider the deal unless they received between 30 and 40 per cent of the equity. I said there was absolutely no chance of that. They needed to reconsider and left the meeting. I immediately said to Simon Boadle and the others from PwC that we were withdrawing our offer for McCarthy & Stone and furthermore I thought that HBOS had been very underhand in the whole affair and that they understood the rules from day one but were trying to bully their way into getting a significant share of the company. I was not prepared to trust them. How right I was.

We asked for our meeting to be confidential, for which undertakings were given, but two days later an article appeared in *The Times*, an obvious leak by McCarthy & Stone, saying that they were not prepared to sell and that the offer was derisory. These press comments lead to a share price rise in anticipation of an improved offer. We put out a statement saying that we'd withdrawn our indicative offer over concerns for the way the housing market was overheating and the disregard the board had shown to its shareholders.

Our press statement on 11th July 2003 ran as follows:

> John McCarthy wishes to announce that, taking into account the responses of the board of McCarthy & Stone to the approach made by the McCarthy family and the current share price, he has decided not to pursue an offer for the company.

> Yesterday's closing price of 520p represents a 38% premium to 277p share price on 7th May 2003, the day prior to initial bid speculation appearing in the press. At this price the company is being valued at a multiple of 2.3 times in its latest reported net asset value of 227.7p per share, which compares to an average for its peer group of 1.2 times.

> John McCarthy said:

> "The housing market is undoubtedly weakening and I expect more difficult times ahead. Given the current share price and unrealistic expectations, driven in part by press speculation, I do not believe it to be sensible to continue to pursue an offer for the company."

I had of course been trying to sound the alarm bells at McCarthy & Stone over my concerns for the over-egged market. I could see a repeat of the 1990s and having lived through the 1980s recession and the struggles of 1973/74 we needed to be prudent. There was no way that we wished to be caught out with large borrowings and reduction in sales as well as prices collapsing: the double whammy for developers.

The board were very upset with our press release and the fact we were withdrawing any offer. I was concerned that they had leaked the proposed offer to the press. The share price had risen significantly the day after our offer for which the Stock Exchange later made an enquiry into potential insider trading. The board were more concerned for their own individual positions than that of the company and its shareholders. They had clearly been implicated as one of the reasons for the failed bid. I resigned as executive chairman but continued to be paid for the next five months until the end of my contract and the prearranged date of my retirement, 31st December 2003. They tried to stop my bonus, and then reduce it by 25 per cent which seemed very petty, but after two court hearings, I won the full entitlement but not before they had gone bust.

The indicative offer had the desired effect of increasing the share price. Keith Lovelock had indicated that the profits for the year would exceed expectations, which in my last year with the company reached £147 million with over £80 million in cash. It was not a bad way to leave the company finances.

Peter Cummings had obviously approached some of his pet investors. Tom Hunter was one and the Ruben Brothers another. He had all the information that I had provided to make our case for an offer. Between them they made an offer of £1.1 billion, valuing McCarthy & Stone at £11 a share. This was double what we had been prepared to go to. It was little wonder that having completed the purchase in 2006 they were unable to meet the interest payments and, as I predicted, the market went into freefall in 2005. The full effect was felt some time later but for every year that went by it only got worse and the business went into administration after Rothschild was called in to advise in June 2008. When this happened the McCarthy family stepped in with another offer at slightly less than its first offer. The banks were to reduce their debt to £400 million plus ratcheted period equity stake of 30 per cent and we would put into the company the equivalent of £105 million. This would mean that the banks, Tom Hunter and the Ruben Brothers would lose something in the region of £700 million. After putting a full offer document together for the business, a pre-package for the company was concocted by the banks. They did not want to be seen to be losing too much from their balance sheets. After going into administration and having excluded Churchill's offer, the banks gave the benefit of doubt to the management leaving the banks running the business.

I did alright out of the sale to HBOS, Tom Hunter and the Ruben Brothers because they bought my bonus shares for £11 each, giving both my daughter and me a profit of £6 million. My daughter had left her McCarthy & Stone shares converted into a loan with HBOS, but on my advice in 2007 she got out because I could see that they too would get into trouble. Sure enough Peter Cummings's over-lending on property brought HBOS down and his ill-judged legacy was passed on to Lloyds. His advice was not to be relied on by his investors. Some very bad decisions were made and buying at the top of the overheated market was simply crazy. His reasoning was fundamentally flawed. He was of the opinion that not enough housing was being built and that land was in very short supply because of planning constraints. That idea was nothing new and if he had been around in the '70s he would have heard the same cry. He had been warned and was privy to all the information that our offer had contained. That wasn't his only mistake. HBOS was oversubscribed in the house building and property market to a massive degree. Before the purchase of McCarthy & Stone they bought Crest Nicholson Plc house builders at well over its value and likewise it ended up in administration. McCarthy & Stone are firmly in the bank's clutches and will find it very difficult to resurrect themselves. It could be third time lucky, but I doubt it.

Why did they not accept a very good offer from us? Churchill and I had offered to put in £105 million pounds of collateral with the only condition being that they wrote their borrowings down to some £400 million. They were probably not prepared to write off such a large amount at that stage and hoped to float the company off for significantly more, thus retrieving some of the losses. The chances of floating the company off in the near future is minimal, especially as the same management are again buying in land at tomorrow's prices and cutting their margin in doing so.

Furthermore, why did they continue to put their faith in a management team whose reluctance to taking action on the very obvious market situation was glaringly obvious? In January 2008 they released a press notice saying that they were expanding. By May a further press release reported that they were making 10 per cent of their employees redundant. By June, Rothschild was called in by the banks and by April 2009 Freshfields, London lawyers, announced a new structured company McCarthy & Stone Lifestyle Ltd., dispensing with all the non-secured creditors.

Churchill, who took action early, had sold a number of sites to McCarthy & Stone including one for £2.5 million that six months later, after completion of the purchase, they immediately put back on the market for £1 million. Their ability to effectively manage their business must be called into question. The margins they had enjoyed in my day of over 30 per cent profit before tax, the highest in the building industry by a very large margin, had gone out of the window. They were doing deals to try and drive up sales that inevitably had a serious and adverse impact on margin. It seemed that the new chairman from Cala, Geoff Ball, and previously David Pretty from Barratts, had introduced conventional house building margins. It was obvious that they were driving for very much higher sales with hopefully higher profits. They would then try to sell the company back to the stock market at a greatly increased price. Higher unit numbers don't necessarily bring increased profit. Sadly the company's ability to manage their affairs properly does a great disservice to the name that we gave to it.

I left McCarthy & Stone on 31st December 2003 and six months later I became a non-executive director in my sons' firm Churchill Retirement Living. It was great to once again be involved with a younger more dynamic company and it brought back memories of McCarthy & Stone when we had floated as a public company twenty-two years previously.

The fall in house prices I predicted at the end of 2003 and start of 2004 didn't materialise until 2005 when Keith Lovelock reported the year 1st September 2004 to 31st August 2005 encompassed what commentators described as the most difficult trading conditions for house builders in the last ten years.

Their profits dropped 14 per cent. He went on to say: "We would not expect volumes to exceed last year's, we anticipate that margins are likely to ease further, we expect another testing year."

Howard Phillips took over as CEO of the company.

It is extraordinary that with these remarks HBOS went on to take the company back into private hands and pay so much over the top with an agreed offer of £1.1 billion in August 2006. By December 2006 Keith Lovelock had resigned as Chairman and Matthew Thorne as Finance Director in April 2007. In January 2007 HBOS were interestingly trying to cut their stake. My contention was that for every year it went on from 2005, the worse the fall in the market would become. That seems to have been right. The banking crisis and the fall in house prices has been a disaster. It is remarkable how many house builders went blindly on in 2006, 2007 and on into 2008 without taking any obvious pre-emptive action. Churchill has gone from strength to strength and with my prudent advice and early action taken by the board in 2007 has emerged in 2010 as a strong business buying back some of the land it sold before the crash, for half what they sold it for pre-crash. A repeat of what happened to McCarthy & Stone in the '90s when I was guiding it through my fourth recession. Some, it seems, will never learn.

If I had my time again I don't think that I would have floated the company in the first place. The flotation probably cost me £2 million. There were too many constraints put on us by the City and the need for profitability of the company in the short term. The City will say that it's the pressure they put on a company that makes it grow. It may be the case with some old or staid companies that need a nudge but it isn't true of younger, entrepreneurial driven and forward-looking firms. The need for funds to expand a business is vital but I question whether there is a need to go to the market for funds that are slightly cheaper than those raised on borrowings from other sources. Borrowing from banks can be a problem in itself but in the short term and for secondary expansion and provided that it's not over-borrowed this is the best route.

Private investors are looking for an out and the out leads to a public offering of the shares of the company. The significant costs in becoming a public company weigh down very heavily on a new entrepreneurial company. It is said that it is easier to raise a rights issue when a company is having trouble than it is to go to the bank and ask for an extension of a loan. This may be the case where insufficient prudence has been practised in the first place. Not to over-borrow and to read the market on a daily basis is vital. There are enough so-called expert analysts out there who will form opinions according to their judgement of the market movement. I have seen, on numerous occasions, where these analysts have got things completely wrong in the building market. In this last recession they were pushing, along with the banks, the property sector which had grown out of all proportion to the market generally. Earnings ratios had climbed well above the normal trends, savings had virtually disappeared, construction was rampant in the market and house prices were increasing well above incomes for many years. The old adage of what goes up must come down was written for the housing and property market.

17. McCarthy on Stone

I've been asked why our partnership lasted so long and did so well. It's quite simple really. Bill gave me carte blanche in running the business. His penchant for business management was of little interest and he left me to manage the business. I do believe it is important that in partnerships each plays to his or her strengths. This same philosophy applied to my two sons, Clinton and Spencer, in the formation of their business. From day one with Bill I ran the little red book which documented our finances. I would do the investigations and estimates for all the jobs and I would be instrumental in driving the business in the direction I'd identified. I don't think Bill ever visited a bank other than when we went public and as a director he had to be present for the due diligence for the prospectus. Even this bored him to tears. In the early days Bill was responsible for the construction on site. His attention to detail was welcome. It was always down to me to find something for which Bill could take responsibility. To include him in the running of the business I'd give him some less important responsibilities in areas that invariably needed close attention.

Why did I put up with this? In the early subcontracting days we both put in the same number of hours and perhaps it was loyalty and respect for each other. Later, when the business took off and became more structured, Bill's interest waned. He did come into my office once and said he'd like to be involved with more of the meetings I was attending in London and elsewhere. I suggested that he should come to the next meeting with me which meant leaving the following morning at six o'clock to travel to London. He found some reason not to make it. I suggested others and these too he couldn't attend so I gave up. Later Bill was put in charge of handling the complaints procedure or, as we called it, "areas of concern". I was approached by other managers in the business saying that the letters he had sent were causing more problems than the original concern. I read some of them and could see that Bill's tact in dealing with the issues was not what it should be. I therefore arranged for others to take over the role.

During the recessions of the mid sixties, seventies and eighties I kept him abreast of what was going on but very little came out of his office that could be used to help in any negotiations. While I was going to training on various different aspects of business management Bill was conspicuous by his absence. We set up a plant department early on and Bill was put in charge. Once again I had to bring in another manager, Uncle Alec, who took over that role in plant and manufacturing which were becoming very important for the growing business.

Bill's love for cars has always been for the more exotic. He drove a German Borgward and his Zephyr 4 was in British racing green. I did persuade him to get a van when we first started subcontracting but this soon changed to a Cortina. He had a DB5 and a DB6 when I was driving something far more sedate. In the early days we did mix socially and one year we went on holiday to Spain. By then I had my E-Type and he had his DB6. We raced each other down to San Sebastián where we stayed overnight, and then on to San Pedro. We had been lent a villa by my father's friend. Gwen's sister and her boyfriend arrived and we all stayed in the large villa for two weeks.

At a restaurant run by two delightful gays Bill discovered that he'd left his money back at the villa. He returned and disturbed some villains during a burglary. There was a sheet in the middle of the main room with some loot from the house but the thieves had escaped with some of our possessions. They'd tried to get into Gwen's and my bedroom but the door was stiff and they thought that it was locked so left it alone. It needed a decent shove to open it. The local police arrived and they were convinced that the attempted burglary was an inside job.

Because I hadn't been robbed I was marched off and interrogated in the local police station for two hours as the main suspect. It was a bit like something from a spaghetti western. My inquisitors sat me on a rough wooden chair in the middle of a stark room with guns on the wall and fired questions at me. Some I understood but most I didn't. My alibis arrived eventually and confirmed that I had been in the restaurant at the time of the break-in and I was released. The finger of blame was then pointed at local gypsies but nothing was ever recovered.

After my Bruce Farr designed yacht won the Yacht of the Year title in 1976 we decided that we were going into commercial yacht production. Bill was put in charge while I was concentrating on our first sheltered home project at the Waverley site. The way forward for the business was soon clear and I told Bill to drop the boat-building idea and scrap the moulds. He was reluctant but eventually agreed. I had instructed agents to sell all our undeveloped land. I was convinced that a step change of direction was required. When it became obvious that the business of private sheltered housing was going to grow at speed I was introduced to County Bank for flotation, on the unlisted market or the AIM market as it is now commonly known, by our bank manager at NatWest, David Giddings. The idea of this route was that I was convinced that the City was undervaluing the company and such a listing only required 10 per cent or more of the ordinary shares to be placed to the public compared with 25 per cent on a full listing on the main market. I did not and still do not trust the City. How right I was. We floated on the 18th June 1982 at a share price of 137p and by January 1984 after a rights issue raising £12.1 million, we fully listed on the Stock Exchange at a share price which had over doubled.

The sole object of the placing was to raise funds, reputation and grab the core market share across the UK. We'd started by opening a regional office in Eastbourne run by Fred Andress. I had introduced other directors on to our board. Trevor Foan ran sales and marketing, John Gray as the Financial Director and Harry (Rodney) Harrison, as Building Director. The fifty-fifty share we had was going to be a problem when we floated. I had a meeting with him. He was planning to sell a significant number of his shares at the flotation. I couldn't accept this. His proposed sale would dilute my own shareholding and over time this would affect my position. I suggested that he sell me twenty per cent of his shares giving me a seventy per cent stake. John Gray agreed with Bill what the payment should be and the freeholds of Admirals Court, Osborne House and £230,000 were given to Bill for his twenty per cent share prior to the flotation. Bill asked me what was going to be expected of him now we were going to be a public company. I said he'd have to have a higher profile and visit the City more often and take on greater responsibility. He replied he wasn't interested in having more work. In 1984 Bill retired from the company as an executive director. I said he could remain as a non-executive director which he did for a number of years. However this role lacked commitment and after not turning up for numerous board meetings, I suggested to him that he should resign from the company, which he accepted. This was in 1993.

Since then Bill has done some small-scale development of his own with an ex-McCarthy & Stone employee, Martin Young. Their company is called Archstone and built up-market £2 million homes in Sandbanks and later went into building houses for the elderly. Bill remained a shareholder for a number of years and was always loyal to me. When the boys and I tried to take over McCarthy & Stone in 2003 Bill agreed to back us and with his 5 per cent shareholding. With mine at 21 per cent we were trying to do a deal and push the undervalued share price up from 350p. Our indicative offer was for 505p.

Bill had a beautiful wife, Janet, but very sadly she died from breast cancer in the early eighties. They didn't have any children. Bill is now married to Sally and lives close to Lymington not far from where we spent our early years together.

We still speak from time to time.

18. Any Other Business?

Some of my best decisions were made in the morning bath. Sometimes, after a fitful night thinking of a problem that keeps going over in your mind time and again, you wake up with a clear head and in taking that dip, naked, unshackled by the trappings of office, on your own apart from your misty reflection, in your own environment, you can cut to the chase very quickly and make up your own mind. It might be something simple like not wearing a tie to the office on a Friday. That would really piss off some of the other directors. It might be the content of the warning letter I sent to Matthew Thorne on 12th November 1998. It might be the way I had to tell Harry Harrison he no longer had a job with me although I don't count that as one of my best decisions. It might be the decision to up the offer for Squalls or it might be to put in an objection and fight that unfair decision.

In 1999 I was asked by our brokers what I did all day. The reply ran to a five-page memorandum. Here is part of my reply:

I have always been proactive in my management style and decisions in that I abhor having to say, "I told you so". This has led me to first suggesting, then persuading and finally insisting on my requirements to ensure that things happened. For example I undertook to review and look at and report on certain aspects of the business.

I fired the director in charge of sales and marketing who had made a number of inaccurate assumptions particularly on the assurance schemes and who had sanctioned a significant over-run in the marketing budget which was approaching 9%. I also fired the agency whose idea it was to continuously reinvent the wheel. I introduced the matrix system of budget control for every site, looking at each of the components to ensure we received value for money. I axed the national advertising and took this in-house, reducing the size and moving back to fundamentals. There were instant benefits compared with a campaign that needed an IQ of over 100 to understand it. I reduced the number of ads nationally and regionally from twenty to a standard five for each and linked the national and regional campaigns into one with one focused campaign for each year, agreed with the regions and tested before implementation.

Brochures and other printed matter were axed as there was too much new work being produced with no relation to the strategy of the campaigns. I instituted a standard brochure and leaflets reducing output by 70%. All this meant that we could reduce significantly the in-house design time and costs.

I reviewed and overhauled the corporate presentation as each region had their own idea of what should be presented with no co-ordination on a group basis due to the hands-off approach by previous management.

I completely reviewed sales training, covering the basics. This is a continuous assessment with changes of staff and the need to introduce a more focused bonus system for team effort.

At the same time I started a push for the IT sales progressing system. I had tried to implement this in 1985 and again in 1990 but it was a total failure with a lack of conviction by those assigned to the job. This time I undertook a very close role even to the point of having the system installed in my home to ensure that momentum was maintained. The system continues to evolve to meet the overall strategy of giving the sales consultants and the sales managers the information to respond quickly and accurately to events while monitoring the success or otherwise of a development or an individual. This system has borne out my enthusiasm for it to be a significant benefit to the business. There is no other house building company with such an all-embracing system from the point of enquiry to completion of a sale. The system has a lot more potential for being more hands-on in austere times while giving the ability to make more cost efficient sales.

After the sale of Peverel in 1993 it was I who introduced the charge for the house manager's flat in each development on a rental basis reviewed each year. I had a dickens of a job to convince the board that the value should be treated the same as the FRIs and in fact it wasn't until the second year of running before it was agreed by Ernst & Young, the accountants, and the FD, that it was acceptable. This has improved the profitability of the Group significantly.

Upon the sale of FRI (Freehold Revisionary Investment or ground rents) to Roche in 1996 it was I who retained at the last minute the Careline connection for the benefit of McCarthy & Stone with a reduction of £300,000 from the purchase price. We now sell to Peverel each year this right which brings in approximately £120,000. These rights are also extended to all new units as they are sold, which will increase by a further £60,000 p.a. In due course as the stock builds up we will be in a position to create our own Careline system. It was I who introduced into Peverel in the late '80s the Careline system after Peverel put up barriers of why not and eventually I ordered the system personally to be installed in our office in 1987/88 while they built the accommodation in New Milton. Finally I instigated the procedure of switching from our old emergency system to the new system in schemes we had completed and sold.

It was I who instigated the connection of the fire alarm system and burglar system into the Careline in 1995 without any further cost to us or the customer. This gave us a unique selling point for the business. If ever there was concern that the costs of Careline were excessive compared to other providers it could be relatively easy to explain the extended service that we were providing.

In 1990 at a volume house builders meeting a Department of the Environment minister informed the meeting that there was going to be a fundamental switch in planning policy. Instead of the "presumption in favour of development" proposals, permission for planning would not be given unless it "complied to the local development plan" which would be approved by the Department of the Environment. I therefore instigated the Group expanding its planning bureau in order to make representations on all the 600 local development plans proposed in the

UK. The importance of this strategy cannot be over emphasised as we have been able to change and modify over 205 local plans with over 500 specific objections to date. On twenty-two occasions we have had to pursue a policy change to a public inquiry.

In the last year and a half I have been promoting and introducing a Corporate Plan system which was originally devised by Ernst & Young. Having identified the five important aspects of the business – finance performance, employee satisfaction, group's reputation, quality satisfaction and customer satisfaction – each of these has a measure or milestone of success with a list of strategic initiatives along with critical action steps to achieve the goals. These are reviewed every three or four months by the board taking two days away from the office and reviewing the action plans on who, what and when. These are then passed down to the regional boards who then compile their action plans to co-ordinate with those of the Plc board. This system ensures that we continually move towards our goals with all participating and this really does make things happen.

Within the last year I have widened the introduction of psychometric testing for all key staff starting with the key area sales managers. This has been followed by the personnel manager being trained to undertake the system in-house and all new appointees are tested. I still sit on the executive committee although I have less and less input, however, I do look very closely at what I perceive as the critical measure and that is the "DISH", a single page, that tells me on the four key points of development what the latest is on the minimum measures of performance for each development on which I then make my comments and recommendations. The more detailed questions are dealt with by the team. The 'DISH' (Development Information Schedule History) is something that I introduced early on with the formation of the Executive Committee.

I still attend development board meetings and chair the Plc board in between researching overseas opportunities such as, the review of customer care, assisted living product and the trial of the super site manager as used in the USA all in the last year.

Other than that I don't do too much!!

The reply also explained that I was trying to move focus away from me, especially in the City's eyes, and on to other board members to give assurance that the company was not just based round one person. History will show that I did a lot and that when McCarthy left McCarthy & Stone the business foundered accordingly. In his book on British Housebuilders, Fred Wellings said as much. He credits the survival of McCarthy & Stone in the 1990s to the dedicated management not the least being its founder. I suppose I could have given the brokers a five-word reply instead of five pages: Back me and make money.

In my youth my driving ambition was to get into business as soon as possible and I was greatly relieved at not being called up for National Service. I had three principles which I stuck to. One was the work ethic, two was recognising luck and acting on it and three was using common sense.

My uncles had a significant influence on establishing the work ethic in me early on. The way they did things instilled in me the good practice for getting things done in a certain way. This was applied equally to work and play. The work ethic was coupled with an eye for detail and once the business had built up I never let this go. I would look at every department and over some months, scrutinise the policies, the work practices and the people to ensure that we received the best output possible. This assessment process was conducted on a recurring basis so that improvement could be fostered. Individuals would often try to put their own stamp on how things should be done and while entrepreneurship was to be encouraged, it was important that any changes to company systems or products did not lose sight of the original goals. The devil is in the detail and my nickname, at least one of them, was Mr Trivia. On entering the full lift one morning it was me that bent down to pick up the scrap of paper lying discarded on the floor. I like to set an example. Evaluate, Plan, Do, Check and Amend was the company song. It was played in the lift for all to hear. Take pride in what you do and it will show.

Delegation is imperative for company growth but only when the person has been proved to be capable of taking on the task and when one has full respect for that individual. They may make mistakes but by understanding and controlling the size and cost of the risk involved you can mitigate any errors. I kept a firm grip on policies and development as well as the corporate shape and strategy of the company. Delegation shouldn't be undertaken too early or on a whim. From my experience, a person who is good at his profession is not always good at management.

I used to work from 7am to 11pm. I then took up playing squash which forced me from the office at 7.30pm. Often after-hours ACOT meetings (arse on corner of table) would be most useful and there were no minutes. These casual meetings with John Gray, our Financial Director, or Harry Harrison, Construction Director, would help shape the company thinking. Harry now works with my boys, Clinton and Spencer, and his experience helps to shape their thinking. He also acts as the peacemaker on the occasions when father and sons disagree. When I used to leave the office I would often see the cars of new employees still working to meet deadlines. After I left the company the car park was empty by 5.30pm. The example I set with my work ethic was eroded.

We all have luck. We don't all recognise luck. When luck comes along it's what you do with it that counts. People have said to me, "Oh but you've been lucky in business." How do you recognise luck when it comes your way? It's the will to succeed that turns the lucky break into something positive. Uncle Peter always thought that the windscreen wiper could be improved. He was right but did nothing about it. Chrysler did and incorporated the intermittent and variable speed blade into their vehicles before any other motor maker. They nicked the idea off an impoverished inventor who did nothing about it and Chrysler had the motivation to use a lucky break to their financial advantage. It could be said that when I read the four-line article in the Home Builders

Federation newsletter suggesting that developers should consider looking at the sheltered housing in the private sector, every other major builder in the land could have read the same article. I appreciated the significance of it. It led me to do some research on the requirements of sheltered accommodation. I identified that if the accommodation was built in the right place, close to shopping facilities, then the already reduced need of the elderly for a car would mean less space for parking, leaving more space for housing. I saw the opportunity and actually did something about it. With my research I persuaded the planning authorities that my scheme was doable. Was it luck? Was it my motivation? It was the combination of both. It was luck that the federation printed a small paragraph about sheltered accommodation and it was my willingness to explore that idea that put me on the right road to fortune. It was luck and the dedication to build on it.

What They Don't Teach You At Harvard Business School is a book written by Mark McCormack and I would recommend it as essential reading for all budding entrepreneurs.

Common sense is being streetwise. People find reasons to change things or make improvements as a way of avoiding good decision-making. Management can complicate things by making decisions so confused in the first place with over-analysis that their thinking becomes clouded and their decision-making a reluctant process. How many times have I sat at board meetings where a particular question was being passed around in a never-ending circle when the answer was blindingly obvious at least to me? I would override needless discussion and make the decision. Some might say that I was being dictatorial. I'd say that I was taking the common sense view and moving on. Common sense and street wisdom comes into its own with every aspect of the business. The buying manager whose wife had run off with another man was not focused on his job. He was double and even triple ordering materials. At first sight this could have been fraud but my PA, whose other job it was to keep her ear to the ground, told me his news. A similar thing happened to our chief land buyer. He too had marital problems and all of a sudden land was not coming forward to be purchased. Land is the lifeblood of any developer. What happens at home has a direct effect on what happens at work. It's common sense. I was asked to deliver a lecture to the CBI and I made it a point to ask all the delegates if any of them had a policy which took account of their senior employees having matrimonial trouble at home. Not one of them had. I suggested an open door policy where these issues could be raised without fear of any discrimination and to give backup to that individual which would help them through the trouble. Common sense told me that every business suffered. Troubled home lives could adversely affect bottom line statistics.

Never believe what you are told. My instinct is to always be suspicious on any proposal. This has made me query several. I have come across con men on many occasions. They always stand out. They talk too much and repeat themselves in the effort to persuade. They have an answer for everything. I have been told that I don't trust anybody. I don't until they have proved themselves worthy of my trust and respect. For example, the guy who said he could fix the steering mechanism on my yacht and was an engineer of great experience but needed several days to do the job. He was wrong. I tightened a loose screw and it was fine. Another wanted to rent my polo grounds after I'd given up. Instead of telling me he had no money he pretended that he had. His front was as flimsy as his bank balance and I smelt him out early on and didn't lose any sleep or money over what could have been a sour deal. My early dealings with the Newtons, our rogue tenants in Osborne House, was another example of common sense and street wisdom coming into play to prevent any harm.

I became a great advocate for psychometric testing after having my son and a colleague tested. Knowing these two already and comparing the results of the tests left me gobsmacked by its accuracy. There is a great difficulty with interviewing and identifying people of quality and ability by what you are told and what is reality can be totally different. The CV and references can often not be worth the paper they're written on. A phone call can often elucidate on what can't be written. The tests are really all about common sense. Watching the TV programme *The Apprentice* makes me cringe. If Lord Sugar made all his aspiring, and to my mind useless, candidates take a psychometric test, he'd have his winner in no time at all. That wouldn't make for very exciting television though.

Common sense tells me that to withdraw is often a better tactic than to carry on regardless. Our experience in court with *The Daily Telegraph* was one such and there have been many others where it made perfect sense to cut and run. Reputation of the company is very important and must be preserved, especially in the elderly business.

Awards can be a fatuous token of an industry's self-gratification or the recognised mark of a job genuinely well done. I had received several in 1975, 1976 and 1977 for my yachting achievements. We thoroughly deserved all of ours in business too and had a cabinet full of trophies from 1989 up to 2004 from a wide cross-section of those interested in promoting such things. They included the *Daily Express* for British House Builder of the Year to *Building* magazine's accolades for thirteen years, to an award from *What House?* pats on the back from National Opinion Polls and MORI and praise from *Site* magazine and the National House-Building Council. There were personal handshakes too from organisations like Pricewaterhouse and Midland Bank, all of which confirmed our unique position at the top of our industry.

My personal trophy room is filled with the taxidermy already described and in my office I have the framed bits of paper and photographs to remind me that I was Director of the Year in 1996 according to Pricewaterhouse and Entrepreneur of the Year as judged by Ernst & Young. More important than any of these was the honour from the Queen.

At first I wasn't really sure what I received my MBE for. I told Her Majesty that I believed it was for services to the elderly. It could just as easily come from my sailing efforts but then I probably upset too many from the old school of yachting to be a serious candidate for any decoration. An MBE is a great honour. Sarcastically it stands for "my bloody efforts". An OBE is "other bugger's efforts". It was wholly appropriate therefore that in 1984, on my return from skiing, I opened the letter that asked me if I would like to accept a Member of the British Empire honour. I did, with very great pleasure.

On the day we went to the Palace it seemed very appropriate that Uncle Alex drove us in the Rolls. You're allowed to take a maximum of three people with you so I asked Gwen, Clinton and Claire, the oldest and the youngest. There were hundreds of us at the Palace with most in some uniform or other. You are briefed about what is going to happen and then when your name is called out you step up to the mark and bow, Her Majesty hangs the decoration on the prepared hook on your lapel and there is a very brief question and answer session, then you shake her hand. It's a brief handshake with the very firm message that your time is up. You then back up, bow, turn and march off. We then had our photograph taken, bedecked as we were in our morning suits and fine attire, and we then withdrew to The Savoy for a celebration lunch.

The following Christmas when we entertained a lot of the management and staff at the Royal Bath Hotel in Bournemouth for a seasonal lunch, Uncle Alex arranged a surprise giant MBE and the thing was paraded through the assembled gathering and presented to me with far less formality than the real thing and with a lot more laughter too.

The fear of failing has kept me on the road to success. I take a keen interest and still play an active part in my sons' business. I am the clear voice of experience that can read the tea leaves and sound the alarm bells when I see choppy waters ahead. There are several examples but one in particular, an email dated 6th March 2007 and titled "Property Crash", was addressed to Spencer with copies to Clinton, Harry Harrison and Dean Marlow the FD. It was a warning to Churchill as follows:

"The IMF of all people are saying that the UK is paying too much tax (highest since 1988) and that there will be a property crash this year, further they are advocating an increase in interest rates (such comments only come from the IMF when they are really concerned on the future prospects). This is but another warning of impending doom and points to the need to close the hatches even more so. The fact that Greenspan is forecasting a recession in the USA and the continued loss on the stock exchanges, the call for increase in interest rates even further, must tell even the more optimistic that we are heading for a bumpy road. Now is the time to pull back.

The longer we leave it the more costly it will be. The prolonged run on an expanding economy must come to an end sometime. The fact that sales continue does not stand up to the reduction in enquiries and visitors for the future. To see the slide this time of the year is NOT good.

I would suggest that if at the end of this month if visitors and enquiries have not improved beyond 10% down, we take drastic action to downsize or at least restrict growth. For my part I would not even entertain 'Petrus' but withdraw now and swallow the pill. To even consider buying in this market is a mistake.

A message must go out that we are consolidating."

We would give potential acquisition projects a code name. Petrus was the code name for our look at Pegasus, the upmarket builders run by Peter Askew, the manager I'd fired from McCarthy & Stone and the one that Matthew Thorne had also invested in. I told my boys that this particular wine had gone off.

My experience with our competitors, such as they were, was considerable. In 1989 the MP Steve Norris came to see me with Peter Edmondson from Anglia Secure Homes. They had been stealing some of our people and copying our lease arrangements and I wasn't happy. They wanted to work with us and their approach was an attempt to save them from their eventual downfall.

A lot of the others had a go at trying to do what I'd started: Barratt, Wimpey, Laing and even Saga. But it's not like normal housing and they hadn't got the detail right, used outside architects and couldn't achieve the margins. English Courtyard run by Noel Shuttleworth were double our sale prices and they too went bust.

Between 1988 and 1995 nearly every month the top ten house builders in the land would gather in a private room at The Ritz for dinner. We called ourselves the Volume House Builder Study Group. We didn't study very much at all apart from the wine list and the menu although it was a useful get together. I suggested that we should perhaps put up some money and do some useful research but the idea was shouted down. It was really a meeting for moaning. Terry Roydon of Comben Homes was the secretary and he probably spent more time looking after business at the Federation of Home Builders and for our meetings than he did minding his own business. The usual suspects attended with Duncan Davidson from Persimmon, Nelson Oliver from Wimpey, Lawrie Barratt from Barratts, Eric Pountain from McLean, Lynn Wilson of Wilson Connolly, David Calverley from Ideal Homes, Philip Warner from Bovis and Sam Pickstock from Taylor Woodrow. Much of the dinner time talk between us concerned planning issues. It was always the common problem. We did invite guest speakers to come and talk to us. Some were memorable and Michael Heseltine in particular impressed me, as did Lord Young and William Waldegrave. On the other hand, Frank Dobson said he'd be there but just didn't show up and he didn't contact us. We were livid. How ignorant of him. When Michael Howard was our guest he had his ear bent on planning regulations and how they were an unnecessary obstruction. Mary Archer was a good friend to the elderly and was pushing hard for house builders to measure the loss of heat from their new buildings.

Outside of the group I met the very bright John Redwood and a subdued Norman Tebbit when he came to our London office just off Barclay Square. The Brighton bomb episode had mellowed him a lot. I met John Major when he was Prime Minister after we sent a donation to the Tory party. I always thought he had a body language problem. He was known as the man in the grey suit, although we were later to learn of his misdemeanours with the egg lady, Edwina Curry, which didn't really seem in keeping with his more sober public image. He was a pleasant enough fellow but modelled as a "yes" man. I also had the pleasure of going to No. 10 and meeting Prime Minister Maggie

Thatcher. When she entered the room, armed with her handbag, the diminutive woman would hold sway. A woman of my heart, she knew what she wanted, got things done and made things happen much to the displeasure of some of her so-called friends. She is famously a grocer's daughter and I, less famously, am the son of a jack-of-all-trades.

I've met people and done things that any poorly educated dyslexic carpenter with drive, passion and determination could do. But I've built a billion. I have been fortunate but I've worked hard. I suppose that I have all the trappings of success. The Aston Martin, my fourth, the Range Rover, my seventh, the 110-foot cruiser Dreamcatcher and the windsurfing, diving, water skiing and sailing I can enjoy around it. I have my eleven-seat Beechcraft Kingair aeroplane that can whisk me from Bournemouth to holiday in Majorca in three hours, or stalking and shooting in Scotland in a lot less. There are my homes, Squalls Estate, the house in Guernsey and a ski lodge in the Alps. I have an enviable wine cellar started when I used to buy from Farr's in London including some '83 Petrus and '96 Haut-Brion and '86 and '96 Lafite. Then not far away there's the log cabin trophy room where I can surround myself with memories of my shooting exploits. I have the hand engraved Purdeys and the Perazzis. I have the drawings of the yachts I built and raced and the photographs of their victories. I have the polo field and Claire's horses all around the place to remind me of my own time in the saddle. There are always dogs wandering around the yard and ducks and geese around the water.

On approaching retirement I decided to build a workshop in the grounds of the estate and go back to my grassroots. I built a twelve by sixteen foot workshop, starting fairly small, but extended it to ten times the size so as to take the woodworking machinery. Modern equipment certainly speeds up the process. I built a store for the dried wood and a spray and finishing shop. I built a drying kiln so that I can use oak cut from trees on the estate. The kiln brings the water content down to between 8 and 15 per cent. I have replaced all the windows to the main house and cottages, a number of the panelled doors and special fitments and the outside octagonal loggia. The furniture I make started when my son Scott asked me to build a family crib for the grandchildren. I French-polished it and the curved panels on the corner were hand-painted in oils with scenes from an old Winnie the Pooh book. The crib led to a cot with oil-painted panels. Clinton required a fifteen-foot table for his dining room with Carver chairs and a sideboard, all in 15th century design style. After that I've made tables galore for my grandchildren, my daughter and friends including a large round table to seat sixteen for Jamie and Lydia Lee. It sits in their glass-roofed dining area and with underfloor heating and the sun; I knew that the wood would move due to its burr nature and would need some refinishing work to its top. That is the problem with locally grown special woods.

I designed and built the eight-foot waterwheel that turns and aerates the water outside the front of our home for the Koi carp. I really enjoy designing and creating something that will hopefully last for many, many years. I love the feel and smell of the wood and sawdust and being able to use my skills, re-honed from the past, that let me turn a rough plank of wood into something my grandchildren will rock themselves to sleep in or my friends and family can sit around and share good meals and conversation.

I have my health. I used to smoke twenty Players a day but when I was twenty-one I packed it in and took up cigars. Initially they were small Panatelas but as my income increased so did the size of the cigar. I love a good cigar like a Montecristo No 2 or my favourite, a Cohiba Robusto, a proper cigar. I smoke one every day and on the odd occasion more. When I'm in the workshop I'm forever lighting a cigar while concentrating, then putting it down to carry out the operation, so one cigar can last me the whole day provided that I don't run out of matches.

The family use a GP just off Harley Street called Renee Kellerman. a lovely woman and who I regard as a friend of the family. She's a South African and as soon as the company floated in 1982 and I could afford it I went to see her every other year until I was fifty and every year since. She carries out the consultation after a rigorous three-hour test on every aspect of my well-being. In 2002 she discovered that I had prostate cancer. I read the books about it. I met a consultant in Salisbury and after having biopsies, which confirmed the problem, he set up a date for a radical surgery operation there and then. Radical surgery it seemed carried the risks of incontinence and impotence, both of which were 60 per cent likely. I did not like that prognosis so I went on the Internet and searched the web. In the USA at the John Hopkins Hospital in Seattle, where they specialised in prostate cancer, they had been perfecting something called Brachytherapy, a type of internal radioactive treatment. I sent them my information and was preparing to fly out for them to carry out the operation when I discovered that there was one urologist in the UK who'd performed fifteen such operations. Renee then gave me the address of Dr Ash in Leeds who'd trained in Seattle at the John Hopkins. After a thorough investigation and research, which he kindly sent me, it was evident that he'd carried out over three hundred successful operations using the system. He was the man for me.

He gave me thirty-six injections with eighty-six radioactive seeds. Prior to the operation they cleared me out, they really did, and then I spent one hour in theatre and three hours sitting in bed working on my laptop. You're home the same day with a warning that everything will be fine for a week and then it will hit you. How right they were. I was getting on the plane for Guernsey two weeks later when I felt as if I was going to die. They got me over to the island and luckily Tim Betley was there to meet me and drive me to our house. I went to bed for two days. My PSA count, a measure of the protein or the prostate specific antigen, went down from 11.8 to .04. The operation cost the insurance company nearly £15,000 and it worked. Surgery would have cost about £30,000 with a 60 per cent risk of impotence and a 50/50 chance of incontinence. With Brachytherapy your sperm count is lower but I'm not planning on having any more children just yet.

I have my leisure time and invariably read books on holiday, Winston Churchill and biographies and autobiographies of Thatcher and Blair as well as business and the history of IBM and Henry Ford of course. Jamie Lee gave me a book on Churchill cigars. I take great interest reading about big game hunting as it once was and books about the war. Stalingrad was particularly well written by Antony Beevor and Douglas Bader, Nelson and Hornblower all have a place on my bookshelves.

I first swung a golf club at Barton-on-Sea and played once with Bill Stone at Lyndhurst. He got so frustrated and cross with his game that on his second round by the end of the first hole he threw his brand new set of clubs into the water hazard. I retrieved them after he marched off. The next day he asked about them but he never played again. Golf is a good social exercise and I've met some like-minded people through the game. Arthur Griffiths and Ken Stone were just two such. Ken was the CEO of C F Taylor in Christchurch and he had an almost paranoid fear of heart disease. There was a history of it in his family and he was worried that he would be next in the grim line up. Very sadly he died of cancer. I built him a wooden bench which sits on the course in his memory. One of his unmistakable traits was to end nearly every sentence with the word, "Indeed". He said it a lot. The inscription on the bench reads, "Golfer indeed".

I play off 16 now and enjoy a round locally either at Salisbury, Rushmore, Guernsey or Remedy Oak or on trips to southern Ireland and Mount Juliet where I stay with Uncle Peter's son, Mark. He runs a B&B which he has converted into a really lovely place to live. Not satisfied with that, like his father, he is building a massive house for himself and his new partner, Anne Marie, and family.

There's the shooting of course which keeps me busy for at least seventy days a year or more and no matter how many times I try to bring down that high curling pheasant or the lead bird in that covey, there will always be room for some improvement. Apart from the competitive nature of the days, there is the wonderful fun of being out with like-minded people, rain or shine, in the countryside, sharing the experience.

I'm not a foodie and hate cooking for myself. When Gwen was ill I cooked a roast once but never again. I have a dislike for rice and pasta. I was not a big fan of liver and bacon but once, back in the '80s, Gwen and I went to the Green House in London where Gary Rhodes cooked us his version. It changed my belief in it. When we came out of the restaurant Chef Rhodes was posing for some photographs outside and leaning up against my Rolls-Royce as though he owned it. After the excellent liver and bacon he'd just served up I didn't care two hoots.

I have my family. I regard myself as being very lucky to have Gwen. We've known each other for over five decades. I found her, lost her and got her back again. She's been at my side through thick and thin with that warm smile.

We used to listen to one of our favourite songs, "Clair", sung by Gilbert O'Sullivan on the radio in 1972. Our own Claire was born on 26th March 1976. Back in the '60s we'd share a bottle of Mateus Rosé at the Sweet Lass Grill on Richmond Hill in Bournemouth. We celebrated Gwen's fifty glorious years with a party at the Gritti Palace in Venice and when I turned seventy we enjoyed the lavish birthday celebrations in Grenada with the whole family, twenty-four of us over Christmas and the New Year.

There are two very happy addendums to our relationship. We married on 13th July 1982 at the Lymington registry office and after a quick drink at the Rising Sun, had a blessing at St Michael and All Angels in Hinton Admiral near Highcliffe in Dorset. There was a celebration lunch at Watton's Farm with friends and family and an evening party. Our wedding was a day I shall always be thankful for as this brought us very much closer together if that is at all possible. Gwen looked stunning and radiant with Claire as the beautiful bridesmaid. Many of the family and our friends old and new were there. Tim Ham, who brought us back together from those earlier, darker days, was there. Harry Harrison was best man and Trevor Foan, another director from the company, was an honoured guest. Gwen's brother, Mike a submariner from the navy and sister Tricia were there. I had managed to persuade a quartet we met in the Royal Garden Hotel in London to serenade the guests.

In July 2004 a letter arrived at Squalls. It was from someone called Gerald Michael Holmes. Having had no luck tracing Gwen through adoption societies, he had Gwen's name from the original birth certificate as some years ago adopted children were allowed access to these. He knew that Gwen's father was a dental surgeon and had been in the Royal Navy so by process of elimination and through researching census and birth and marriage certificates he narrowed his search down to about three ladies with the same name. But there was only one with a father in the Royal Navy. He found Gwen's address as her name was listed at Companies House in connection with a small building company that Gwen and I were directors of. His letter to Gwen was carefully worded suggesting that Gwen may be a relative if indeed she was the Gwendolyn Holmes, daughter of a naval dentist. Only five months previously Gwen had received a letter from an unknown second cousin in New Zealand who was researching her family tree, so she thought that this latest letter was just another family member doing the same. But then she looked at the end of the letter which was signed with the name Gerard Michael Holmes. This was the name that she had given to her son before he was adopted.

So there followed many letters between Gwen and her son, then emails but no photos or phone calls. He had had a happy life with his parents but sadly both had passed away so he had felt it was time to find his birth mother. He said he would feel at ease with whatever reasons Gwen had had for giving him up for adoption. After a month of communication Gwen felt that she should arrange a meeting with her son. So on 1st August mother and son met at Westover Hall in Milford on Sea, just the two of them. They talked and talked, laughed and cried and when Gwen looked at his face it was like looking into her own eyes. When I first met him I was astounded by how much he looked like Gwen's father. They get on really well and have continued a really wonderful relationship ever since. Richard Baker, as Gerald Holmes is known, has a wife Paula and there is the bonus of three grandchildren. Richard and his family have been welcomed by all three boys and Claire and it's as if he has always been with us. There is little doubt that the reconciliation was an enormous high point. Every year on the date of Richard's birthday Gwen would often shed a tear and wonder what had happened to her son. The reconnection, trying to catch up the missed years and meeting her grandchildren brought Gwen the happiness that she longed for.

I am extremely proud of my three boys and my daughter. Their achievements and the children they have raised give me a great sense of legacy. Clinton and his wife Kathryn have two beautiful daughters Laura, 25 and Emma, 21. Laura has three children, Hugo, Rosie and Molly. Spencer is married to Bridget and they have Helen (Ellie), 11, who rides dressage horses, and James, 10, taller than me and plays rugby and polo. Scott and his wife Lisa have Aston, 13, a serious golfer, Grace, 9 and Max, 8. Claire has two children Cody, 2 and three-month-old Coco. Gwen's son Richard is married to Paula and has three boys, William, 10, Luke, 9 and Matt who is 6.

I have my memories and my ambitions for the future. If my boys, all my children, grandchildren or great-grandchildren do better than me and in a quicker time, then I will be very happy. There is no good in doing worse than your father and there is little point in doing as well. The children have got to do better than the parents and that's surely how man improves. "Doing better" is judgmental. If your children can run faster then they are "doing better". If they can play polo more skilfully then they are "doing better". My own benchmark is how they do in business and the sign of a good businessman is how successful, how profitable he has made his business and how well he looks after the people involved with it.

When Churchill achieved the "*Daily Express* House Builder of the Year Gold Award 1995" it was a tremendous achievement against all the house builders in the country. How proud I was to read that the Churchill business was short-listed by *The Daily Telegraph* Business Awards for 2010 under the category Employer of the Year Award. This is another accolade in a string of others that the boys have clocked up with their business.

Spencer is more like me than any of my children. He'll probably be the one to go further than I have. Clinton is one of the most endearing people to be with and he has a lot more wit and more friends than I will ever have. Scott certainly tries hard and has a wonderful ability at bringing family and friends together. Claire's patience is more like mine, short, and her determination is like mine too. She is never slow in coming forward and this applies to her horses. On top of this she is a superb mother.

My parents' ashes are buried by the lake at Squalls. Father died in 1987, aged 78, and Mother went on Christmas Day 1995 aged 82. They are on the opposite bank from the crosses for the dogs and there's a bench where I can sit and talk to them if I need to. I treat them with the respect they deserve. You need to show respect and you certainly have to earn it. After over seventy years I hope I've done my share of both.

I don't believe in an afterlife. I am an atheist. Darwin proved for me that there is birth and death and in-between evolution and that is all there is to it. My early Sunday school experience was boring and not engaging. Churches are for christenings, weddings and funerals, a meeting place for the families and friends to celebrate. I do believe in the marriage contract which brings together certain morals which one is expected to love and live by. In my life I have never had to turn to anyone or anything else for what is termed "spiritual inspiration".

I don't believe in God or some greater being than mortal man here on earth. In the end we're just like the leaves on the trees. They start as little green shoots, grow into dense foliage, turn golden and then drop off and fall to the ground. They are gathered up for the bonfire or rot to provide nourishment for the next generation. All the while the tree trunk grows stronger. I believe that's what happens to us but just in case they get it wrong I want to be buried with my mobile.

As for my belief, I believe in me.